BUILDING ORGANIZATIONAL DECISION SUPPORT SYSTEMS

BUILDING ORGANIZATIONAL DECISION SUPPORT SYSTEMS

Grace M. Carter
Michael P. Murray
Robert G. Walker
Warren E. Walker

with Robert A. Reding, Allan Abrahamse,
and Daniel Relles

A RAND Research Study

ACADEMIC PRESS, INC.
Harcourt Brace Jovanovich, Publishers
Boston   San Diego   New York
London   Sydney   Tokyo   Toronto

Composition   *Professional Book Center*

This book is printed on acid-free paper.

ACADEMIC PRESS, INC.
1250 Sixth Avenue, San Diego, CA 92101

United Kingdom Edition published by
ACADEMIC PRESS LIMITED
24–28 Oval Road, London NW1 7DX

RAND books are available on a wide variety of topics. To receive a list of RAND books,
write or call Distribution Services, RAND, 1700 Main Street, P.O. Box 2138, Santa
Monica, CA 90407-2138, (310) 393-0411, extension 6686.

Library of Congress Cataloging-in-Publication Data:
Building organizational decision support systems / Grace M. Carter ...
    [et al.].
        p.   cm
    Includes bibliographic references.
    ISBN 0-12-732070-9 (alk. paper)
    1. Decision support systems.   I. Carter, Grace M.
    T58.62.B86   1992
    658.4'03--dc20   92-19077
                                                                        CIP

PRINTED IN THE UNITED STATES OF AMERICA

92 93 94 95 BC 9 8 7 6 5 4 3 2 1

Contents

v

Contents

Chapter 7 Loss Modules in the EFMS

Chapter 8 Decision Support Models in the EFMS

Chapter 9 Data for Analysis and Model Building

Chapter 10 The Use of Prototype Models and Staged Implementation

Chapter 11 Test and Evaluation of ODSS Models and Modules

PART V IMPLEMENTATION

Chapter 12 Principles for Implementing an ODSS

Chapter 13 Passing the Baton: Implementing New Models

Chapter 14 Selecting the System's Software and Hardware

Chapter 15 Database Design and Management

Contents

Chapter 16 Building Applications

Chapter 17 User Interfaces

Chapter 18 Updating and Maintaining the Models of an ODSS

Preface

OVERVIEW

Early descriptions of decision support systems (DSSs) were based on the paradigm of a single decisionmaker at a stand-alone terminal or microcomputer who had a specific decision (nonrepetitive, semi-structured) to make. (Some of the early literature even recommended matching the user interface to the "cognitive style" of the decisionmaker). However, recent advances in computer technology, information systems, and telecommunications (collectively referred to as *information technology*, or IT) have facilitated a broadening of the scope of a DSS to include organizational units and, in some cases, entire organizations. Such systems are called "organizational decision support systems" (ODSSs).

Successful designing and implementation of ODSSs will be increasingly critical to the success of organizations—especially large ones with geographically dispersed operations or foreign subsidiaries. Organizations have been evolving to take advantage of the capabilities offered by IT, and, conversely, IT has facilitated dramatic changes in how organizations operate. The multinational corporations of the 1970s, which were really separate companies loosely coupled at the top, have given way to truly integrated global corporations, structured as a global web of operations instead of a multinational pyramid. IT makes such an organization possible. Organizational decision support systems help make it successful.

ODSSs are not simply larger versions of a single-user DSS. There are important differences. These differences lead to critical differences in how ODSSs should be designed, developed, and maintained. This book highlights the differences and provides guidance to those who are engaged in building an ODSS. The guidance is not only theoretical (e.g., based on recommended approaches in the DSS and MIS literature), but is based on the authors' experience in building an ODSS for the United States Air Force. The system, called the Enlisted Force Management System (EFMS), is being used to help members of the Air Staff in the Pentagon make decisions related to their enlisted personnel. The three basic building blocks of an ODSS are the same as those of a traditional DSS (TDSS):

- model base (and model management system)
- database (and database management system)
- user interface (a dialog system that manages the interaction between the user and the other two components)

But an ODSS includes two additional components: a case management system, to facilitate assembling and cataloging the input data for model runs and to keep track of the output from the runs, and a communications system that allows users to communicate and cooperate with each other and with the models and data in the process of organizational decisionmaking.

An ODSS involves many users in loosely-linked parts of an organization operating a multitude of models that are fed by a number of databases. A well designed ODSS can provide central guidance and generalized control from top management to the individual decisionmakers, while permitting them (and helping them) to make their separate decisions. As a result, decisions made throughout the organization will be consistent with organizational goals and management's shared interpretation of its operational environment, while individual decisionmakers will simultaneously enjoy a maximum degree of freedom and independence.

The size, scope, and cost of an ODSS makes it very visible, and requires that its development be more carefully planned and managed than a TDSS. Because it is so visible and crosses organizational boundaries, successful implementation of an ODSS depends as much on political considerations as on technological considerations.

The key to a successful information system, as a growing body of applied research on organizations suggests, is the process by which the technology is introduced. This book deals with the process of building an organizational decision support system, from needs assessment and project formation, through conceptual design, to system implementation, maintenance, and updating. It addresses the technical issues involved in building models, creating databases, and choosing hardware and software. In fact, most of the book is devoted to these issues. But it also addresses political issues that have to be faced, such as the roles of the various organizational units, turf battles, and the composition and management of the project team. As Woolsey [1989] has said: "I have never seen an OR/MS/MIS system fail because of an insufficient level of technology, but I have seen such systems fail—big time—because the level of expertise related to people issues was nowhere near that dealing with technical matters."

The book has been written for those who are, or may become, involved in the development of an ODSS. This includes ODSS users, the analysts who may be developing the models for an ODSS, the programmers and information systems personnel who may be writing its programs or developing its databases, the information systems managers who might be leading the ODSS development project, and the top managers who might be considering introducing an ODSS into their organization. Much of the book is written in clear, nontechnical language. However, some of the information for the analysts and implementors is slightly more technical. These parts can be skipped by nontechnical readers.

This book is unique in the DSS literature, for three reasons. First, although there are many books that treat the concepts of decision support systems and how to build a DSS, there are no "how-to" books that are based on the experience of actually building one. Second, although there are many books on decision support systems, there are no books on ODSS's. Third, this book treats many issues concerned with the building of a DSS that are not treated together in any other DSS book. These include:

- The effort and pitfalls in managing the development of a large ODSS
- Organizational and political issues
- Relationships among modeler, implementor, and user
- Data gathering and cleaning
- Building analytical databases
- Modeling

- Integrating models
- Implementation
- Documentation
- Maintenance
- Updating and refitting models

The book provides step-by-step guidance to those who are engaged in building an ODSS. The guidance is not only theoretical (e.g., based on recommended approaches in the DSS and MIS literature), but is based on the experiences that the authors had in building an ODSS for the United States Air Force. The system, called the Enlisted Force Management System (EFMS), is being used to help members of the Air Staff in the Pentagon make decisions related to their enlisted personnel. The book weaves together principles for designing and building an ODSS with illustrative examples from the EFMS that show how the principles were applied. Because of its size and scope, the EFMS presented the development team with almost every conceivable challenge that might be faced in building an ODSS. We hope that the use of EFMS examples brings the ODSS development process alive for the reader.

ORGANIZATION

The book is divided into five major parts. Part I is primarily definitional and conceptual. It describes the decisionmaking environment within which an ODSS must function, decision aids in general, and ODSSs in particular. It specifies some principles that underlie the design of an ODSS, and the implications of those principles for the components of the system. Part II provides information on the Air Force's EFMS that is needed later to illustrate the points being made. Some of this discussion may be somewhat arcane to the general reader with little interest in Air Force personnel matters. But we feel that the gains of becoming familiar with this material outweigh the costs. Among the important gains is that the illustrations can delve into technical problems and political issues in a way that would be impossible if they were based on artificial examples with a less rich context.

Part III describes the process of building an organizational decision support system. It discusses the activities that are required and the issues (technical and managerial) that must be dealt with. It compares this process to those used to develop a traditional DSS and to develop a traditional management information system (the "System Development Life Cycle" approach).

Part IV deals with building models for inclusion in an ODSS. It begins with first principles concerning decision models—what they are and how they vary. It then discusses more complicated issues, such as how many models the system should contain, simplicity vs. realism, fitting the models, prototyping, and test and evaluation. Models are at the heart of an ODSS. As Brennan and Elam [1986] wrote:

"All decision making involves predicting the likely consequences of decisions, which suggests that the decision maker should have a "model" of the problem situation being faced. The majority of DSS in use today do not attempt to represent this model explicitly, but rather provide access to data that can be utilized by an implicit, internalized model. One way to increase the quality of solutions produced by DSS is by incorporating explicit models of the decision making environment."

While portions of Part IV are aimed at the analyst and modeler, Part IV's basic intention is to present for all readers the core concerns about models essential to building an ODSS.

Part V focuses on issues related to the implementation of an ODSS. It deals with the technical issues of programming, designing user interfaces, building the system's databases, preparing documentation, and updating the system. But it also covers less technical issues, such as project management, relationships with users, and transferring models from the analysts to the implementors. An understanding of these issues and a sensitivity to their importance will go far to determining whether the ODSS will be successfully implemented and used.

ACKNOWLEDGMENTS

The EFMS was a joint product of the RAND Corporation and the U.S. Air Force. Warren Walker was RAND's project leader throughout the ten-year EFMP effort and Robert Walker was the Air Force's project leader during the EFMP's first seven years. Murray and Carter were senior researchers on the project from its inception to its end. In all, more than 100 individuals contributed to the building of the EFMS. (Their names are listed in the final report on the EFMP [Walker and the Enlisted Force Management Project Team, 1991].) The lessons we draw in this book are further fruits of those individuals' labors. The authors are indebted to all who worked to build the EFMS, but several people deserve special mention.

Jan Chaiken participated in the conceptual design of the EFMS and his work left a mark on the project throughout its life. Marygail Brauner joined the project in its early days and set a high standard for carefulness and insight. Col. Robert Barnhardt played an early key leadership role across a wide range of project functions and activities. Peter Rydell joined the EFMP midstream and infused the project with a concern for users' views of the unfolding system. Generals J.B. Davis, W. Scott Harpe, and Robert Oaks supported the EFMP effort at critical junctures. Col. James Sampson succeeded Robert Walker as the Air Force's project leader for the EFMP and successfully brought the system through its final transition from development to full implementation. The collaborative research efforts of three Air Force officers, Joseph Cafarella, Glenn Clemens and Kevin Lawson, with their RAND counterparts, were essential to the integration of the RAND and Air Force system development work. Barbara Like masterfully cast our many drafts into a manuscript with a single format and coherent appearance. Robert Anderson and Gene Fisher made significant contributions to the content and organization of the book through their reviews of an early manuscript.

The book is truly a joint effort of the four primary authors. The outlines of the chapters were created at group brainstorming sessions. Draft chapters were critiqued and revised by us all. Robert Reding contributed extensive raw material for Part IV of the book. Allan Abrahamse co-authored Chapter 11. Dan Relles authored Chapter 9.

The creative exercise of writing a book is quite satisfying. The nitty gritty details of putting a book together are another matter altogether. The rest of us are grateful to Warren Walker for handling the myriad managerial details required for assembling this book, and for his fulfilling that same essential task throughout the EFMP. Warren managed our budgets, our staffs and our creative tensions while simultaneously conveying first to the EFMP and then to the book project the pulse of progress in the literature on Decision Support Systems.

Carter and Murray also want to note that the Walkers were from the outset the key champions of the EFMP. Few researchers would have had Warren's persistence in the face of the early difficulties with the client over specifying the initial models or the courage to continuously defend the project to management during the first few years when developing some early models took much longer than planned. Few Air Force officers would have had Robert's independence of spirit to press the EFMP within the Air Force in the face of the substantial skepticism from several powerful individuals.

Grace M. Carter
Michael P. Murray
Robert G. Walker
Warren E. Walker

January 1992

List of Acronyms

AFMPC	Air Force Military Personnel Center
AFSC	Air Force Specialty Code
APM	Authorization Projection Model
ATC	Air Training Command
BEM	Bonus Effects Model
BMT	Basic Military Training
CJR	Career Job Reservation
CMS	Case Management System
CPU	Central Processing Unit
CSCW	Computer-Supported Cooperative Work
DBA	Database Administrator
DBMS	Database Management System
DMDC	Defense Manpower Data Center
DMI	Disaggregate Middle-term Inventory Projection Model
DoD	Department of Defense
DOS	Date of Separation
DP	Deputy Chief of Staff for Personnel
DPP	Directorate of Personnel Programs
DPX	Directorate of Personnel Plans
DSS	Decision Support System

EAGL	Enriched Airman Gain/Loss (data file)
EFMP	Enlisted Force Management Project
EFMS	Enlisted Force Management System
EIS	Executive Information System
EMS	Electronic Meeting System
ESO	Equal Selection Opportunity
ETS	Expiration of Term of Service
GDSS	Group Decision Support System
GLS	Generalized Least Squares
HYT	High year of tenure
IPM	Inventory Projection Model
IT	Information Technology
MAJCOMs	Major Commands
MBMS	Model Base Management System
MIS	Management Information System
MMS	Model Management System
MTL	Middle-term Disaggregate Loss Module
NCO	Non-commissioned Officer
NPS	Non-prior Service
ODSS	Organizational Decision Support System
OETS	Original Expiration of Term of Service
OLS	Ordinary Least Squares
PACE	Processing and Classification of Enlistees (data file)
PDGL	Promotion, Demotion, Gain, Loss (data file)
PE	Prediction Error
PEPNR	Percent of Number at Risk
PPB	Planning, Programming, and Budgeting
PR	Programs and Resources
PRE	Percent Relative Error
PRM	Directorate of Manpower and Organization
RAM	Random Access Memory
SAM	Short-term Aggregate Inventory Projection Model
SAMFBYL	Short-term Aggregate Model, Force by Year Listing
SDLC	System Development Life Cycle
SMO	System Management Office
SPE	Standardized Prediction Error
SQL	Structured Query Language
SRB	Selective Reenlistment Bonus
T&E	Test and Evaluation

TDSS	Traditional Decision Support System
TIG	Time in Grade
TIS	Time in Service
TOPCAP	Total Objective Plan for Career Airman Personnel
TPR	Trained Personnel Requirements
UAR	Uniform Airman Record (data file)
YAR	Year at Risk (data file)
YETS	Years to ETS
YOS	Year of Service
YOSTG	Year of Service Target Generator

PART I

THE CONTEXT OF ORGANIZATIONAL DECISION SUPPORT SYSTEMS

Chapter 1 | Organizational Decision Support Systems

1.1 INTRODUCTION

As the pace of technological change continues unabated into the 1990s, the focus is shifting from office automation and traditional computer applications to the development of tools for using the enormous potential of technology to increase the speed and the quality of organizational decisionmaking. One such tool is the *decision support system* (DSS).

Early descriptions of DSSs were based on the paradigm of a single decisionmaker at a stand-alone terminal or microcomputer who had a specific decision to make. However, recent advances in computer technology, information systems, and telecommunications (which, taken together, we will refer to as *information technology* [IT]) have made it possible to broaden the scope of a DSS to include organizational units and even entire organizations. In fact, some computer system designers and theorists have begun to characterize certain technologies as "groupware" hardware and software complexes that are designed from the perspective of the role they will play in the dynamics of action and coordination among a group of people interacting with one another. The actors may be operating independently, but they are interdependent and are working toward mutually defined goals. In the case of an organizational DSS (ODSS), these goals are the goals of the organization.

Organizations have also been evolving to take advantage of the capabilities offered by IT and, conversely, IT has facilitated dramatic changes in how organizations operate. The multinationals of the 1970s, which were really separate companies loosely coupled at the top, are becoming truly integrated global corporations, structured as a global web of operations instead of a multinational pyramid. According to Eom [1990], the global corporation "does research wherever necessary, develops products in several countries, [and] promotes key executives regardless of nationality." But, although decentralized, it is fully integrated in all its activities, including product design, fabrication, accounting, marketing, and finance. In fact, many successful companies now are facades "behind which teems an array of decentralized groups and subgroups continuously contracting with similarly diffuse working units all over the world. The threads of the global web are computers, facsimile machines, satellites, high-resolution monitors, and modems—all of them linking designers, engineers, contractors, licensees, and dealers worldwide" [Reich, 1991]. IT makes such an organization possible. Organizational decision support systems (or the subset that Eom [1990] calls "global decision support systems") make such a corporation successful.

The potential for developing and benefiting from large integrated ODSSs results from the complementary organizational and technological trends alluded to above. Organizationally, large corporations have moved toward globalization and decentralization of their management and operations. Also, modern business and governmental organizations have demonstrated an insatiable demand for information, along with the desire to automate routine operational functions, such as payroll, billing, inventory management, etc., which in turn generate tremendous amounts of data. Technologically, a revolution has occurred in the way information is gathered, stored, and processed within organizations. Price and performance improvements in IT have brought most organizational functions within the reach of automation on a cost-effective basis. Expanded file and database management system capabilities have allowed the gathering and manipulation of larger and larger amounts of data, which increasingly cross the functional and organizational boundaries. End-user computing, driven largely by the rapid growth in personal computers and workstations, has opened up previously unimagined areas for computerization. With the continued maturation of networking technology, physical distances, geographic borders, and organizational or functional boundaries are becoming less constraining in the movement of information to those points where it is needed. In addition, powerful new tools for building systems are becoming increasingly available. As Huber [1990] summarizes these trends, "The availability of the advanced information technologies increases the communicating or decision-aiding options for the potential user, and thus in the long run, unless the selected technology is inappropriately employed, the effect is to increase the quality (broadly defined) of the user's communication or decision-making processes." He then concludes, "For advancement of their own interests, organizational participants will use advanced information technologies in ways that increase their effectiveness in fulfilling organizational goals."

Over the past few years, many types of decision support systems and groupware have been developed. To provide the reader with a clear idea of what this book is about, we provide brief definitions of some of these. There may not be universal agreement on these definitions, but we will use them consistently within the book.

Decision support system (DSS). An interactive IT-based system that helps decisionmakers utilize data and models in making their decisions.

Traditional decision support system (TDSS). A DSS built around a single decisionmaker, utilizing a stand-alone microcomputer or a terminal (or microcomputer) linked to a larger computer, that is designed to help that decisionmaker make certain specific decisions (see Keen and Scott Morton [1978]).

Executive information system (EIS). A TDSS designed to be used by top executives or managers. (See Reck and Hall [1986].)

Group decision support system (GDSS). A DSS that supports a group of people collectively engaged in making decisions. GDSSs are used by committees, review panels, task forces, etc., which involve several decisionmakers working together on the same problems (see DeSanctis and Gallupe [1987]).

Electronic meeting system (EMS). An IT-based environment that supports group meetings and group interactions. An EMS provides an environment within which group decisionmaking can take place (see Dennis et al. [1988]).

Computer-supported cooperative work (CSCW). An inclusive label for practically any use of IT support for work group collaboration. CSCW includes EMS, GDSS, and other terms. (See Olson [1989].)

Organizational decision support system (ODSS). A DSS that is used by individuals or groups at several workstations in more than one organizational unit who make varied (interrelated but autonomous) decisions using a common set of tools. An ODSS is designed to coordinate and disseminate decisionmaking across functional areas and hierarchical levels such that the decisions are congruent with organizational goals.

An ODSS is more than a computer system. As pointed out by Bots and Sol [1988], it is "a collection of hardware, software, people and procedures that keeps the organization *alive.*" For an ODSS to be effective and to realize its potential requires solving an enormous array of compatibility and coordination problems (technical, organizational, and behavioral). It requires "a clear perception of the structure of the target organization,...adequate knowledge of the theories and the techniques that can be applied in order to solve the myriad of specific problems that may arise in that organization...[and] thorough understanding of the process of information systems design in general." [Bots and Sol, 1988]. In short, it requires new approaches to designing, building, and maintaining information systems.

This book is a first step.

1.2   THE DECISIONMAKING PROCESS

To explain what ODSSs are and their role in an organization, we must explore briefly the nature of decisionmaking and decision aiding. Decisionmaking is a process in which one or more persons identify a problem (a dissatisfaction with the present state) and then design, choose, implement, and monitor a solution. Baccus [1991], van Schaik [1988], and others regard decisionmaking as synonymous with problem solving, and we will do so in this book. (Simon [1960] understands decisionmaking to be synonymous with managing.)

Many models of the decisionmaking process have been proposed in the literature. (A review of the literature on decisionmaking in the context of decision support systems is given by van Schaik [1988, Section 1.2].) In fact, different decisionmakers use different processes, and different decision situations call for different processes. What must be remembered when building a DSS is that decisionmaking is a process and that the DSS should be designed to mesh with that process.

In this book, we assume an organizational process model of decisionmaking that is based on common models in the management science literature. As opposed to behavioral models of decisionmaking, it explicitly considers the environment within which the decisions are to be made.

For illustrative purposes, we use a combination of the "rational actor" model of decisionmaking as described by Allison [1971] and Simon's [1969] satisfying model. Our model assumes an individual decisionmaker who wants to make decisions that will improve the existing situation by taking into consideration the probable consequences of a number of alternative courses of action—selecting the alternative to implement by comparing its costs and the extent to which it helps to achieve objectives and possible other benefits against those of the other alternatives. This view of the decisionmaking process is not required by a DSS or by the approach to developing a DSS that is described in this book. It just makes it easier to provide illustrative examples.

The rational actor model is normative and focuses on the logic of optimal choice. The decisionmaker is assumed to have a system of preferences or "utilities" that permit the consequences of alternatives to be ranked. He or she can then choose the alternative that ranks highest. The term "economic man" summarizes this conception of how choices are made. This view of decisionmaking, although an idealization, has played a major part in the development of operations research and management science over the years, and still represents a useful guide to the direction in which one may wish a given DSS to move.

Simon [1969] argued that the rational conception does not represent the world as it really is and suggested a definition of "satisficing man," who does the best he can but does not even attempt optimization. His argument is clear and convincing [Simon, 1969, p. 64]:

> In the real world we usually do not have a choice between satisfactory and optimal solutions, for we only rarely have a method of finding the optimum. We satisfice by looking for alternatives in such a way that we can find an acceptable one after only moderate search.

We are dealing with large organizations, where satisficing is much more realistic than optimization (unstructured problems, multiple criteria, no utility function for producing a ranking, subjective judgments, which are a necessary part of choice, political considerations, multiple interested parties, multiple decisionmakers). However, as we will see in Chapter 4, optimization models still have a role to play in this environment and may be included in the DSS.

Practically all of the process models of decisionmaking view it as involving a series of steps. Different versions of this model list different numbers of steps and give them different names. For our purposes, we view the process as progressing through the following eight steps (the steps are not necessarily sequential, and there are feedback loops that can return the process to an earlier step at any point in the process):

1. Identify problem. Decisionmaking begins with the identification of a dissatisfaction with the present state (a *problem situation*). Simon [1960] claims that most managers devote a large fraction of their time to surveying the environment (economic, technical, political, and social) to identify conditions calling for action. This step includes *problem formulation*, which is the translation of a problem situation into a specific problem. "We fail more often because we solve the wrong problem than because we get the wrong solution to the right problem" [Ackoff, 1974, p. 8].

2. Identify objectives. These are what the decisionmaker wishes to achieve. Objectives are needed in order to choose among alternatives. (A different objective implies a different preference among alternatives.) An objective may be turned into a *constraint* by requiring the solution to have a certain characteristic.

3. Decide on measures of benefits and costs. A benefit measure indicates the degree to which an alternative will meet an objective. A cost is a negative benefit (what must be given up to acquire the alternative). Sometimes an objective may be difficult or impossible to quantify. In this case, it may be possible to define a *proxy* measure (a consequence that can be measured and is directly related to the objective). Unquantifiable factors should not be left out of the analysis. They should be recognized and their effects factored in later. We divide benefit measures into three categories, and cost measures into two categories:

- Efficiency: how well scarce resources are being used
- Effectiveness: how well the alternative achieves stated goals
- Equity (mainly in the public sector): how fairly the alternative's costs and benefits are distributed
- Economic costs: benefits lost or opportunities foregone
- Social costs: negative impacts on the quality of life.

4. Select alternatives. Alternatives are the possible ways of achieving the objectives. This is an important step, since, if an alternative is not examined, it cannot be chosen, even if it is a good one. Design of a good new alternative is likely to be worth more than a thorough evaluation of an unsatisfactory old one. Specification of alternatives is a creative act—much like the design stage in architecture. The more varied the alternatives, the better (the more diverse, the better the chance of finding a good solution). Some rules of thumb for selecting alternatives:

- Specify a wide range of alternatives.
- Include the current situation as the base case.
- Consider implementation (e.g., legal, political, and physical constraints).

If the set of alternatives is too big, reduce the number to be examined in detail by using screening [Walker, 1988].

5.   Evaluate each alternative.   This has been the most important use of model-based DSSs. Models are abstractions of the real world. *Descriptive* models are used to predict the consequences of implementing an alternative. The input is a description of the alternative (and the environment it will have to operate in); the output is the value of the performance measures. *Prescriptive* models are used to generate good alternatives ("best" according to some criteria). Most decisionmakers use *mental* models (unstated, implicit, held in the mind). A DSS includes *computer* models, which may be descriptive or prescriptive.

6.   Compare alternatives and choose one.   Assemble   information from as many sources (decision aiders) as possible. Each may have a different perspective. The purpose of using decision aids for this step is to reduce the risk and uncertainty involved in the decisionmaking process. (A choice must be made on the basis of incomplete knowledge among alternatives that do not yet physically exist and whose consequences will occur if at all only in the unknown future.) Information from the DSS is only one source. Others are the decisionmaker's own judgment, advisors, lobbyists, media, etc. One way of comparing alternatives is to use colored scorecards (see Findeisen and Quade [1985, Section 4.7]).

7.   Implement chosen alternative.   Decisions and actions must be taken to flesh out the decision. In this step concrete details are added and open issues resolved. Some activities in this step are preparing an implementation plan, constructing or procuring facilities and equipment, hiring and training personnel, and developing rules, regulations, and guidelines.

8.   Monitor and evaluate results.   What was the impact of the decision on the problem situation? Sometimes the result is consistent with the decisionmaker's intent, but it may differ substantially. Some differences result from the implemented policy being different from the chosen one (e.g., because the policy was adapted to make it more practical or to accommodate new political concerns). Others occur because the decisionmaker and the implementors are usually different. Also, the environment may have changed from the one that was modeled or the model may have been inaccurate. Models are only abstractions of reality, so results in the real world may be different. This step in the process is often forgotten, but it is of critical importance. These and other issues in the evaluation of the success of a decision are discussed by Goeller [1988].

Simon [1969] and many other authors, group the first six steps into three stages; the last two steps can be viewed as a fourth stage.

1. *Intelligence*—scanning the environment for situations demanding a decision.
2. *Design*—generating, developing, and analyzing alternative courses of action.
3. *Choice*—selecting a course of action.
4. *Implementation and review*—implementing the decision and monitoring its performance.

To simplify even further, decisionmaking consists of (1) a mechanism for deciding (e.g., objectives and performance measures) and (2) the processing of information to inform, feed, and satisfy this mechanism.

1.3 COMPUTERIZED DECISION AIDS: TOOLS IN THE DECISIONMAKING PROCESS

1.3.1 Decision Aids and Decision Support

According to Baccus [1991], decision aids are procedures, techniques, or presentational forms that enhance the performance of a decisionmaker by making one or more problem parts and interim steps in the decisionmaking process more clear or manageable. They are tools for displaying, looking at, examining, playing with, simulating, testing, and assessing the various pieces of a decision problem. There are tools for looking at raw data (charts, graphics), for interrelating problem elements (diagrams), for leading the decisionmaker through problem considerations (argument, negotiation), etc. Many decision aids are unrelated to computers (e.g., maps), and some are computerized (e.g., expert systems).

Decision aids can help a decisionmaker minimize the chances of (1) making a poor decision, (2) missing a good alternative, (3) making a decision at a bad time, or (4) focusing on the wrong issues or problems. They can also be used to reduce complexity to manageable proportions, seek robustness so as to hedge against uncertainties, or provide intuition, insight, and understanding. Perhaps most important, decision aids are designed to enhance the performance of the decisionmaker (by, for example, overcoming human information processing limitations, speeding up the processing of information needed for problem solving, and increasing the quantity of usable information).

Different types of decision aids help a decisionmaker in different ways:

- Procedures (e.g., checklists) to organize his or her thinking or provide a framework within which specific analytic methods can be used.
- Methods and techniques (e.g., simulation) to help examine alternative solutions.
- Presentational forms (e.g., charts and graphs) to help display and review data, interrelationships, and output.

So, several decision aids might be used in any given decision situation. The more complex and uncertain the situation, the more helpful a decision aid can be.

A decision aid becomes a device for decision support if it becomes a reliable, acceptable, and integral part of the decisionmaking process in an organizational environment. Once firmly integrated and routinely applied, some even lose their character as "decision aids" ; they become part of standard operating procedures and are no longer visible as aiding devices.

A DSS is a computerized decision aid. This book discusses how DSSs can be designed, developed, and implemented so as to become devices for decision support.

1.3.2 Relationship to Decisionmaking Process

A clear distinction exists between decisionmaking processes and analytic processes. Decision support models do not make decisions. Decision support systems do not make decisions. Both aid decisionmakers. Their outputs are only one input into the decisionmaking process.

To paraphrase Majone [Majone and Quade, 1980, p. 8], the role of mathematical modeling and DSS in assisting decisionmaking is generally discussed in a language that tends to obliterate the distinction between *decision aiding* and *decisionmaking*. The same categories—performance measures, alternatives, optimization, etc.—are used in both cases, thus setting up a one-to-one correspondence between the stages of the decision process and the stages of the analytic process. This approach has considerable intuitive appeal and economizes on terminology, but it can lead to a great deal of confusion and misunderstanding. Specifically, it leads some to believe that DSSs can and should be used to produce "the solution" to a decision problem. It may also lead to rejection of the tools by decisionmakers who need help but want to retain control of the decisionmaking process.

For nonautomated decision support, the relationship of the steps offers little difficulty: People can just ignore the supposed sequence and use the support at will, working within their own decisionmaking process model. Thus, management information system (MIS) reports can be consulted early, late—whenever—in the decisionmaking task. Automated decision support poses a different problem. Some systems may actually enforce the stepwise progression through computer program design. Using an analytic process model to prescribe actual decisionmaking analysis steps confuses a specific methodology with an approach to general decision problem solving. In our view of modeling and decision support, the notions of a single decision model and a prescriptive decision process must be abandoned if decision support is to proceed.

The key to understanding how decision aids fit into the decisionmaking process is the realization that decision aids can help in each of the steps, that different problems require different amounts of different tools in each step, and that, for successful and sustained use, the choice of the tools should remain under the control of the decisionmaker. (See Baccus [1991, Section 1] for a discussion that links various types of decision aids to the steps of the decisionmaking process.) To paraphrase Quade [Majone and Quade, 1980, p. 31], decision aids are tools in the decisionmaking process, just as brushes and palettes are tools in painting. They are means to an end, not an end in themselves.

1.3.3 Examples of Computerized Decision Aids

Decision aids can take many forms and can reside in many delivery systems—from mental models people carry around in their heads, through hardcopy manuals, to expert systems. Prior to the computer age, decisionmakers relied on a wide variety of decision aids, many of which are still in widespread use. Examples of these "low-tech" aids include graphs, maps, flowcharts, tables, checklists, and briefings. With the advent of the computer, which coincided with an increase in the complexity of problems that government and corporate decisionmakers deal with, the computer has been used increasingly as the delivery system for decision aids.

Some of these computerized decision aids merely automate versions of previous aids:

- Procedural: computerized checklist
- Methodological: statistics package (e.g., SAS)
- Presentational: computer graphics, flowcharts.

However, some take advantage of the unique capabilities of the computer to provide support to the decisionmaking process in new ways:

- Real-time decision support: Real-time DSSs that can support (for example) military field decision problems. Such systems can be used to correlate incoming intelligence and sensor data, perform a rapid evaluation of alternative options, and suggest the best route or weapons mix for a specific mission objective.
- Expert systems: These simulate decisionmaking itself, using rule sets representing actual decisionmakers' judgments and heuristics in a problem domain. Linked to simulation models representing the real-world environment, such an approach can potentially support all aspects of decisionmaking.
- Group decision support systems (GDSSs): These facilitate the solution of decision problems by a set of decisionmakers working together as a group (often in the context of a decision-related meeting).

Organizational decision support systems (ODSSs) are one type of computerized decision aid. In fact, by their very nature, they probably require more computer and data resources than practically any other type of decision aid.

ODSSs are also one type of MIS. The approach to the design, development, and maintenance of an ODSS that we will be recommending in this book is closely related to that recommended for MISs. Therefore, in the next section, we provide a brief overview of MISs.

1.4 MANAGEMENT INFORMATION SYSTEMS

1.4.1 Definition and Major Features

Our discussion of management information systems (MISs) is based in large part on Davis and Olson [1985]. They define an MIS as "an integrated, user-machine system for providing information to support operations, management, and decision-making functions in an organization. The system utilizes computer hardware and software; manual procedures; models for analysis, planning, control and decision making; and a database."

An MIS is often described in terms of a pyramid (see Fig. 1.1), in which the bottom layer consists of transactional data and tools for accessing and processing them; the next level consists of information resources in support of day-to-day operations and control; the third level consists of information system resources to aid in tactical planning and decisionmaking for management control; and the top level consists of information resources to support strategic planning and policymaking by higher levels of management. In ODSSs, we are concerned with the top three levels of

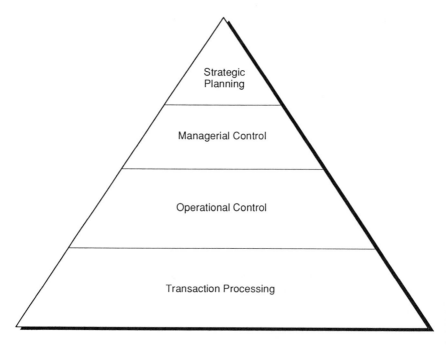

Fig. 1.1 The Management Information System Pyramid

the pyramid. Some of the information to support management and decisionmaking at these three levels comes from the transactional data, while some may be new data about activities external to the organization.

One of the important benefits from a well-designed MIS is that it provides the basis for integration of organizational information processing. The trend in information system design is toward separate application processing from the data used to support it. The separate database is the mechanism by which data items are integrated across many applications and made consistently available to a variety of users.

Another trend in MISs is the inclusion of decision models. For example, an MIS for inventory control might include a model that computes safety stock under a variety of assumptions, or a financial management system might include a budgetary control model. In fact, Davis and Olson [1985] define a decision support system as "an information system application that assists decision making" and state that they "represent a significant class of MIS applications."

Although we agree that an ODSS can be considered a type of MIS, we believe that they are a very special type, which require their own principles and procedures for design, development, and maintenance. However, some MIS principles and procedures are perfectly applicable to ODSSs. In particular, many aspects of the System Development Life Cycle (SDLC) approach used to build MISs apply to the building of an ODSS. We, therefore, describe the SDLC in the next section.

1.4.2   The System Development Life Cycle Approach to Information System Development

The basic idea of the SDLC process model is that a well-defined, linear, structured process is provided by which an application is conceived, developed, and implemented. The criteria for progressing from one stage to the next in the process are also provided. The activities in the SDLC provide a basis for management and control. They define segments of the flow of work that can be identified for managerial purposes and specify the documents or other deliverables to be produced by each activity.

The SDLC is described differently by different writers, but the differences are primarily in amount of detail and manner of categorization. There is general agreement on the flow. We summarize Davis and Olson's [1985, pp. 570–591] specification of the three stages of the approach, within each of which we specify a number of activities.

1. Defining the system and the project. This is the organizational and design stage. It is basically carried out the same way for DSSs as for MISs. It includes the following activities:

- *Assessing needs (or "problem definition").* What is wrong with the existing system and what would it take to correct it? What would be the objectives and goals of the new system? Does building a new system for these purposes make sense?
- *Getting management support (or "feasibility").* This means formulating functional recommendations for the system, selling the idea to top management (e.g., with a "feasibility study" showing its technical, economic, schedule, and operational feasibility), and obtaining a commitment (and resources) to build the system.
- *Getting organized.* This involves setting up a steering committee, choosing a project leader, and identifying the members of the project team.
- *Getting a plan of action ("analysis").* This involves laying out the plan for the development process. What steps must be carried out? What specific problems would the system address (and what would it not address)? In what order should the problems be addressed? How will team members communicate with each other? How will work get documented? How will decisions get made?
- *Developing the conceptual design.* This activity produces a blueprint for the system, which serves to guide subsequent decisions made by the system's builders. As Brooks [1975, p. 42] says: "It is better to have a system omit certain anomalous features and improvements, but to reflect one set of design ideas, than to have one that contains many good but independent and uncoordinated ideas." The conceptual design emphasizes the system as seen by those who will operate it or use its outputs.

2. Developing the system. This stage includes two types of activities:

- *Designing the physical system.* This activity includes choosing the software, choosing the hardware, and designing the database. It results in a detailed technical design of the system. Part V of the book is devoted to describing this activity in detail.

- *Developing the system's models and analytical database.* Models are usually a more important factor in a DSS than in an MIS. Part IV of the book is devoted to describing this activity in detail.

The way in which these activities are carried out for an ODSS differs greatly from the way they are carried out for an MIS. These differences will be spelled out in Part III of the book. The differences primarily relate to the fact that development of an ODSS is an iterating, evolutionary, adaptive process, while most MIS are developed using a more linear process.

3.   Installing and operating the system. This stage includes:

- Installing the physical system.
- Programming the system's computer models. (For clarity we sometimes refer to the mathematical specifications as models and their implementations as computer models.) In this activity, the application programs are coded and tested.
- Creating the database. This activity refers to the collection and conversion to machine-readable form all of the data required by the system.
- Documenting the computer models and database.
- Training users.

At the completion of each activity, formal approval sign-offs are usually required from the users as well as from the leader of the project. Each activity also results in formal documentation. The SDLC can follow an iterative assurance strategy, in which review may result in returning to a previous step (e.g., review after the physical design might result in going back to prepare a new conceptual design), but the iteration is normally a negative indication (e.g., an indication of an error or problem) rather than a positive indication of an adaptive, improving system. See Davis and Olson [1985] for a more complete description of each of the stages and activities of the SDLC approach.

The approach that we recommend to building an ODSS combines the structure of the SDLC method with the adaptive/iterative features of prototyping. The approach is discussed in Chapter 3.

1.5 TRADITIONAL DECISION SUPPORT SYSTEMS AND ORGANIZATIONAL DSSs

1.5.1 Decision Support Systems

We define a Decision Support System (DSS) to be an interactive IT-based system that helps decisionmakers utilize data and models in making their decisions.

The basic paradigm for a traditional DSS (see Sprague and Carlson [1982, p. 29]) is that it consists of three major components:

- model base
- database
- human interface

each of which interacts with the other and with the decisionmaker. Thus, the set of integrated computer-based tools that form a DSS (see Fig. 1.2) can be viewed as consisting of:

- a model base and software to manage it
- a database and software to manage it
- a dialog system that manages the interaction between the user and the model base and database.

The purpose of a DSS is to improve the quality of the user's decisionmaking. This means improving either the decisionmaker's efficiency or effectiveness. Improving the efficiency of decisionmaking means performing a given task in the decisionmaking process more quickly or with fewer resources (i.e., faster or cheaper decisions). Improving the effectiveness of decisionmaking means improving the quality of the outcome of the decisionmaking process (i.e., better decisions).

Each of the words that make up the phrase "decision support system" is critical to understanding what a DSS is. "Decision" indicates that a DSS is problem oriented. Its success will be measured in terms of its contribution to the decisionmaking process.

"Support" reminds us that a DSS is a decision *aid*. That is, it aids (but does not replace) the decisionmaker. The user is always in control and guides the solution process. As Thierauf [1988, p. 35] put it:

> The main thrust of decision support systems is on decisions in which there is sufficient structure for the computer and quantitative models to be of value but where the user's judgment is essential. DSS extends

the range and capability of a user's decision process to improve *effectiveness*. The relevance for the user is the creation of a supportive tool, under personal control, that does not attempt to redefine objectives, automate the decision process, or impose solutions directly. With DSS, the user employs the computer's capabilities as an extension of her or his mind.

A DSS is a decision aid for decisionmakers much as an x ray or blood test is a decision aid for doctors. X rays provide a better basis for a doctor's exercise of his or her judgment. A DSS provides this better basis by (among other things) clarifying the problem, suggesting alternatives, and predicting their consequences.

Even though they have been primarily designed to support the selection and evaluation of alternative decisions, it is possible to design a DSS to support any or all of the steps of the decisionmaking process. For example, a DSS can be used to help identify a problem situation that requires a response. It can also be used to help monitor the performance of a chosen alternative.

The word "system" in the term DSS reminds us that a DSS integrates a user with machines, data, and models. We should also comment on two of the other words that are found in our definition of a decision support system. First, the word "models." Models are crucial elements in a DSS (particularly in an organizational DSS). They are one of the key elements that distinguish DSSs from traditional MISs. (As Ariav and Ginzberg [1985] say: "The mechanism for explicit management of models and modeling activity is what distinguishes DSS from more traditional information-processing systems. The ability to invoke, run, change, combine, and inspect models is a key capability in DSS and therefore a core service.") Models provide ways of understanding and organizing data (e.g., statistical models), evaluating alternatives (descriptive models) and suggesting reasonable decisions (prescriptive models). They are so important that we devote a large portion of the book to them (see Part IV).

Second, the word "interactive." Man-machine interaction (and interactive computer graphics) is a vital part of a DSS. It helps make the system easy to use ("user friendly"), helps make the results easy to understand and to display, and enables the decisionmaker to control the solution process.

To sum up, the following attributes of a DSS distinguish it from a traditional management information system. A DSS is:

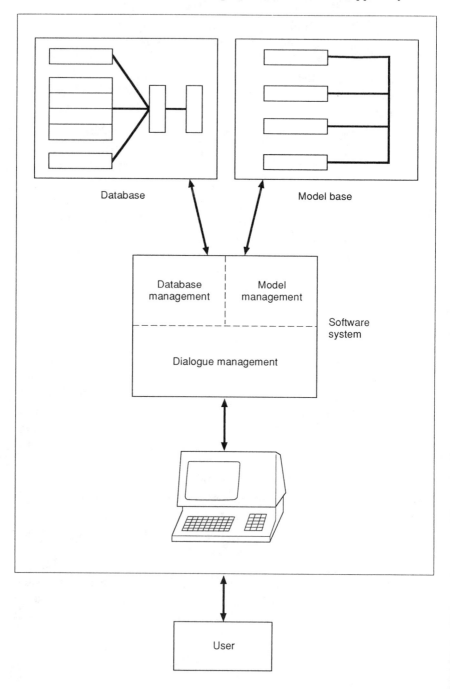

Fig. 1.2 Components of a Traditional DSS

- decision focused
- easy to use by noncomputer people interactively
- user initiated and controlled
- emphasizes flexibility, adaptability, and quick response
- combines the use of models and analytic techniques with traditional data access and retrieval functions.

1.5.2   Organizational Decision Support Systems

In Section 1.1, we defined an ODSS to be "a DSS that is used by individuals or groups at several workstations in more than one organizational unit who make varied (interrelated but autonomous) decisions using a common set of tools." It brings to bear the full array of information technology to facilitate the work of the organization. What distinguishes an ODSS from other types of information systems is its focus on decisionmaking. It is designed to coordinate decisionmaking and disseminate decisions across functional areas, hierarchical layers, and geographically dispersed units. It provides a mechanism for a large, geographically dispersed, decentralized organization to allow individual managers to make decisions within their domains while maintaining consistency with organizational goals and the decisions being made by other managers. In short, it provides distributed decision support to distributed decisionmaking.

Figure 1.1 shows the traditional decisionmaking pyramid in an organization. An ODSS is designed to assist all of the decisionmakers represented in the pyramid by facilitating the flow of information (from the top to the bottom, from the bottom to the top, and horizontally), and by providing decision-aiding models to each of the decisionmakers.

The need for an ODSS increases as the size of an organization grows and as its operations become decentralized and geographically dispersed. As Eom [1990] predicts, global decision support systems (one type of ODSS) "will emerge as a key element in management decisions and as an essential weapon against global competitors. The global DSS [will] integrate organizational decision making across functional fields, planning horizons, and national boundaries to create a coordinated global strategy."

If designed and used correctly, an ODSS can provide the glue that holds a large organization together and keeps its parts marching to the beat of the same drummer toward common goals. The two key factors for obtaining this outcome are (1) transmittal of consistent, timely information up and down the organizational hierarchy in forms that are appropriate to each decisionmaker and (2) a set of decision-aiding models that use this information and that are appropriate for the decisions being made by each decisionmaker.

As discussed in Part V of this book, the system's databases, database management system, and data administration are the keys to realizing factor 1. An ODSS requires that data be viewed as an organizational resource, not as an application resource (tied to a specific computer program, organizational unit, or decisionmaker). Viewing information as an application resource inhibits the ability to provide integrated information by allowing each application to stipulate its own standards for data. Databases must be defined that can be shared and that can support multiple applications. The *Information Engineering Management Guide* [Pacific Information Management, Inc., 1989] shows how an organization can set up an integrated information resource management system. Ozsu and Valduriez [1991] explain the data management and computer system choices that must be made in setting up and operating distributed database systems.

As discussed in Part IV of this book, the system's models and model management system are the keys to realizing factor 2. The models must be designed to address the particular problems of the individual decisionmakers. But the variables must be consistently defined and applied, and their current values and current constraints on possible solutions must be passed through the shared database. The models are the mechanism for helping the organization respond to changes in its environment and for exercising the control and coordination needed to direct the organization toward common goals.

1.5.3   Differences Between a TDSS and an ODSS

ODSSs are not simply big TDSSs. There are important differences, which lead to differences in how ODSSs should be designed, developed, and maintained. The main differences fall into the following five categories:

- purposes
- politics
- approach to building
- focus on functions
- components.

The first four categories are discussed in the remainder of this subsection. The components of an ODSS are discussed in Section 1.6.

PURPOSES

The primary purpose of a traditional decision support system (TDSS) is to improve the performance of an individual decisionmaker—to improve the quality of his or her decisionmaking by improving its effectiveness and efficiency. This is certainly one of the purposes of an ODSS. However, an ODSS serves other purposes that are broader and more far-reaching. A well-designed ODSS can benefit a multitude of organizational goals.

The performance of the organization can be enhanced if its decisionmakers share common data and models. An ODSS facilitates such sharing, thereby providing a means for communication and coordination among personnel at the same or different levels in the same organizational unit, and at the same or different levels across organizational boundaries. As soon as a decision is made (e.g., the list of Air Force occupations that will be offered a bonus), the database is updated and the latest information can begin to be used immediately by others in the organization. This helps to integrate and unify an organization, and improves control and consistency. It also improves the efficiency and effectiveness of organizational decisionmaking (in addition to individual decisionmaking).

Bidgoli [1989, p. 60] offers the example of a high-tech company that implemented a cost-based ODSS. Before implementation, different division managers provided different prices for a finished product. The establishment of an on-line cost-based ODSS significantly improved the interpersonal communication and the intergroup coordination of these executives. His conclusion is that, by providing comprehensive information regarding the entire organization, "the overall control of the organization, including control over costs, inventory, and personnel, will be improved."

In the Air Force case, discussed in detail in Chapter 2, before the Air Staff had an ODSS, different organizations used different models for projecting the future composition of the enlisted force. It was impossible to determine whether differences in the projections were due to different policies, data, or models. Now, when the different organizations use the same model and data, it is clear that differences in projections are due to differences in policies.

POLITICS

Because an ODSS involves the interaction of two or more organizational groups, it will necessarily involve organizational politics. This complicates the process of building the system. Since a TDSS is often built around a single decisionmaker and the system is meant primarily to provide cognitive support to that single individual, psychological issues (e.g., appropriate design of the user interface) are major concerns. An ODSS is more a political beast. The success or failure of an ODSS is largely dependent on how well the political issues were handled. That is why this book deals with political issues at great length.

The concept of a DSS is new; the idea of building an ODSS might encounter resistance and some managers might require education before the idea gains acceptance in an organization. Managers are familiar with the concepts of transaction processing and management information systems, but DSS has a set of unique properties (e.g., flexibility, user control, analytic capabilities, responsiveness), some of which may be unfamiliar. A TDSS is usually built around an enlightened user. Thus, little new education is required. In building an ODSS, at least one individual in the organization is likely to be encountered whose cooperation is essential, but who is unenlightened. Gaining the cooperation of such individuals is an important part of building an ODSS. Thus, a major difference between building a TDSS and building an ODSS is that in the former, the system must be sold to an individual; in ODSS development, the system must be sold to an organization.

Since an ODSS will affect the turfs of a much larger number of powerful people in an organization, attention must be given to political concerns in every stage of its development. Also, since an ODSS will take much longer to develop than a TDSS, support for building it must be a firm personal commitment from the top level of the organization, not just a commitment of resources. All parties involved must be prepared for the long haul.

Maintenance of political support for the project is as important as maintaining the system's database. Since the project will last for a long time, commitments can wane, alliances can lapse, leaders can come and go from various organizational units. To ensure the continued flow of resources and the ultimate acceptance of the system into user organizations, political acceptance of the ODSS must be lobbied for over and over during the development process. Interested parties at all levels must be briefed, their concerns answered, and their involvement obtained, over and over. The political aspects of building an ODSS are discussed more fully in Chapter 12.

Much of the job of maintaining political support will fall on the shoulders of the project leader. That is why the choice of project leader is so important (and more difficult than the choice of project leader for a traditional MIS development project). We discuss this and other management issues in Section 3.2.

APPROACH TO BUILDING

A TDSS is almost invariably looked on as a single entity, the building of which can be approached on an *ad hoc* basis. However, an ODSS might better be viewed as being composed of two separate but related systems. First, we have the models themselves—sets of mathematical equations designed to produce a variety of results based on a range of parameter values determined by its users. Second, is the physical system, which includes all of the other software and hardware elements of the system—computers, networks, data entry/display services, printers, jobs, programs, data sets, interfaces, etc., which provide the mechanism for transforming the mathematical equations into useful products, such as on-line computer displays or printed reports. Because of its size and complexity, an ODSS should not be built on an *ad hoc* basis. It demands a more structured and disciplined approach to development.

The development of an ODSS can be thought of as somewhat analogous to the production of a new line of automobiles. In such a case, a design effort occurs that does not produce the actual cars themselves, but a precise set of specifications that describe in great detail all of the pieces that make up the automobile and how they fit together, as well as defining the various combinations of models, options, and colors. This effort may also lead to the building of mock-ups in the form of prototypes to test the design concepts for their validity and provide a physical representation of what the final product may look like. A second effort is required to design and build, or modify, the factory to manufacture the production version of that particular line of automobiles. It encompasses processes that relate not only to the actual assembly of the cars, but an entire infrastructure that, among other things, must ensure that the appropriate components are manufactured, made available, and moved to the production line for assembly at exactly the right moment to produce the car that has been specified by a particular order.

An ODSS development project might consist of two development teams: first, a team of mathematical modelers who work with the users and the builders to specify the form and content of the individual models making up the system and validate their work through the user of working prototypes of those models. Second, a team of information engineers who build the information system that links those models together and provides the data and other elements and processes necessary to control and assemble the information produced by the system.

Just as in the case of producing a new automobile, the more closely these two teams work, the more closely the final system will match the design concept and meet the needs of the users. Close cooperation also means that the concept and the implementation will more likely be in harmony with each other, i.e., objectives such as ease of use, operational efficiency, and maintainability will be incorporated in model design.

There are situations in which the two teams may function so closely that they almost become a single entity for a specific purpose, such as the development of the conceptual design or creation of the user interfaces for the system. Each team may be looking for different things from these tasks, but much is gained by combining separate objectives within a single endeavor. There is also a need for project management and a clearly defined process for building the system.

We describe a recommended approach to building an ODSS in Part III of the book. Part IV deals with the development of the system of models. Part V deals with designing and building the physical system.

FOCUS ON FUNCTIONS

Another major difference between a TDSS and an ODSS is that the focus in the development of a TDSS is usually on the individual decisionmaker, while that of an ODSS is on the functions to be performed. This is the view of a TDSS that Wagner [1981] refers to as Executive Mind Support. According to him, "Executive Mind Support is the intimate coupling of a system (a DSS) with the mind of an executive, with close rapport and two-way communication, for the executive's own purposes and on his own terms. It is a special relationship by which the system actually supports and extends the manager's own thinking processes." The ODSS is part of a unified, organizational approach to problem solving. It must, therefore, be designed with a consistency and unity that is inconsistent with a focus on individual differences. Also, as Huber [1983, p. 575] suggests, each function in an ODSS is likely to have different users over time, as job incumbents move through a position. "Thus a flexible rather than an idiosyncratically constrained design seems called for." In the words of Carlson [1983, p. 19], "if a DSS is to support varying styles, skills, and knowledge, it should not attempt to enforce or to capture a particular pattern."

Thus, for the Air Force's Enlisted Force Management Project (EFMP), the conceptual design document was devoted almost exclusively to a functional description of the system—the constituent computer models and their interconnections. The user interfaces were designed in conjunction with the incumbents in the user positions, but the idea was to make sure that all of the information needed by a person in that position would be available in an understandable and usable format. Screens were designed assuming "average" user behavior, so the models would be useful to practically any user (of course, the screens can be changed if a new user does not like something). Because of officer rotation, several of the models have already had several "owners."

By focusing on functions, the builder of on ODSS can avoid two other pitfalls that can lead to the failure of the system. First, we must consider the pitfall of designing the system to reflect current organizational responsibilities and interactions. Some systems are designed too closely around an existing organizational configuration. Organizations change frequently (e.g., departments move around on the organization chart), but the functions that have to be carried out within the organization are more stable. So, if models are designed for functions—not organizational units—use of the models can be transferred to new organizational units when the functions are transferred. At the beginning of the EFMP, the Directorate of Manpower and Organization (see Fig. 1.3) reported to the same three-star general as all of the other organizations using the Enlisted Force Management System (EFMS). In the middle of the project, the "manpower" functions were split off from the "personnel" functions and assigned to a different three-star general. This had no effect on the design or implementation of the EFMS.

Second, focusing on functions can avoid the pitfall of using the implementation of a system for rationalizing decisionmaking as an excuse for trying to rationalize the structure of the organization. In studying the existing system during stage 1 of the system development process, it will probably become clear that improvements in the efficiency and effectiveness of decisionmaking can be made by changing the structure of the organization. It is tempting to write a report that recommends that this be done in addition to the construction of an ODSS, and that the design of the ODSS be made dependent on the new structure. Unless the tasking for stage 1 explicitly includes a requirement for producing recommendations on organizational design, this is something to steer clear of. Focusing on functions accomplishes this. The first RAND project leader on the EFMP recommended a consolidation of the three directorates responsible for manpower and personnel decisionmaking as part of the EFMS design. As a result, the general in charge of one of the directorates tried to cancel the entire project. (A separate report making some suggestions for organizational changes might be submitted, but this should not be tied to the ODSS development effort.)

1.6 COMPONENTS OF AN ORGANIZATIONAL DECISION SUPPORT SYSTEM

By "components" of an ODSS we mean its functional breakdown, not its modules or formal subsystems. Three of the components of ODSS are the same as those of a TDSS, although there may be big differences in how the components are designed and used. The DSS literature (see, for example, Turban [1988, Section 3.5]) identifies three major system elements and three major functions necessary for a TDSS (see Fig. 1.2):

Elements	Functions
User	Dialogue management
Models	Model management
Data	Database management

An ODSS requires two additional elements and functions:

Network	Communication
Model runs (cases)	Case management

The basic paradigm for an ODSS (see Fig. 1.4) would have one or more users with interactive computer workstations linked to a mainframe computer or one or more "servers" through a local-area network or wide-area network (using telephone lines, satellites, etc.). The dialogue management subsystem would allow the user to interact with both the database (through the database management subsystem) and an interlinked system of models (through the model management subsystem). A case management subsystem would keep track of the models and data that are used.

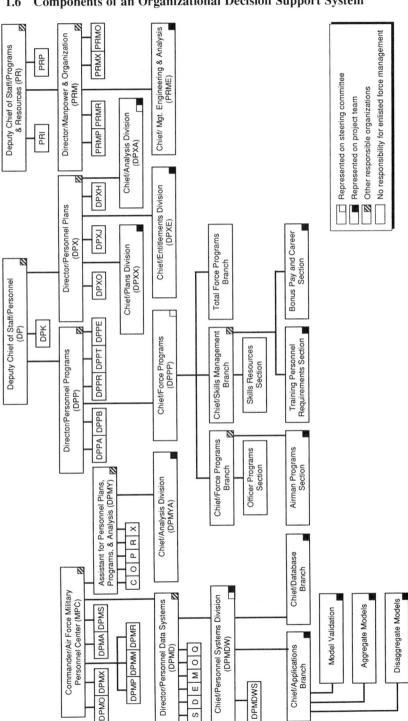

Fig. 1.3 Organizations Responsible for Enlisted Force Management in the USAF

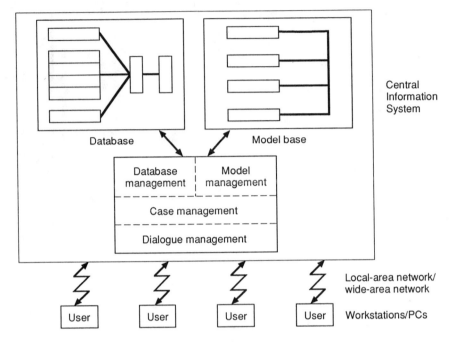

Fig. 1.4 **Components of an ODSS**

The primary differences between this paradigm and the paradigm for a TDSS are that we assume there will be many users and that the users will be geographically distributed (perhaps even in different cities). We have also added a case management subsystem to the traditional DSS paradigm. But this addition would probably help a TDSS user as much as it would help an ODSS user. We discuss each of these components in the following subsections.

1.6.1 Dialogue Management

The first principle of decision support systems is to place the user in control. The dialogue management component of an ODSS embodies the specialized functionality necessary to handle the system's interaction with its users. The dialogue between the user and the system establishes the context for user inputs, the environment for running models, and the framework in which outputs are presented. Poorly designed user interfaces are one of the major reasons why managers fail to take advantage of the power of computers in their decisionmaking. As Brennan and Elam [1986] have said, a DSS "requires a user interface that allows managers to define models and to view their results in a framework—a conceptual model—that makes sense to them."

There are three parts to the dialogue management system:

1. the hardware devices (e.g., keyboard, light pen, mouse, screen)
2. the user interface, which includes the semantics (e.g., user commands) and the style (e.g., menus, command language)
3. the software that provides the necessary (two-way) translation between users' vocabularies and the system's internal modeling and data access vocabulary.

We discuss some elements of good user interfaces in Chapter 17. For additional information, see Stohr and White [1982].

It is generally unnecessary to develop special software for dialogue management. Most DSS generators include adequate capabilities for creating effective dialogue management systems. This is fortunate, since, if a DSS generator is not used, the largest costs in developing the software for a DSS are likely to be for the dialogue management system. According to Sprague and Carlson [1982, p. 209], about 60 percent of the code written for a DSS they were associated with was for the dialogue component, and about 75 percent of the changes made to the system over a four-year period were changes to that code.

1.6.2   Model Management

As already mentioned, the central role of models and provision of mechanisms for the management of models are what distinguish decision support systems from more traditional information processing systems. Any support beyond direct access to raw data requires the application of a model.

Following Turban [1988, Section 3.7], we view the model management system (MMS) of a DSS as composed of four elements. These elements, their relationships to each other, and their interface with the other DSS components are illustrated in Fig. 1.5. The elements are:

• *Model base*, which consists of the quantitative models that provide the analytical capabilities in the DSS. We discuss issues related to the design, development, testing, and updating of models in Part IV.

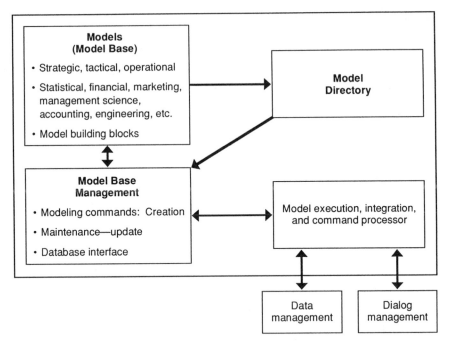

Fig. 1.5 The Structure of Model Management

- *Model base management system (MBMS)*, which integrates the models and makes them easy to use. We discuss functions and capabilities of an MBMS below.
- *Model directory*, which is a catalog of the models in the model base. Its main function is to answer questions about the availability and capabilities of the models.
- *Model execution, integration, and command processor*, which controls the actual running of the models, combines the operations of several models when needed, and is the interface between the MMS and the other components of the DSS.

According to Turban [1988, p. 85] and Sprague and Carlson [1982, p. 33], the MBMS should provide the following capabilities:

- Facilitate the creation of new models.
- Allow users to manipulate the models so they can conduct experiments and sensitivity analyses.
- Interrelate models with appropriate linkages through the database.
- Manage the model base with functions analogous to database management (e.g., store, access, run, update, link, catalog, and query).

For example, the MBMS should give users the ability to invoke a model, modify it, change its parameters, specify its inputs, run it, save it, and (in some cases) delete it. The MBMS can also include access to model building blocks, such as random number generators and regression subroutines.

Miller and Katz [1986] list some principles for MBMS design, which include:

- *Flexibility*: This is the ability to change models without making extensive modifications to large programs and with little danger of introducing errors. (They suggest using many small models, called modules, instead of one big one model.)
- *Separation of modeling and analysis*: Procedures to analyze and display results should be kept separate from the model. This is why the MBMS is separate from the models.

Miller and Katz [1986] also list seven steps for using a model management system, which are useful for clarifying the specific capabilities that a model management system should have. The steps, which are carried out by various combinations of the elements of the model management system, are:

1. Introduce new models (or modules) into the model base.
2. Select appropriate modules to comprise a model. (This assumes that a model to be executed is a combination of several smaller modules.)
3. Arrange for information transfers among the modules and for controlling their execution.
4. Locate the data needed by the modules in the database and arrange for its extraction and transmission to the modules.
5. Identify the user's specific inputs and arrange for them to be transmitted to the model.
6. Run the model and arrange for saving the inputs and outputs.
7. Analyze the inputs and outputs.

As Sprague and Carlson [1982, pp. 258–260] point out, models have generally not lived up to their potential for improving decisionmaking by managers. They say that most reasons for the nonuse of models by managers can be traced to "the lack of a set of integrated models and an easy way to manage their use in the decision-making process." Brennan and Elam [1986] also point out that improving the quality of the models would increase the quality of the solutions produced by a DSS. The goal of Part IV of this book is to improve the quality of models used in a DSS.

1.6.3 Database Management

The database management component of a DSS provides access to the raw material needed for decisionmaking. Following Turban [1988, Section 3.6], we see the data management element of a DSS as composed of four elements (see Fig. 1.6):

- *Database*, which is a collection of interrelated data organized in such a way that it corresponds to the needs and structure of the organization and can be used by many persons and many models for many applications. The system need not have a single, integrated database. Each model could have its own data files. But the data must be consistent, centrally managed, easy to access, and easy to update.
- *Database Management System* (DBMS), which provides the mechanism for the creation, storage, retrieval, and updating of the database. The DBMS also provides data security.
- *Query facility*, which accepts requests for data from other DSS components, determines how these requests can be filled, formulates the detailed requests, and returns the results to the issuer of the request.
- *Data directory* (sometimes called the *data dictionary*), which is a catalog of all the data in the database. Its main function is to answer questions about the availability of data items, their source, and their meaning in order to facilitate the sharing of data among applications.

We discuss issues related to the design and development of the data management component of an ODSS in Chapter 15.

1.6.4 Communications

The single most important distinction between a TDSS and an ODSS is the linkage among the various users. A TDSS generally involves a single user. In an ODSS, multiple users are making interrelated but autonomous decisions. Without an ODSS, the shared information needed for decisionmaking would be passed among the decisionmakers through memos, telephone calls, meetings, etc. In an ODSS, individual decisionmakers make their local databases accessible to each other. The mecha-

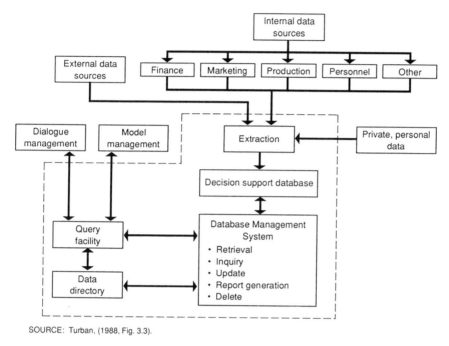

SOURCE: Turban, (1988, Fig. 3.3).

Fig. 1.6 The Database Management Subsystem

nism for such interconnection and coordination is the local-area network (LAN), where users are generally connected by dedicated equipment (e.g., cable) or a wide-area network, which utilizes general-purpose technologies such as telephones, satellites, and microwave transmission. Malone and Rockart [1991] refer to organizations that are restructured to be more interactive and coordination-intensive as "networked organizations." Rash [1991] explains that these organization-wide networks (which he calls "enterprise networks") create a "platform for the centralization and control of vital corporate data while providing access for people throughout an organization."

ODSSs are, therefore, one type of distributed computing system. (According to Ozsu and Valduriez [1991], a distributed computing system is "a number of autonomous processing elements (not necessarily homogeneous) that are interconnected by a computer network and that cooperate in performing their assigned tasks.") The implications of distributed computing for design of an ODSS's hardware and software architecture are discussed in Ananda and Srinivasan [1990].

More specifically, ODSSs make extensive use of a model of distributed computing called the client/server model. Francis [1990] distinguishes three styles of client/server computing, any or all of which can be effectively used in an ODSS, depending on the particular situation:

- *Client/server computing*, which splits the processing of an application between a front-end portion (local data manipulation and user interface), which is executed on a PC or workstation, and a back-end portion (database manipulation and numerical intensive processing), which is executed on a server (mainframe, minicomputer, or dedicated server).
- *Cooperative processing*, which spreads data for a given application across several systems. This style makes efficient use of all systems on a network and makes data available to any user connected to it.
- *Distributed computing*, which allows an application to run on more than one system—a PC and a mainframe, for example.

The EFMS makes use of client/server and distributed computing.

1.6.5   Case Management

A single user of an ODSS will often run a model many times, each time with inputs that are only slightly different from the previous run. He or she will generally create large amounts of output and many computer files. In the past, the effort to create input data files, to keep track of runs made, and to catalog output data files overwhelmed the user. As a result, his use of the DSS gradually decreased. It has recently been recognized by builders of DSSs that the user needs help in all of these areas. So, just as DBMSs were developed to manage large databases and MBMSs are being developed to manage systems containing large numbers of models, case management systems (CMSs) are being developed to help the user who wants to make large numbers of runs.

We define a case to be a specific run of a computer model. The case is identified by a case name. A case includes a specification of all of the input data used in the run (names of data files, parameters supplied by user), the names of the output files generated, and (optionally) a brief description of the run.

A CMS performs three main functions:

1. It acts as an accounting system for the runs made by a user, facilitating the creation, deletion, copying, documenting, and cataloging of model cases.
2. It provides the user with simple ways to modify the input data for a given model from one run to the next (by specifying changes only), and keeps track of the differences. As a result, it can also report on the differences in inputs between two runs.
3. It facilitates the comparison of outputs from various runs of the model.

A good CMS can provide the user with clarity and control of what he or she is doing. An example of a CMS is found in a DSS package called MathPro. MathPro,[1] which was developed by MathPro, Inc., is a DSS for solving mathematical programming problems. In MathPro, the case manager establishes a hierarchical (tree-structured) case bank for each distinct model/user combination. In this hierarchy, each case is subordinate to a parent case, logically "inherits" all elements from its parent, and physically contains only elements that differ from those of its parent. Each case is named, time stamped, and documented.

1.7 CENTRALIZED SUPPORT FOR DECENTRALIZED ORGANIZATIONS

Organizations come in a variety of shapes and sizes. ODSSs can be designed to fit the needs of any of them. For example, some organizations are pyramidal hierarchies, with a CEO on top and expanding numbers of managers and workers at progressively lower levels. Control is imposed from the top; middle managers convey orders downward and carry information upward. In such organizations computers have been primarily used for data processing and large-scale repetitive functions, such as the management of routine operations (e.g., production planning). ODSSs can be used to speed the conveyance of orders and information. They can also be used to provide decisionmaking tools to middle and lower level managers that allow them to make their decisions autonomously, but in a coherent, consistent manner.

Hierarchical organizations are increasingly being replaced by new, more flexible, transnational organizations, which Toffler [1970] referred

---

[1] MathPro is available from MathPro, Inc. 2501 M Street, NW, Suite 550, Washington, D.C. 20037.

to as "adhocracies," Hedlund and Rolander [1990] call "hetarchical" organizations, Applegate [1988] calls "cluster organizations," and Reich [1991] calls "global webs." Such organizations are international partnerships of skilled people who work in small teams or clusters anywhere in the world, whose insights and talents are combined with one another to solve business problems or define processes, and whose teams may disband when their job is finished. Coordination is the key to the success of such organizations. Advanced information technologies, such as computers, facsimile machines, satellites, high-resolution monitors, and modems, provide the glue that holds such organizations together and coordinate and facilitate their operations. Such organizations would be unable to function without them.

Advanced information technologies also provide the necessary mechanisms for decisionmaking in these organizations. Geographically dispersed lower and middle level managers can use computer-assisted communication technologies to stay informed about the organization's overall situation and about its current problems, policies, and priorities. As a result, these managers can make better, less parochial decisions than they could if such technologies were not available.

According to Huber [1990], in large organizations high-level managers are encouraging the decentralization of decisionmaking because of their "desire to decrease the time for organizational units to respond to problems or the desire to provide autonomy for subordinates." After observing the implementation of networked personal computers in the General Motors' Environmental Activities Staff, Foster and Flynn [1984, pp. 231–232] concluded that "from the former hierarchy of position power there is developing instead a hierarchy of competency . . . . Power and resources now flow increasingly to the obvious centers of competence instead of to the traditional hierarchical loci."

Placing responsibility and authority in the hands of those at the working level, who have knowledge and enthusiasm for the tasks at hand, can be very rewarding for the organization. But it can also be very risky. The lower level managers need direction and guidance. There must be a mechanism for assuring that the decisions being made by the many different persons in the many different locations are consistent with each other and with the overall goals of the organization. An organizational decision support system provides such a mechanism—enabling the flexibility and responsiveness of a decentralized organization to be combined with the integration and control of a centralized organization.

The way in which an ODSS can offer both flexibility and control involves taking advantage of several of the combined benefits of advanced information technologies, including the ability for geographically dispersed individuals to access the same databases, the rapid transmission of information, and the ubiquity of microcomputers. In this setting, high-level managers use aggregate models for making decisions that reflect overall organizational goals and that provide guidance to lower level managers. The resulting information and guidance do not dictate the decisions to be made by the lower level managers, but they do limit the options that are available them. These parameters (e.g., costs, targets, constraints) are instantly and (if desired) automatically passed to the lower levels through the ODSS database. The models that the lower level managers use for their decisionmaking will then take these parameters into account and will produce results that are consistent with them. As a result, the lower level managers throughout the organization will be given considerable freedom to make decisions in their areas of responsibility, but their decisions will reflect a shared vision, shared goals, and common purpose.[2]

Drucker [1988] compares this decisionmaking process to what happens in an information-based organization like a hospital, where there are many specialists and little middle management. A good deal of the work is done in *ad hoc* teams as required by an individual patient's diagnosis and condition. The specialists cannot be told how to do their work, but their performance is based on management's clearly-stated goals for the enterprise and for each specialist, and on "organized feedback that compares results with these performance expectations so that every member can exercise self-control."

Some researchers (see, for example, Kaula and Dumdum [1991] and King and Star [1990]) argue that an ODSS should be designed using an "open system" architecture, in which each user's autonomous subsystem would communicate with the others and would share data, but in which there would be no attempt at global consistency. "Consequently, there is perpetual inconsistency and incompleteness among various subsystem knowledge bases" [Kaula and Dumdum, 1991, p. 169]. It is certainly difficult to build a consistent system. The cost of doing so should be balanced against the desired benefits.

---

[2] This process is similar to the way George Dantzig [1963, p. 462] envisioned the decomposition principle of linear programming being used for "central planning without complete information at the center."

This tradeoff depends to a large extent on whether the decisions being made are tightly or loosely coupled. As discussed by Swanson [1990], if the decisions are tightly coupled, few such constraints tend to exist, and a more open system would be suitable. Tightly coupled decisions are more likely in pyramidal organizations, such as the U.S. Air Force. Loosely coupled decisions are more likely in an environment of voluntary bottom-up collaboration, such as in a brokerage house.

In any event, it is not an all or nothing decision. There will always be areas in which users operate with their own programs and data. In this book, we focus on those functions of the organization for which global consistency is important. The remaining functions (and databases) can be viewed as being autonomous TDSSs that are loosely connected for purposes of sharing information (with no guarantees concerning the quality of that information). Global consistency does not mean tight central control. Each user has the autonomy within his or her area of responsibility that he or she always had. But the user is supplied with the guidance (and data and models) to enable him or her to operate effectively and efficiently while making decisions that are consistent with the goals of the organization.

PART II

Chapter 2	Building an Enlisted Force Management System for the United States Air Force

Before proceeding with a discussion of the process of building an ODSS, we divert to a discussion of a particular ODSS that was designed and developed during much of the 1980s by the authors: the Enlisted Force Management System (EFMS). Much of our later discussion of ODSS design is illustrated by examples from the development of the EFMS, so an introduction to its concepts and terminology is necessary at this point.

2.1 ENLISTED FORCE MANAGEMENT

Effective management of its enlisted force is of increasing importance to the U.S. Air Force as it tries to carry out its mission in the face of higher costs and constrained budgets. The enlisted component of approximately 415,000 airmen spread over 369 occupations (identified by Air Force Specialty Codes [AFSCs]) and nine pay grades (labeled E–1 through E–9) constitutes more than 80 percent of the Air Force's active-duty manpower and accounts for expenditures of more than $13 billion per year. Planning for, programming, budgeting, and managing these resources to provide enough of the right kinds of people in the right grades and occupations in the right places at the right times to carry out the Air Force's missions is a

39

monumental task. This task is the responsibility of the Deputy Chief of Staff for Personnel, Headquarters, U.S. Air Force, and the Director, Manpower and Organization, Headquarters, U.S. Air Force.

Management of the enlisted force involves making decisions about force structure, promotion policies, and the procurement, assignment, training, compensation, separation, and retirement of personnel. In 1981, when the Enlisted Force Management Project (EFMP) began, these decisions were being made by the Air Staff using tools that had both conceptual and operational shortcomings. The set of models being used was called TOPCAP (Total Objective Plan for Career Airman Personnel).

2.1.1   TOPCAP

TOPCAP was approved by Office of the Secretary of Defense in May 1971. It was the first comprehensive computerized system for supporting enlisted force planning and programming activities of any of the military services. TOPCAP is both a management philosophy and a set of computerized management models that translate that philosophy into practice. Under the EFMS, the TOPCAP philosophy remains; the models are changed.

One of the key elements of the TOPCAP philosophy is a visible career progression system. Until 1981 the system provided for equal selection opportunity (ESO) in all occupations. That is, the probability of being promoted out of a given grade would be identical in all occupations and independent of grade authorizations in individual occupations. A high-year-of-tenure (HYT) policy (specifying the highest year of service an airman is permitted to attain and still remain on active duty in a grade) was established for the five highest grades. In October 1981, ESO was modified to allow slightly faster promotion rates in some critical skills.

TOPCAP includes two mechanisms for controlling the occupation structure: establishment of career entry quotas by AFSC and centralized retraining. In the early TOPCAP years, retraining was voluntary for all personnel beyond the first enlistment point. However, ESO is incompatible with authorizations based on requirements, because authorizations and continuation rates vary by specialty. As overages and shortages in higher skill personnel have developed over time, more aggressive retraining programs have been implemented.

TOPCAP was designed for conditions of relative stability. But, since its implementation in 1971, the environment in which it has had to operate has changed considerably. The political environment has seen a change from enlistments in the face of a Selective Service draft to enlistments into an All-Volunteer Force. The economic environment has changed from one of relative stability to one of wide variations in unemployment rates and inflation. The technological environment has seen spectacular gains in raw computing power and the widespread introduction of microcomputers.

The TOPCAP models and their operational environment did not change with the times. For example, our examination of the system as it was operating in 1982 revealed the following systemic and modeling problems.

- *Multiple computers.* The TOPCAP models were spread over three geographically dispersed third-generation, large mainframe computer systems,[3] with no direct (computer-to-computer) links. This led to time delays and database management problems.
- *Lack of system integration and consistency.* The data and assumptions were different in the different models.
- *Time delays.* The information flows and data management procedures in TOPCAP often resulted in long time delays. (For example, magnetic tapes were sent through the mail from one computer system to another.)
- *Manual data manipulation.* The reports produced by the computer programs sometimes did not contain the specific information desired by the users. As a result, users made manual calculations to obtain the desired information, which led to mistakes and additional time delays.
- *Little documentation and maintenance.* Documentation for the TOPCAP models was largely nonexistent and there was no central group responsible for maintaining all of the models. As a result, the models were rarely updated to reflect changing situations.
- *Inadequate attention to personnel costs.* Practically none of the TOPCAP models considered personnel costs.
- *Future loss rates based solely on past rates.* There is an implicit assumption in the TOPCAP models that future loss patterns will be the same as the patterns during the past year. The system included no routinely used models for predicting the effects of policy changes or

---

[3]The computers were located in the Pentagon, at Randolph Air Force Base (San Antonio, Texas), and at the San Antonio Data Services Center (San Antonio, Texas). They included Honeywell and IBM mainframes.

the effect of external conditions on loss rates. Loss rates depend on such things as basic compensation, bonuses, promotion opportunities, retirement options, and civilian opportunities. TOPCAP provided no support for the analyst trying to assess, for example, the effects of a change in bonuses or in the unemployment rate on loss rates.

• *Limited gaming capabilities.* One of the most important activities of personnel planners and programmers is to examine the implications of alternative parameters and policies. However, many of the TOPCAP models were difficult to use in this manner.

The RAND Corporation was therefore asked to take a fresh look at the Air Force's approach to enlisted force management and to provide a conceptual and mathematical design for a new Enlisted Force Management System (EFMS) that would overcome the deficiencies and enhance the capabilities of TOPCAP.

The following subsections provide a brief introduction to the activities related to management of the enlisted force that the EFMS will be supporting.

2.1.2   Activities Related to Enlisted Force Management

Enlisted force management embraces all activities that relate to the supply of and demand for enlisted personnel. For simplicity, the activities can be viewed as beginning with the determination of the manpower ("spaces") needed to accomplish the service's missions and ending with the assignment of personnel to each of the positions ("matching faces to spaces"). The activities include:

• *Requirements determination.* Determination of the levels and types of manpower required to carry out the Air Force's mission objectives, for several years into the future, unconstrained by either budget or the personnel inventory.

• *Authorization management.* Determination of personnel assignment targets by (among other dimensions) AFSC and grade, based on applying constraints (e.g., budget) to the unconstrained manpower requirements.

- *Personnel planning*. The set of activities that determine the policies under which the enlisted force will be recruited, trained, promoted, and separated.

- *Personnel programming*. The set of activities that determine the quantity of and schedule for accessions, initial training, reclassification (of occupational specialty), retraining, bonuses, promotions, reenlistments, and separations. We divide these these activities into two groups: (1) skills management, and (2) aggregate programming and oversight. Skills management relates to programming decisions at the AFSC level. Aggregate programming and oversight is concerned with management of the force at a more aggregate level.

- *Personnel requisition and assignment*. Recruiting and enlisting airmen, and assigning them to authorized positions. These are management tasks that deal with individual enlisted members rather than with aggregates.

- *Total force planning*. Planning for the entire enlisted force, including the Reserves and Air National Guard, as well as for the active force.

The EFMS has been designed to support management activities in authorization management and personnel planning and programming. Although it is technically feasible to develop an integrated system to support all of the above activities, it is not necessarily worthwhile. Among the many reasons for not including all the activities within the scope of the Air Force's new EFMS are: (1) Some of the activities are already well supported by existing systems (e.g., personnel requisition and assignment) and (2) the well-known problems of developing and implementing large, multifunction, multiuser distributed data processing systems.

To assure that enlisted force management activities are carried out in an integrated and consistent manner, the EFMS includes manual and computer interfaces with other enlisted force management activities. For example, the system reserves data on manpower authorizations from an entirely different management system, it receives data on the current inventory of airmen from the Air Force's transaction-based personnel system (which maintains data on individual airmen), and it supplies trained personnel requirements to a computerized system that helps manage the training pipeline.

Since the EFMS will be used to illustrate many of the points being made throughout the remainder of the book, we provide brief summaries of each of the sets of management activities supported by the EFMS below. Additional information on the EFMS is provided by Carter *et al.* [1983] and Walker and the Enlisted Force Management Project Team [1991].

AUTHORIZATION MANAGEMENT

Authorizations result from applying constraints derived from funding decisions to the unconstrained manpower requirements. They specify the desired allocation of manpower at the command, base, and unit levels by occupational specialty, skill level, and grade. They are the targets for the personnel planning, programming, and assignment systems.

During the planning, programming, and budgeting (PPB) process, the unconstrained manpower requirements are constrained to fit within fiscal and end-strength limits placed on the Air Force by Congress, the Office of the Secretary of Defense, and the Office of Management and Budget. Among the outputs from this process are the levels of manpower authorized by major command (MAJCOM). The distribution of authorized manpower to units by occupation (identified by Air Force Specialty Code, or AFSC) and grade is then determined by the MAJCOMs. The EFMS uses an Authorization Projection Model (APM) to provide personnel planners and programmers with information about expected skill and grade allocations by AFSC before MAJCOM decisions are available.

PERSONNEL PLANNING

Personnel planning is the set of activities that determines the policies under which the enlisted force will be recruited, trained, promoted, and separated. The distinction between personnel planning and personnel programming relates primarily to the level of detail of policy specification rather than to organizational arrangement. Planning is responsible for policy guidance (usually at the total force level), and programming is responsible for the translation of the guidance into detailed program specifications for each occupational specialty and grade. Usually planning is concerned with a longer time frame than programming.

One of the major tasks of personnel planning is to choose a target force structure, including its composition by grade, year of service, and (sometimes) occupational specialty. Personnel programmers then use this target force to choose policy parameters. The EFMS includes several modules that can be used to determine and evaluate alternative target force structures.

PERSONNEL PROGRAMMING

Personnel programming is the set of activities that determines the quantity of and schedule for (1) accessions, (2) initial training, (3) reclassification (of occupational specialty), (4) retraining, (5) bonuses, (6) promotions, (7) reenlistments, and (8) separations. Except for initial training, these need to be determined for each of the 369 occupational specialties (AFSCs) by grade and year of service.

The models for personnel programming are the key modules of the EFMS. Detailed inventory projection models (IPMs) are at the heart of the personnel programming portion of the EFMS. The gap between the total number of enlisted personnel in the projected inventory and the target force helps to define accession goals. At the occupation-specific level, a comparison of projected inventories with targets may show the need to change bonus levels, retrain part of the force, or restrict reenlistments.

For example, a comparison by occupation of the target inventory to the projected inventory provides information that is compiled into the *Trained Personnel Requirements* (TPR), which is published quarterly. Most of the training requirements are subsequently filled through recruiting. Alternatives to recruiting for occupational shortages include increasing retention (e.g., through the use of reenlistment bonuses) and cross-training (i.e., training an airman in an overage specialty for a job in a shortage specialty). One way that personnel programmers encourage cross-training out of overage specialties into shortage specialties is to use a Career Job Reservation (CJR) system. CJR quotas are established for reenlistees in particular occupations. Airmen who wish to reenlist in one of these occupations but who are in excess of the CJR quota for the specialty must retrain into a specialty where a CJR is available (or leave the service).

The inventory projection models depend on predictions of reenlistment and loss rates, which are subject to considerable uncertainty. As inventory is monitored during the year, the original projections may turn out to be very wrong, in which case large changes in programs (e.g., early outs or accessions) must be made during the operating year. Because the programmer's options are limited by the short time horizon, the final program decisions may be inefficient compared with the decisions that would have been made if more accurate loss predictions had been available. Considerable effort on the EFMP was devoted to developing models that produced good predictions of reenlistments and losses. The models include the effect of changes in the environment (such as different bonuses), so programmers can evaluate the effect of policies given different assumptions about the future. Much of our experience in specifying, building, and testing these models is reflected in the contents of Part IV of this book.

2.1.3   The Life Cycle of an Airman

To understand the structure, concepts, and models of the EFMS, it is helpful to have a general knowledge of the life cycle of an airman,[4] from when he enters the force until he retires. The following is a broad overview, which is true for most but not all airmen.

Non-prior service (NPS) accessions sign an enlistment contract of four, five, or six years, which defines their first term of service. Their expiration of term of service (ETS) is the date they report for duty plus the length of their enlistment contract. Virtually all NPS accessions go through basic military training (BMT), which lasts about six weeks. (The exceptions are reservists who enlist in the active force.) Formal technical training follows BMT. Some skills receive no technical training (they are trained on the job), while the technical training for others takes more than a year.

Each enlistee has a five-digit Air Force Specialty Code (AFSC). The code designates the particular job the airman is trained to do. An airman's pay is based on his grade. The grades are E–1 through E–9, with E–5 through E–9 being non-commissioned officer (NCO) grades.

For promotion to any NCO grade, a minimum time in service (TIS) and time in grade (TIG) is required. For every grade there is also a maximum time in service, called the high year of tenure (HYT). The range between the minimum and maximum TIS is called the promotion zone.

Airmen who leave the service before the end of their term of service are classified under the general categories of attrition losses or early releases. Attrition includes such separation reasons as disability, hardship (including pregnancy), quality (e.g., poor performance in BMT), and death.

---

[4] The Air Force uses the term "airman" to refer to both male and female members of the service.

Three Air Force personnel programs release airmen before the end of their obligated term of service:

- Palace Chase: Early release for the purpose of joining the Air Reserve Force.
- Early Out: Early release during a fiscal year of airmen who otherwise would have left next fiscal year, for the purpose of reducing the earlier year's end strength.
- Rollup: Early release during a fiscal year of people who otherwise would have left in a later month during the same fiscal year, for the purpose of reducing total personnel costs in the year.

As an airman approaches his ETS, he has several choices. He can choose to leave the service (this is a loss to the Air Force called an ETS loss); he may ask to extend his term of service; or he may reenlist. A reenlistment is routinely granted to airmen in their second and later terms of service. However, the Air Force has quotas (called CJRs) for first termers who wish to reenlist in a given AFSC. If a CJR is not available in his specialty, the airman might be allowed (or even encouraged) to retrain into a related specialty for which a CJR is available. The CJR system gives enlisted force managers a way to shape the force or to meet end strength or budget constraints.

To stay in the force, airmen must continue the process of extending their contracts and/or reenlisting. In the EFMS, the force is divided into four categories of enlistment:

- first term
- second term (reenlisted once)
- career (reenlisted more than once but is not yet eligible for retirement)
- retirement eligible (airmen are eligible to retire and receive retirement benefits after 20 years of service).

To summarize the life cycle behaviors suggested above, Fig. 2.1 shows the pattern of losses for a representative cohort of 60,000 four-year enlistees who enter the service together. The abscissa of the figure is the number of full years of service (YOS) an airman in the cohort has already completed in the Air Force. For simplicity, the figure assumes that all reenlistments are for four-year terms, which include as part of the four years any period of extended service in the previous term. Nearly three-quarters of the airmen leave the service before the second term, and more

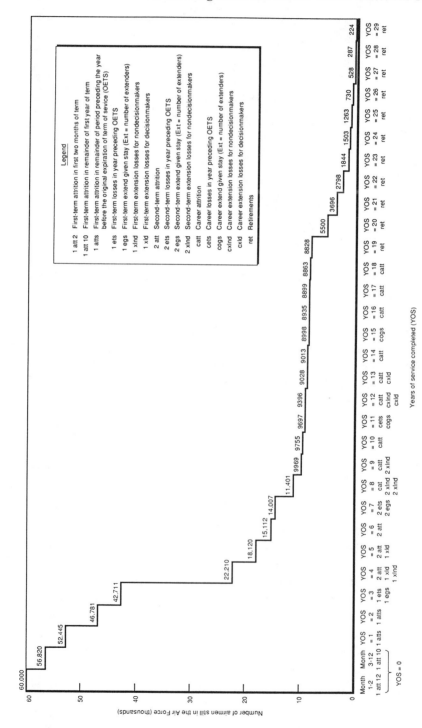

Fig. 2.1 Progression of a Representative Cohort of 60,000 Four-Year Enlistees

than half of these losses occur right at the end of the first term. In relative terms, losses at the end of the second term and at the 20-year point (first opportunity for retirement) are also especially large, with nearly a third of the airmen reaching each of these decision points choosing to leave the service.

2.1.4 Organizations Involved in Enlisted Force Management

The Air Force breaks the tasks related to enlisted force management into three functional areas: "manpower," which is associated with determining manpower requirements and allocating authorizations; "personnel," which is associated with managing the organization's personnel; and "training," which is associated with properly training (or retraining) Air Force personnel. The manpower functions at the Air Staff level are the responsibility of the Directorate of Manpower and Organization (PRM), which is one of the directorates reporting to the Deputy Chief of Staff for Programs and Resources (PR) (see Fig. 1.3). The Director of PRM is a major general (two stars). The head of PR is a lieutenant general (three stars).

Policymaking with respect to personnel planning and programming is carried out by both the Directorate of Personnel Plans (DPX) and the Directorate of Personnel Programs (DPP). Implementation of these plans and programs is the responsibility of the Air Force Military Personnel Center (AFMPC). These three organizations are led by major generals, who report to the Deputy Chief of Staff for Personnel (DP), a lieutenant general (see Fig. 1.3).

Most of the formal military and technical training is provided by the Air Training Command (ATC), which is led by a four-star general. The roles and interactions among these organizations, as they existed in 1980, are documented in Armstrong and Moore [1980]. As suggested above, the primary users of both the TOPCAP models and their replacements are the personnel planners in DPX (in particular, the analysts in DPXA), the personnel programmers in the Force Programs Division of DPP (in particular, those in the Airman Programs Section, the Training Personnel Requirements Section, and the Bonus Pay and Career Section), and members of the Management Engineering and Analysis Division of PRME.

2.2 THE ENLISTED FORCE MANAGEMENT PROJECT (EFMP)

In 1981, the Air Force's Deputy Chief of Staff for Manpower and Personnel asked RAND to design a new system for enlisted force management that would overcome the deficiencies and enhance the capabilities of TOPCAP (see Section 2.1.1). This was the beginning of the Enlisted Force Management Project (EFMP). Between 1981 and 1983 RAND worked jointly with the Air Staff to determine the scope and functions that should be included in a new Enlisted Force Management System (EFMS). The approach to this task involved the following steps:

- Specifying all activities related to management of the enlisted force.
- Reviewing the methods used by the various armed services to accomplish these activities.
- Identifying the scope of activities that would be supported by the EFMS.
- Developing the conceptual design for an EFMS that would support those activities. (This design is presented in Carter *et al.* [1983].)

The Air Force adopted the conceptual design for the EFMS in 1983. A joint RAND/Air Force effort to develop the system was then begun. In addition to RAND staff, the project team included Air Force analysts from DPPP, DPXA, DPMDW, DPMYA, and PRME. Overall control and direction of the project was provided by a steering committee composed of representatives from the participating organizations, including the team leaders from RAND and the Air Force. Meetings of the steering committee were generally held quarterly. Responsibility for implementation and operation of the EFMS was assigned to the Washington Area Personnel Systems Division of the Air Force Military Personnel Center (AFMPC/DPMDW). (In the remainder of the book, we refer to AFMPC/DPMDW as the System Management Office or SMO.)

Although work was often performed jointly, there was a clear division of responsibility and differentiation of roles between RAND and the Air Force. Tasks were assigned to one or the other based on comparative advantage. In most cases, responsibility for a task was assigned to one of the two partners, but the other partner provided assistance in carrying out the task. In general, RAND was responsible for developing the conceptual and mathematical specification for the system's modules, and the Air Force (primarily the SMO) was responsible for the information systems tasks associated with the project, including transforming the specifications into operational programs and integrating them into the overall information system architecture.

In particular, RAND's major roles and responsibilities were to:

- develop a conceptual design for the EFMS
- develop the mathematical specification of the models
- create data files to facilitate designing, building, and testing the models
- refine the mathematical specification of the models as needed during the testing and implementation phases
- provide system programmers with advice on input formats and output reports
- provide advice on desirable hardware capabilities
- help the Air Force to implement the system and set up procedures for operating and maintaining it.

The roles and responsibilities of the SMO were to:

- identify the specific needs of the various users of the system
- choose the system's software and hardware
- supply source data to RAND for building analysis files
- design and build the system's software architecture, including processes, subsystems, interfaces, databases, and data management facilities
- design and implement the hardware architecture—the computers and communication facilities
- transform mathematical specifications and model prototypes into operational programs and integrate them into the architecture of the system
- test and evaluate the performance of the models
- document the system.

RAND's project team included persons with a range of backgrounds. Most of the members fell into one of the following categories: economist, statistician, operations researcher, computer programmer.

Figure 2.2 traces the history of the EFMP from fiscal year (FY) 1981 through FY 1989. It highlights how the composition of the joint project team changed over time. The early years (1981–1985) were primarily devoted to conceptual design, model development, information system architecture design, and hardware and software selection and acquisition. RAND expended considerably more manpower resources than the Air Force during these years. In 1986, the emphasis shifted toward im-

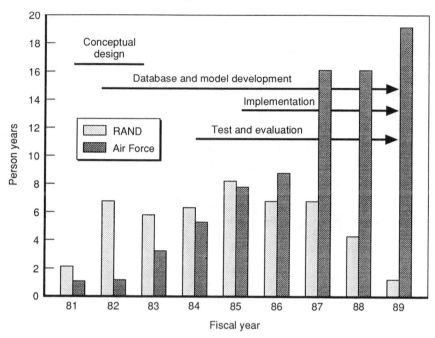

Fig. 2.2 Size of the EFMP over Time

plementation and the Air Force began to expend considerably more manpower resources than RAND. Through FY 1989 the project involved
approximately 125 man-years of effort.

2.3 THE ENLISTED FORCE MANAGEMENT SYSTEM (EFMS)

2.3.1 Overview

The EFMS is a computer-based system whose purpose is to improve
the effectiveness and efficiency of the efforts of Air Staff members
engaged in managing the enlisted force in carrying out their decisionmaking and information processing responsibilities. The objective in managing the enlisted force is to provide a group of airmen that is best able to
support the missions and operational programs that the Air Force must
execute. This is an iterative, continuous task, because the Air Force's
needs and resources change in response to congressional, presidential, and
Department of Defense decisions, decisions by the Air Force, and exogenous labor market forces. The task is becoming increasingly difficult as

the technology of weapons systems becomes more sophisticated and as budget pressures force the Air Force to make more effective use of its resources.

The EFMS is designed to support many of the functions related to the enlisted force that are carried out by PRM, DPX, and DPP. There are data exchanges between the EFMS and the computer systems used by PRM, AFMPC, and ATC that permit the EFMS to obtain inputs from these systems and to supply information to them.

As of this writing, the EFMP is still under way. The project was begun in 1981. Some of the more important milestones have included the following:

- 1983—conceptual design completed
- 1985—hardware and software installed
- 1986—first models operational
- 1990—all critical components implemented and tested.

As of the end of 1991, there were the equivalent of 21 full time Air Force people working on the development, operation, and maintenance of the EFMS.

2.3.2   Models

Figure 2.3 is a simplified flowchart showing the four major sets of models in the EFMS, their interrelationships, and their most important inputs and outputs. The sets are:

- authorization projection
- grade allocation
- aggregate planning, programming, and oversight
- skills management.

The last two sets constitute the bulk of the EFMS models and consumed the bulk of the EFMP's effort. Figure 2.4 shows the skills management models in the EFMS and their most important inputs and outputs. Figure 2.5 shows the aggregate planning, programming, and oversight models in the EFMS and their most important inputs and outputs.

The models in the EFMS can be divided into two categories: screening and impact assessment. Screening models are generally designed for rapid comparison of many alternative plans or programs using summary or

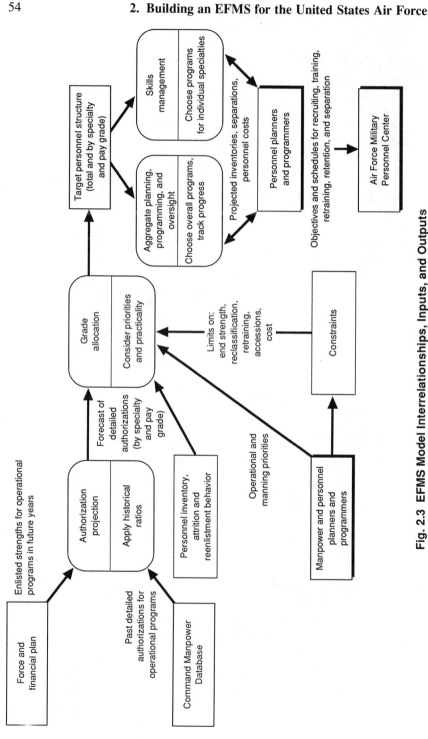

Fig. 2.3 EFMS Model Interrelationships, Inputs, and Outputs

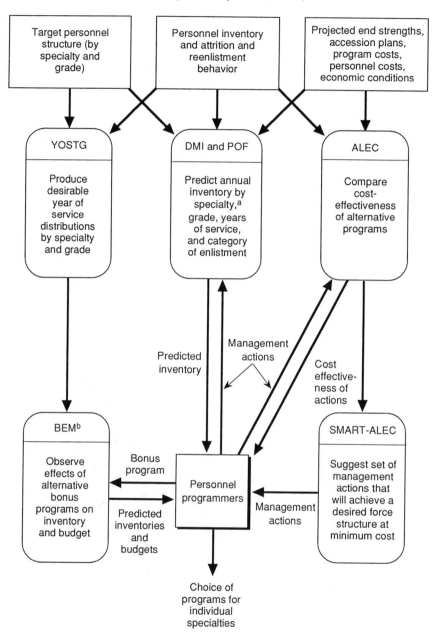

aThe POF predicts the inventory for a group of specialties.
bScreening model.

Fig. 2.4 Skills Management Models in the EFMS

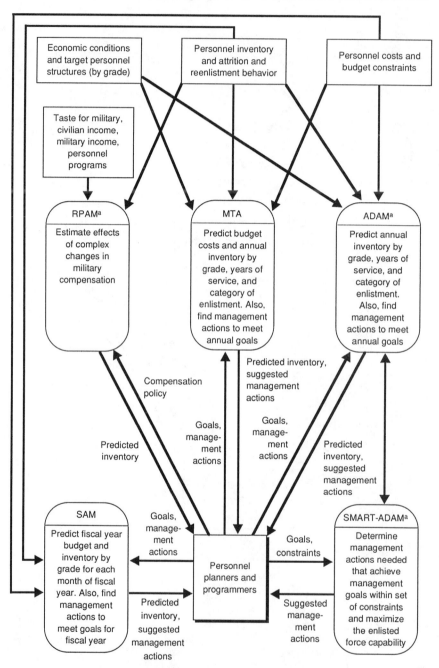

aThe POF predicts the inventory for a group of specialties.

Fig. 2.5 Aggregate Planning, Programming, and Oversight Models in the EFMS

approximate measures of performance. Impact assessment models are used when more detailed or more accurate calculations are required. The impact assessment models form the core of the ODSS proposed in the conceptual design (see Carter *et al.* [1983, Sec, 3.2]). These models and their databases reside on the EFMS's mainframe computer. Most are programmed in the system's DSS generator language EXPRESS. Users at microcomputer workstations have access to these models and their databases, but they are run on the mainframe. Output reports are displayed at the user's workstation. The databases are centrally updated and maintained by the System Management Office (SMO) at Bolling Air Force Base.

Most of the screening models are microcomputer models that are installed on the microcomputer workstations of their users. They do not reside on the mainframe computer and are not programmed in EXPRESS.

The databases for the models include three types of data:

- output from another EFMS model
- data supplied by other branches of the Air Force (e.g., information on the current airman inventory comes from AFMPC)
- external data (e.g., projected unemployment rates).

The major inputs to the system are projected end strengths and counts of authorizations by AFSC and grade for several years into the future. Another major set of inputs are the current inventory and recent actual experience (e.g., losses and reenlistments). Other inputs needed by one or more of the system's models include program costs (e.g., training costs), manpower cost factors, and budget constraints.

The remainder of this section provides brief introductions to a few of the EFMS models that are used as examples throughout the remainder of the book.

SHORT-TERM AGGREGATE INVENTORY PROJECTION MODEL

The Short-term Aggregate Inventory Projection Model (SAM) is the component of the EFMS that supports aggregate planning within a fiscal year. SAM provides one- to twelve-month projections for the aggregate force (across all AFSCs). It consists of five modules. One of them (called SAM1) estimates for each month, how many airmen will reenlist, be lost, become retirement eligible, or simply continue in retirement. The ETS, loss projections are "policy-free" i.e., the ETS losses that would occur if there were no early release programs.

SAM1 begins any given month with the inventory in each of a large number of airman classes (the actual number and their defining attributes depending on the loss model being used). It then estimates the number of each type of transition that will occur within each class. Given these transition estimates, SAM1 updates the size and composition of the airman classes for each projection month. Output from SAM1 becomes input to the next module.

DISAGGREGATE MIDDLE-TERM INVENTORY PROJECTION MODEL

The Disaggregate Middle-term Inventory Projection Model (DMI) makes annual predictions of Air Force enlisted force levels by AFSC for one to six years into the future. The predictions are conditional on specific management policies (for example, reenlistment bonuses) and on economic conditions (such as unemployment rates). Losses and extensions in the DMI are predicted using a set of middle-term disaggregate models (see Section 7.3).

The primary purpose of the DMI is to help managers match the personnel inventory to manpower targets. The targets are specified by time (end of fiscal year), job (AFSC), and grade. If the model is run with existing policies and plans, its projections will warn of future mismatches between the projected inventory and the targets. Then additional runs can be made using alternative management programs to test ways to reduce the mismatches. The model also provides forecasts of training requirements for the Air Training Command and forecasts of accession requirements for Air Force recruiters.

YEAR-OF-SERVICE TARGET GENERATOR

The Year-of-Service Target Generator (YOSTG) adds a year of service dimension to the manpower targets. The YOSTG produces desirable year-of-service distributions (for each AFSC) that are designed to meet mission needs as reflected in the targets and to be attainable with current personnel policies. The need for the YOSTG arises from two considerations. First, some personnel programs act by increasing or decreasing the number of personnel in specific year groups. To decide how to manage these programs, it is necessary to know how many people one wants in each occupation and year group—i.e., it is necessary to have year-of-service targets. Second, authorizations are created without explicit attention to feasibility. It may be that, given personnel constraints, it is impossible to meet both this year's authorizations and future years' authorizations in both grade and AFSC detail. Thus, personnel managers must trade off today's overages and shortages against future overages and shortages. The YOSTG calculates the optimal trade-off point, given the user's time preferences.

BONUS EFFECTS MODEL

The Bonus Effects Model (BEM) is designed to help bonus managers develop the Air Force's selective reenlistment bonus (SRB) program. It provides the capability to examine the effects of alternative bonus program decisions on projected inventory and projected bonus expenditures. Bonus managers can quickly and easily obtain information about the impacts of a variety of potential bonus plans on the decisions of individual airmen (e.g., reenlistment choice and occupational choice) as well as on the evolution of the force structure (e.g., projected aggregate force profiles and experience mixes within AFSCs). This information could be obtained from the DMI, but, because of long run times, it would not be feasible to run the DMI to test a variety of bonus plans. The BEM was developed as a simplified analytical tool that retains the DMI features that strongly affect the accuracy of bonus effects (such as the number of airmen facing a reenlistment decision in each specialty and zone during each planning year), but eliminates second-order effects. The model facilitates the identification of good bonus plans. These (few) plans are then run through the DMI to obtain more accurate and detailed predictions of their performance.

2.3.3   Physical Configuration

The general physical configuration specified for the EFMS in the conceptual design is shown in Fig. 2.6. End users in geographically dispersed sites would utilize microcomputer workstations. Through a high-level, English-like command language, each user would interact with both an integrated database and an interlinked system of modules, both of which would reside on a mainframe computer. The system's detailed hardware configuration is shown in Fig. 2.7. Chapter 14 describes the selection of the system hardware and software.

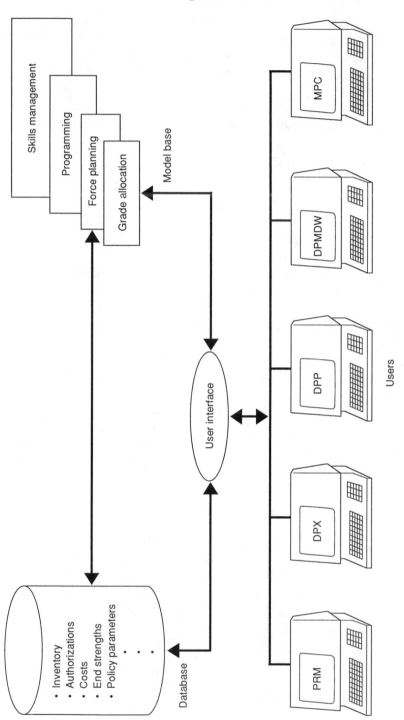

Fig. 2.6 Major Elements of the EFMS

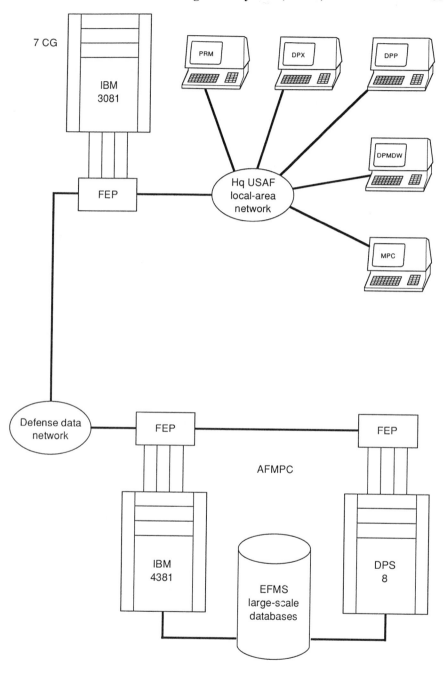

Fig. 2.7 Hardware Architecture of the EFMS

PART III

Chapter 3	The Process of Building an ODSS

3.1 STAGES OF DEVELOPMENT

Research on the introduction of innovative technologies in organizations has concluded that its success is explainable in terms of three components: characteristics of the organization, its information technology, and the implementation process [Bikson, Stasz, and Mankin, 1985]. Of these, the way the technology is developed and introduced is the key determinant of success.

The development of an ODSS requires a formal, structured approach, since we are talking about a large, complex, system programming effort. But this does not mean that it should be developed using the system development life cycle (SDLC) approach for building a management information system (see Section 1.4.2), or that its design needs to be frozen before work is begun. As Boehm [1988] explains, the traditional approach, which requires fully elaborated documentation as completion criteria for the requirements and design phases, pushed many projects "to write elaborate specifications of poorly understood user interfaces and decision-support functions, followed by the design and development of large quantities of unusable code." Such an approach is inappropriate for an environment in which users will learn more about their problem or environment as they

62

use the system, and may identify new and unanticipated information needs. In these situations, an "iterative" [Sprague and Carlson, 1982, p. 139], "adaptive" [Keen, 1980] approach is preferred.

The approach to building an ODSS that we recommend (and that we used on the EFMP) is a combination of the SDLC and iterative/adaptive approaches that we call "staged implementation." Dennis, Burns, and Gallupe [1987] call a similar approach "phased design," and Boehm [1988] describes a related approach that he calls the "spiral model of software development." Staged implementation divides the system development process into the same three stages usually used in the SDLC approach:

1. *Defining the system and the project.* This is the organizational and design stage, which provides a framework and structure that will allow flexible, adaptive, iterative implementation of the system in the final two stages. It is also the stage in which the concept has to be sold to management and users. It is carried out in a structured way, just as if the plan were to build a management information system. This chapter describes stage 1 in the development of an ODSS. Parts IV and V deal with the last two stages. It should be emphasized, however, that implementation and maintenance of the system must be considered in both stage 1 and stage 2 (see Chapter 12).

2. *Developing the system.* This stage is iterative/adaptive, involving prototyping for the development of the system's models (see Part IV).

3. *Implementing and maintaining the system.* This stage is carried out using a combination of the iterative and SDLC approaches. Because the system will be continually evolving, adapting, and expanding, this stage continues indefinitely (see Part V).

Many MIS and DSS texts provide excellent descriptions of how to carry out stage 1 effectively and efficiently. (See, for example, Davis and Olson [1985, pp. 574–577] and Thierauf [1988, pp. 203–213].) Since we generally agree with their descriptions, we see no need to repeat them here. However, two aspects of this stage deserve special attention, since they are critical determinants of the ultimate success or failure of the system and are not treated fully in other texts. They are (1) management and staffing of the project and (2) the conceptual design of the system. We deal with these two aspects in the following two subsections.

3.2   MANAGEMENT AND STAFFING

Building an ODSS is a much more significant undertaking than build-ing a TDSS. In the latter case, the literature suggests that an *ad hoc* approach can often be used, involving in some cases only the user (a "user-developed DSS" [Turban, 1988, p. 133]), a builder (programmer/ analyst) and a user (see Keen and Gambino [1983, Fig. 7.5]), or a user with some help from an information center [Turban, 1988, p. 121]. In con-trast, an ODSS requires a much more formalized approach—a team effort involving persons with a variety of skills at different levels of the organi-zation and in different organizational units.

This difference can be compared directly to the difference that Brooks [1975] identified between writing a computer program and developing a programming system product. A program is "complete in itself, ready to be run by the author on the system on which it was developed." It might be produced cheaply by one or two programmers in a short amount of time (say y man-months). A programming system product is "a collection of interacting programs, coordinated in function and disciplined in format, so that the assemblage constitutes an entire facility for large tasks." Its indi-vidual programs must have been thoroughly tested and documented. In addition, its programs must be tested together in all expected combina-tions, and it must be designed to use only a prescribed budget of resources (e.g., memory space, computer time). According to Brooks, to make the original program (in this case, a TDSS) into a component of the system product requires $9y$ man-months and, more important, requires the efforts of a team, not just one or two programmers.

What is needed is a structured approach (discussed in this section) involving three possibly overlapping groups of people—a steering com-mittee, a project team, and a System Management Office (SMO)—plus a blueprint for the system, which we call its conceptual design (discussed in Section 3.3). The general management structure that we are suggesting is shown in Fig. 3.1.

3.2.1   Steering Committee

The *steering committee*, composed of top- and middle-level managers from all organizational units that will be involved in building or using the ODSS, or that will be affected by it in some direct way, provides overall control and direction to the project.

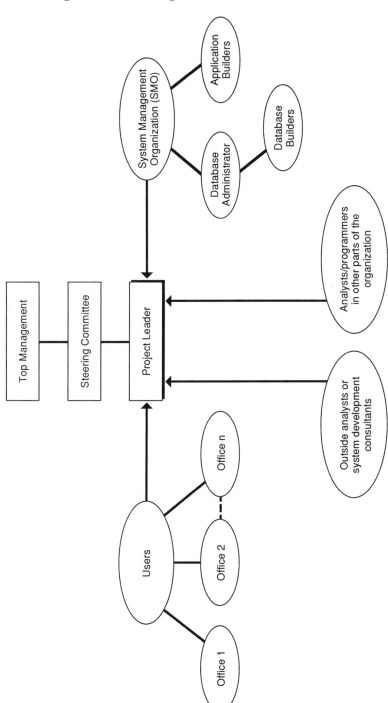

Fig. 3.1 Management Structure for Building an ODSS

It makes policy decisions, assigns priorities, monitors progress, and allocates resources. It meets regularly (on the EFMP, the steering committee met quarterly). At these meetings, participants:

- see presentations by members of the project team (progress reports)
- get an understanding of the status of all work in progress
- decide on the schedule for future work
- resolve problems (e.g., allocate resources, assign priorities, obtain access to data).

The status of the members of the steering committee and its role in the project enables it to serve as a buffer between the project team and the organization's top management. It could easily promote the project with top management, disseminate information on the project's progress, and help smooth implementation of the system.

On the EFMP, the head of the steering committee was the leader of the project team. This may be good for efficient development, but not necessarily for successful implementation. To maintain top management support, it would be better to have the steering committee led by a high-level person in the organization—perhaps a top manager from one of the user organizations.

3.2.2   Project Team

The *project team* is composed of staff members from all of the affected organizations (in roles as builders or users) plus, at its core, builders employed in a technically oriented SMO (see Section 3.2.3). As in the case of a TDSS, development of a successful ODSS requires the active involvement and participation of the users from the very beginning. The system will be designed around them. They need to believe that it is "their system."

Some organizational units (e.g., finance departments) also have their own analysts and programmers. The team should include them, because their knowledge of the users' problems will be helpful and because they may be helpful in updating and maintaining the system.

Some organizations may not have enough internal analytical support to design an ODSS. In this case, they might hire outside analysts to write the mathematical specifications for the system's models. In the case of the EFMS, the Air Force asked RAND to play the lead analytical role.

The talents required are many, which implies a large and diverse project team. Successful design, development, and implementation of an ODSS requires persons with an understanding of the problem area, plus expertise in such areas as mathematical modeling, statistics, database management, computer programming, information systems analysis/design, organizational behavior, and human factors engineering. Neglecting any of these disciplines might lead to problems. Also, all of these perspectives on building the system should ideally be represented on the team from the beginning of the project, since it is hard to change direction once the project is under way.

Bikson, Stasz, and Mankin [1985] describe the development of an ODSS for a company they identify as XYZ. In this case, the director of the project team was a member of top management. The project team included three employees who had a substantial understanding of the corporation. They were not systems professionals, but were comfortable with information technology. It also included a person with recent systems implementation experience. For technical assistance, this internal group relied on advice and consultation from an outside firm providing technical assistance for business systems development to several subsidiary companies in the corporate group of which XYZ is a member.

The head of the XYZ project team emphasized the importance of both employee participation and technical expertise on the project team. The employees were able to identify the functional needs. The leader contended that once the functional needs were known, finding the appropriate tools was easy, but that making good decisions about tools when the task is unclear is impossible. On the other hand, scanning available technologies and making recommendations about what tools would best serve which needs required strong computer system professionals.

Successful functioning of the project team requires continual interaction, good information flow, and close working relationships among team members. This is not so hard in the case of a TDSS, since the members of the team are in only one or two organizational units. But an ODSS project team includes persons from many organizational units who might even be geographically dispersed. The EFMS project team included persons in Washington, D.C., San Antonio, Texas, and Santa Monica, California. We used a wide variety of means for communication and coordination, including:

- trips by team members to other locations
- use of common computing facilities and common databases (via telecommunication)
- numbered memos distributed to all team members, accessible at all times in a book maintained by a designated person at each location
- exchange of information by telephone, overnight mail service, facsimile, and electronic mail
- use of an action plan, defining tasks, schedules, and responsibilities.

In addition to its direct responsibilities for system development, the project team must play the role of a change agent, keeping the users involved throughout the development period and making sure that they understand what is happening and why. The work that this group does before implementation will determine to a large extent how successful the system will be. People in organizations are more or less resistant to change according to the way that change is introduced. To help improve chances for successful implementation, the project team should consider such organizational and behavioral questions as follows:

- How will existing procedures be changed?
- Which jobs will be most affected and in what ways?
- How can the people affected be prepared for these changes?
- What sort of training will the affected people need?
- What is the best timetable for implementing the changes?

3.2.3   System Management Office (SMO)

The SMO is roughly the ODSS counterpart of the group that develops and maintains an MIS. But its unique character (and the issue of where in the organization it should reside) comes from some of the special characteristics of the ODSS environment.

The added dimension of mathematical modeling requires a two-pronged development effort—one part focused on the modeling aspects of development, the other focused on the traditional information system aspects and the integration of the models into an automated system. Depending on how the mathematical modeling is conducted and the way the overall organization distributes its quantitative and information system resources, the SMO may incorporate responsibility for both aspects of development in its charter.

Members seconded from the SMO will constitute a large part of the project team, but the project team contains others (e.g., modelers and representatives of the users). The SMO is not one of the user organizations; it is an organization housing technical experts (software, hardware, statistics, etc.) whose sole *raison d'être* is to build and maintain the system and provide support to its users. This distinction should reduce the potential for conflicts among organizational units. Maintaining the SMO as a separate entity on the project team offers the opportunity to bring on board the potential users of the system and others who might have a stake in its success. If operations research and other quantitative skills reside in other places in the organization, it also allows those personnel to join the team in an advisory capacity or as full members. Membership provides inclusion and a sense of ownership. It fosters a willingness to participate. Establishing a separate entity on the project team also provides visibility for the project within both the information systems and user organizations. This does not diminish the role of the SMO, since many of its personnel will be on the team and it may be responsible for overall project management, or at least play a prominent management role.

The SMO should be set up at the very beginning of the project. There should be a close relationship between the leadership of the SMO and the project leadership. There are good reasons for making the head of the SMO the project leader (e.g., he or she will be knowledgeable about the system, will have a stake in seeing it developed well, and will be able to transition the project easily from development to operation and maintenance). However, being the project leader requires political skills that are not necessarily essential to being the head of the SMO. A better choice as head of the SMO might be the deputy project leader—a person chosen more for technical and administrative skills (see Section 3.2.6).

The SMO's role on the project (and personnel numbers and expertise) will change over the course of the project, but it has things to do during all stages. During the definition stage, most of the work is done by the project team, with major inputs from the users. The development stage initially includes intense interaction with users. It also includes intense interaction between the SMO's system builders and the modelers. Thus, the development stage requires the project team personnel to be engaged with SMO and user organizations to give counsel, help fix bugs, and evaluate prototypes.

Responsibility for implementation would be phased gradually from the project team to the SMO. Upon completion of development, the project team would most likely be disbanded, and the SMO would become the organizational entity responsible for maintenance of the system.

During the definition stage, the SMO would be responsible for:

- identifying the specific needs of the various users of the system.

During the development stage, the SMO would take the lead in:

- designing the information system architecture
- selecting the DSS generator
- selecting the system's hardware.

During implementation, the SMO would:

- procure the hardware and software
- prepare the central computer facility and set up user workstations
- develop standards and procedures for programming, database management, and user interaction
- develop standards for documentation
- program the system's models (including testing the models)
- create the system's database
- document the models and database
- develop training materials
- keep potential users informed of progress.

As soon as one or more of the models of the ODSS has been implemented, the attention of the SMO must begin to shift toward maintenance and updating. During this phase, the SMO would have to:

- train users (and answer questions as they arise)
- distribute hard-copy reports produced by the system
- update documentation of the models and database as changes are made
- maintain and update the database
- maintain and modify the models.

Some organizations already have an information center that may be able to serve as the source for SMO personnel. Several companies (e.g., Northwest Industries, American Airlines, and Sun Oil Company) have formed DSS departments, which contain a group of people who have the necessary skills and capabilities to be DSS builders.

The most efficient and effective way of organizing the programming effort is likely to be the "surgical team" approach recommended by Brooks [1975] for organizing a system programming team. In this approach, a single person (the "surgeon") is made responsible for one of the system's models. He or she personally defines the functional and performance specifications, designs the program, codes it, tests it, and writes its documentation. Other members of the team with specific expertise (e.g., database management, statistics, programming) provide support to this effort. The success of this approach depends on starting out with a conceptual design of the entire system that has "conceptual integrity" i.e., it is clear what the pieces are and how they relate to each other. If this approach is used, it is then possible to have separate teams working independently to develop different models, and still have them integrated into a coherent system.

3.2.4   Location of Project Team and SMO

As discussed above, we strongly believe that the development of an ODSS should be carried out by an *ad hoc* project team, which includes technical persons from an SMO, representatives of user organizations, and perhaps external analysts or other technical persons. Its members would have homes in several organizations, but would be seconded to the team for the design and development effort. This approach not only provides the project with the needed technical expertise, but also, as Mankin *et al.* [1988] point out, facilitates the development of a system "that users will be able to operate successfully" and that provides users with "a feeling of ownership and a stronger commitment to making it work."

We also believe that the SMO should have an identity separate from the general MIS function. That is not to say that the SMO need be a separate department. In most circumstances, it should fall within the normal patterns of information systems support for the organization. However, if located within the main MIS structure, it should have a separate identity because of the unique character of decision support systems. They represent a sharp break from more traditional data processing applications (e.g., payroll, accounts receivable). The individual applications within the DSS may not be organized along functional lines, and the DSS may have data requirements or interfaces that cross the boundaries of several organizational units. Giving the SMO a separate identity within MIS will also give it the visibility and support it may need to break new ground in the uses of information technology.

It may be that the organization already has decision support technology being applied by separate groups in more than one part of the organization. In this case, the project team would include members from each of the SMOs involved. This has its advantages. For example, it may be easier for the SMO personnel to develop closer relationships to the users, which might foster greater familiarity and understanding of the functions supported. But some disadvantages arise as well. It might be harder to undertake projects involving several information systems groups, or the different groups might use different technologies and approaches that are not easy to tie together in an ODSS.

If ODSS development is to be successful in such an environment it requires:

- a strong element of centralization in terms of technology decisions within the organization, so that the technology provides a common foundation around which systems are built
- provision for the type of *ad hoc* project team approach suggested above, where members of the project cross functional and organizational lines
- an organizational commitment to treating data as a corporate resource, with a centrally managed corporate database or organization-wide standards, policies, and procedures to ensure that data are consistent.

3.2.5 Leadership of Project Team and SMO

As discussed above, a likely choice as project leader would be the head of the SMO (or the person targeted to become head). However, several reasons indicate that this might not be the best choice. First, as already pointed out, the criterion for choosing the project leader should be that he or she is qualified to be project leader *and* qualified (and willing) to be the head of the SMO. Being the project leader requires political skills that are not essential to being head of the SMO. Thus, a more technically oriented deputy project leader might be the appropriate choice to head the SMO.

Another possibility is to place the project management function within the user community. In this case, the "champion" of the project in the user community, or one of his or her representatives might assume management of the project. This not only helps ensure that the project gets the emphasis needed, but may also be preferred by the traditional MIS department, which might play a supporting role. The major problem in this case is to get all users—across organizational boundaries—to accept leadership by one user.

Choosing an in-house person as project leader offers the opportunity to select an individual who is already established in the organization, one who has a measure of credibility and an underlying familiarity with internal processes, procedures, and personnel. In addition, an in-house person with day-to-day involvement in the organization can be attuned to important changes taking place within the organization itself or its environment to a degree that would be difficult, if not impossible, for an outsider to achieve. Last, of course, an insider is in a much better position to fight the political battles and potential rivalries that may arise from the system, especially in its early stages when critical issues such as project approval and funding are initially resolved.

Being politically astute and well-connected within the organization are only two of the requirements for the "ideal" project manager. Project management skills are, of course, also necessary. (Since these are equally applicable to many types of projects, they are not discussed further in this book.) Technical skills related to the disciplines used in the project (e.g., operations research, statistics, and system design) are also important. However, remember that we are discussing a management, not a technical, role in the case of the project manager. Often in technical disciplines promotion to a management position is predicated on a person's demonstration of a high degree of proficiency in technical positions, e.g., elevating a highly skilled programmer to a position supervising other programmers. Technical proficiency does not always equate to management proficiency as many organizations have discovered to their dismay. However, some degree of technical proficiency is required for an ODSS project manager.

The project manager has to be a "knower" in this regard, rather than a "doer." That is, he or she has to have a degree of knowledge to be able to give direction to the project, make choices with regard to technology and approaches, be able to discern problems, and know when someone is trying to "snow" them—but the project manager need not be proficient to the point of being able to do the actual work in any of these areas, e.g., code a program or do a specific piece of analysis. For example, the Air Force project manager on the EFMP was instrumental in initiating the search for, managing the selection of, and securing approval for the advanced software tools used in the EFMS, even though he was not a technician and had no programming experience. What was required was an overall knowledge of the technology available, an ability to relate that to the specific needs of the project, both technical and business, and the will and desire to apply it.

The project leader need not embody all of the talent and expertise mentioned above. (Indeed, it would be extremely difficult to find anyone who did.) What is critical is to ensure that the project team includes members at a supervisory or management level who are strong in those areas where the project manager may not have extensive knowledge.

3.3 CONCEPTUAL DESIGN

The conceptual design of an ODSS tells what should happen; implementation tells how it is made to happen. According to Brooks [1975, p. 44]:

> For a given level of function, that system is best in which one can specify things with the most simplicity and straightforwardness. Simplicity and straightforwardness proceed from conceptual integrity. Every part must reflect the same philosophies and the same balancing of desiderata...Ease of use...dictates unity of design...The separation of architectural effort [conceptual design] from implementation is a very powerful way of getting conceptual integrity on very large projects.

Once it has been decided that an ODSS will be built, but before any work is done on specifying hardware, software, or models, a conceptual design must be produced. The design must include at least the following elements:

- design principles, which will guide all decisions for the remainder of the project
- functions to be supported
- models to provide the support, how the models would work (including inputs and outputs), and the relationship among the models (e.g., a flowchart showing interconnections)
- data requirements (generic data; no file names or database layouts)
- hardware and software considerations (hardware configuration and software capabilities, not specific equipment and languages)
- approach to implementation (structure of SMO, priorities, prototyping strategy, documentation rules, responsibilities of participating organizational units).

These elements are discussed in the following subsections.

3.3.1   Design Principles

Five principles guided the design of the EFMS. These principles are widely stated in the DSS literature, but are easier to say than to do. By stating them before any development work began, they guided the entire system development process. The principles were:

1. Improve the effectiveness and efficiency of enlisted force management and decisionmaking.
2. Place the user in control.
3. Make building the system as fast and easy as possible.
4. Make the system flexible, adaptable, and easy to maintain.
5. Coordinate and integrate the decisionmaking environment.

The first four principles apply equally well to TDSSs. Principle 5 is one of the most important reasons for building an ODSS instead of a separate TDSS for each function.

These principles, although traditional and obvious, had important implications for the design of the three basic components of the EFMS: the model base, database, and user interface.

MODEL BASE

The desire for flexibility, adaptability, and easy maintainability suggested the use of an interlinked system of many small models (or modules), each designed for one specific purpose, instead of a few complicated, comprehensive, large models.

The modular approach to modeling is attractive for a variety of reasons. In addition to mitigating the problems inherent in building a single large model, it makes it easier for users to understand (and accept) the models in the system. The modular approach also makes it relatively easy to adapt to a wide variety of circumstances, availability of data, and types of analyses without having to incur large amounts of time, skill, and confusion in reprogramming.

Modules also make it easier to use the "surgical team" approach to writing the DSS computer programs. As Miller and Katz [1986] explain: "The various modelers need communicate about the inputs and outputs of the submodels for which they are responsible, but they do not have to understand each other's submodels in detail."

DATABASE

The desire for coordination and integration originally led to the specification of a common, consistent, easily accessed, centralized database for the system in the conceptual design. The database would provide input to the models, would retain output from the models for management reports, and would be available for direct inquiry by users. Information generated by one model would be automatically (and instantaneously) available to other models. Data both internal and external to the organization would be included. (For example, the EFMS database includes information on the inventory of airmen and data on the U.S. economy.)

But the system need not have a single, unified, integrated database, and the EFMS does not. In the EFMS, each model has its own database. But database administration is centralized (assigned to the SMO). The principle to be followed is that responsibility for updating and maintaining each item of information should be assigned, and each piece of information should be stored in only one place. Also, since the system is being used by different organizational units, privacy and security provisions must be built in. Some users would be unable to access certain information and those permitted to change data in the system's database would be specifically linked to those items of data for which they were responsible.

USER INTERFACE

The primary implication of the design principles for the user interface is that the system have a common interface for all of its elements; that is, that dialogues be managed in a uniform fashion regardless of the particular model being run. Of course, each model would have different specific input and output screens. But each would enable the user to do the same types of things in the same ways. For example, if the user wanted to run a model, modify a parameter value, or name an input data file, he would use the same procedure for all models. Also, since the users of the EFMS were not information system professionals, we decided that the interface should be menu driven, easy to learn, and easy to use. The user (without the help of a programmer) would be able to

- request information from the database
- make temporary or permanent changes to data in the database
- specify parameters and input data for a model
- run a model

- tailor output reports (scope, aggregation, time periods)
- compare outputs from two different runs of the same model.

The distinctions among systems that are easy to learn and easy to use, and some of the tradeoffs needed, are discussed by Anderson and Shapiro [1989].

3.3.2 Functions to Be Supported

As discussed in Chapter 1, the focus in the development of a TDSS is usually on the individual decisionmaker, while the focus in the development of an ODSS should be on the functions to be supported. Thus, the conceptual design should be devoted to a functional description of the system—the constituent models and their interconnections.

3.3.3 Models

The conceptual design of an ODSS should include a listing of the models the system will eventually contain, a short description of the function of each one, their major inputs and outputs, and a flowchart showing their interrelationships. Just as it is useful in forming the project team to forecast the needs to the end of the project and include all necessary skills from the beginning, it is important to try to specify the full functional scope of the system at the conceptual design stage. This will make it easier to construct a coherent, integrated, unified system. Without this framework, it is likely that the system will end up a fragmented patchwork quilt, held together by baling wire. With this framework, the system can be developed in an iterative, adaptive way. Whenever a model is ready to be added to the system, it can be plugged in. To the extent possible, connecting hooks should already be in place to greet it, or additional interface programming should be minor.

Figure 2.3 is the summary flowchart for the EFMS that underlay its conceptual design [Carter et al., 1983]. It indicates the major sets of models in the system, their major inputs and outputs, and their interrelationships. The conceptual design also included more detailed flowcharts for each of the sets of models, which showed each specific model, its inputs, its policy levers (i.e., decision variables), its outputs, and where the outputs were to be sent (e.g., reports to Congress or the Department of Defense).

3.3.4 Data

An ODSS has much more demanding needs for data than does a TDSS, and more attention has to be given to this aspect of the system. In general, four different types of data are used during the course of building an ODSS. These are data

1. to understand or define the problem situation being addressed
2. to estimate the models
3. to test and evaluate the models
4. to run the models (input data).

We call the data for the first two uses "analysis files," since they are primarily used by analysts engaged in defining and building models. The other two types of data are "operational files," which are created and used by the SMO.

A great deal of thought must be given to data issues at the conceptual design stage, and a great deal of time must be allocated to creating these databases during the development of the system. Projects that make extensive use of large data files usually underestimate the amount of effort required to create useful databases. We estimate that between 25 and 40 percent of the effort on the EFMP was devoted to collecting, cleaning, and analyzing data.

The conceptual design document should try to estimate the amount of data that will ultimately be required within the system, where the data would come from, and a strategy by which data files can be added to the system as models are added without affecting the integrity or the consistency of the database.

To make the EFMS easy to update and maintain, we included a principle in the conceptual design that the data required by the models should be as easy to obtain as possible. We said that the input data should not require extensive preparation or previous analysis and should be routinely collected by the Air Force or some stable external source (such as the Census Bureau or Department of Labor).

3.3.5 Hardware and Software

Although the functional specification of an ODSS can be accomplished without considering the physical environment within which it will be implemented, it is still important to include such considerations in the conceptual design document. At this point, only the general outlines of the hardware and software required to support the system are to be specified. This information serves two purposes:

1. The organization's management needs such information to estimate the system's development cost.
2. The system's users need such information to understand how the system will work and how they will fit into it.

Since the system will be supporting users throughout the organization, it is likely that one of two types of distributed data processing approaches would be used: (1) a mainframe linked with PCs or user workstations or (2) user workstations linked with a central file server. The general physical configuration specified for the EFMS is shown in Fig. 2.6. End users in geographically dispersed sites would utilize microcomputer workstations. Through a user-friendly interface, he or she would interact with both an integrated database and an interlinked system of models, both of which would reside on a mainframe computer. The models would be downloaded into PCs for operation. The software would combine a wide range of capabilities in a single package (see Fig. 14.1). Both Figs. 2.6 and 14.1, which are part of the conceptual design, show generic functions and capabilities. The actual selection of the hardware and software comes during the development stage (see Chapter 14).

3.4   THE INTRODUCTION OF NEW TECHNOLOGY

The introduction of new technology can be an important element in the development of an ODSS. In fact, the effective utilization of new technology can be essential to the success of an ODSS project. This was certainly true of the EFMS. The transition from the familiar to the new may involve more than simply learning to use yet another tool. It may require those using the new technology to develop an entirely different conceptual framework. For example, transitioning from the use of third-generation languages such as COBOL and FORTRAN to fourth-generation languages can be very difficult. A significant learning curve may be necessary to lead up to the point of being able to use the new tools with an adequate degree of efficiency and effectiveness. It is not necessarily a matter of mastering the procedural statements or commands of a language, but of conceptualizing a new approach to programming and building information systems.

There is also a psychological component to the introduction of new technologies. Those who will be expected to use them have to be not only trained in their use, but they have to be open to using them. Not every information system person desires to be on the forefront of technology. There are COBOL programmers who do not want to be anything but COBOL programmers, and if given another programming language to use will produce programs that look very much like COBOL. There are those who have done system maintenance for years and have few aspirations to do anything else. Needless to say, these are the types of persons to avoid placing on the ODSS development team.

Educating the system developers in the new technologies should not be neglected. Up-front investments in training can pay off over the life of a project or system. There are a number of alternatives for providing this training. Most software vendors provide some training on the products they sell. Often they will even tailor or create training classes to meet special needs. These can provide a good beginning, but they often fall short of meeting the overall need. Most classes are geared to the novice, because that is where their students are when they start. Unfortunately, many ODSS applications require more sophisticated and creative uses of the software.

Partial remedies can be found by hiring people who already possess the technical skills required. This can work if the technical base you are using has penetrated the market place to the extent that those people are readily available. However, this is not likely to be the case if you are committed to a leading-edge technology. Using consultants who are familiar with the technology can provide a reasonable alternative—one that was used with great success on the EFMS. Where trainers provided by vendors often have more theoretical, general, and shallow expertise, consultants are often survivors who have successfully battled problems similar to the ones that might be faced in an organization implementing an ODSS for the first time. However, if a consultant is used, technical expertise should not be the only selection criterion. Equally important is the capacity to be able to apply that technology in the specific context of the ODSS being built.

3.5 POLITICAL ASPECTS OF BUILDING AN ODSS

One of the most important principles of implementing an ODSS is to always sit with your back to the wall. While this advice might seem more pertinent to a Western gunfighter, it can also be effectively applied to

ODSS development. System development is very much a political process in addition to being driven by technology.

3.5.1   The Problem

Most ODSSs are going to alter the status quo within an organization, and in every organization there are those who will resist change. Some of these have a vested interest in maintaining the status quo. Others are risk averse and are reluctant to try something new for fear of adverse consequences. A third group may see their positions in the organization as being dependent on their exclusive control and dissemination of the information directly related to their jobs. A final group may just find comfort and security in the familiar way of doing business.

None of these types is likely to be influenced by logical arguments or objective evidence. They will continually find reasons why something will not work—although they will rarely be candid about their motivations (if in fact they know them). Often they will demand more information or data, ask for one more feature before they will accept the system, or want to apply standards of performance that exceed anything they currently have and that are beyond the realm of realistic system capabilities. The best course of action may be to influence them through their coworkers and supervisors, finding allies who are more open to, and accepting of, change. The third type may require that the system be designed to make them feel that they have some control over the information produced and its dissemination.

Political problems will be substantial if there are groups in the organization who see the implementation of an ODSS as an encroachment on their "turf," or as a threat to their perceived place in the organization. This is a very real possibility, whose likelihood is increased when the application of an extensive decision support system cuts across traditional organizational lines or when the ODSS requires a wide range of disciplines that reside in different places within the current organizational structure. For example, information systems and analytical or modeling personnel may not be functionally colocated within the organization. Yet, both elements may be required in the system. Acrimony may develop over leadership roles, division of responsibility, and the kudos for success.

Such a problem developed with the EFMS. Opposition began to develop as it became clear that the system was likely to achieve success. It started with passive noncooperation, but quickly escalated to more active forms of political infighting as the system became a perceived threat to the positions of a number of people in the organization. A number of hastily conceived alternatives to selected portions of EFMS were launched at various times in an effort to discredit the project and seek political advantage.

Although the EFMS's opponents failed, the infighting had a debilitating effect on the project. Confusion was created across the staff as people tried to make sense of conflicting claims and alternatives. Time and attention that should have been focused on the project were spent in defusing criticism, rebuilding user support, and forming alliances. The acquisition of critical project personnel was delayed for an extended period as these political issues were resolved, causing delays in implementation.

This story is not an isolated example. Organizational politics and personalities are frequently important factors—often the overriding factors—in determining which systems ultimately get implemented. Although project leaders who are very analytically oriented and expect decisions to be made on a well-ordered and rational basis may find this situation difficult, they must be prepared to deal with it.

3.5.2   A Marketing Approach

Successful launching and implementation of an ODSS project needs to be accompanied by a thorough and effective marketing effort. The idea of having to "sell" a system is not something that is normally covered in an operations research or information systems text, but in a less than perfect world of limited resources and competing interests, effective marketing may make the difference between success and failure. Systems do not get built without resources, and the competition for resources can be extremely fierce. Because of the factors noted above, a rational and objective statement of the arguments for a particular course of action is not likely to be enough to win the day.

Finding out who can influence or make the decisions about issues associated with the project, and knowing their biases and personal agendas, can be extremely important. Once this information is known, presentations can be tailored for those persons and structured to their perceived needs. Since initial approval to proceed is only the first of many favorable decisions that must be made to assure completion of a major project, the marketing effort must continue throughout the entire development effort. Most multiyear projects will require follow-on funding decisions or milestone reviews. These events should be viewed as marketing opportunities, with careful consideration given to the messages to be communicated in addition to "factual" statements of project status.

Often the successes of a project are not self-evident, especially to individuals not directly connected with the day-to-day operations of the project. Many of the early successes represent intermediate steps in the development process and are not amenable to documenting on a screen or report. Since individuals who do not have constant exposure to the project are likely to be among those who are key to having the project continue, a conscious effort needs to be made to ensure that progress and successes are effectively communicated to these key people.

The use of marketing as a project management tool is not to suggest that hyperbole replace substance or that marketing should be used to make up for project deficiencies. Nor are we suggesting that truth be distorted in the pursuit of project goals. But most organizations operate within the confines of an advocacy process, and those most likely to succeed in these circumstances realize this fact of organizational life and use it to their advantage.

3.5.3 Champions and Sponsors

In dealing with the political realities of a project of any significant size, chances of success are greatly enhanced by the presence in the user organization of a "champion" and "sponsor." Champion is a term used at 3M and other corporations. It was publicized in the best selling business book, *In Search of Excellence,* by Peters and Waterman [1982]. To quote from that book, "A champion...[is] the pragmatic one who grabs onto someone else's theoretical construct if necessary and bullheadedly pushes it to fruition." This kind of commitment is most likely to be found in someone who can relate organizational or personal success directly to the system. The champion might be the project manager, or it might be a potential user, who having identified the benefits of the system, is willing to do whatever it takes to ensure the project is completed. We would venture to say that the chances of success are considerably reduced without the commitment of a champion from somewhere within the organization.

A sponsor differs from a champion in level within the organization. A sponsor is normally someone who holds a key executive position. The main functions of the sponsor are to give organizational legitimacy to the project, provide political cover, and secure and protect project funding. Ideally, the sponsor would occupy a position that would give him or her overall responsibility for all of the functions to be supported by the ODSS. This would put the sponsor in a position to minimize organizational friction that might arise over various aspects of the project. If not at that level, the sponsor must be in a position where he or she directly participates in the major decisions that could affect the project (e.g., funding and resources).

How a project is viewed within an organization is often directly tied to the level of its sponsorship, i.e., who in the organization is really behind the effort. Obviously, the higher the level of sponsorship, the more chance the project has to obtain cooperation and support. The project needs to be protected when difficulties arise. A high-level sponsor who has faith and trust in the project team can be the most effective kind of ally—and may at times be the only person standing between the project and its cancellation.

Since all organizations are subject to change through transfer, promotion, resignations, and other factors, expanding the project's support base by cultivating potential backup sponsors or by attempting to add additional sponsors would be a prudent strategy. One of the groups that initiated a "quick fix" alternative to EFMS had sponsorship at the highest levels of Air Force personnel management. But that person was their only constituency. When he departed they were essentially cut adrift with no other organizational ties or elements of support and were eventually absorbed into the EFMS project team.

PART IV

Chapter 4	Decision Support Models

The model base is the heart of any decision support system. In this part of the book we discuss the process of building a model base for an ODSS. We draw conclusions about desirable attributes of both the model base and the process of its creation from our experience with the Enlisted Force Management Project and other large systems of computer-based models.

4.1   WHAT IS A DECISION SUPPORT MODEL?

A decision support model is a rule (or more frequently a large collection of rules) that predicts the outcomes that will occur when particular decisions are implemented in a particular environment; it may incorporate an evaluation of its predictions in terms of user-selected criteria. The purpose of the evaluation would generally be to suggest decisions that meet the criteria. The rules are built from a set of hypothesized relationships among elements of the environment. The relationships are often expressed as equations—for example, an equation describes the probability that an airman will leave the Air Force during his first year of service as a function of his education, test scores, and demographic characteristics. The equations are then programmed in a computer language or on a spreadsheet so that one can observe how the dependent variables change with changes in the independent variables.

Decision support models are one of the sets of basic units of the DSS as seen by the users. Each such model supports a planning, decisionmaking, or policymaking activity by estimating the consequences of an action that might be proposed. We reserve the word *model* to refer to such a decision support model. Much of the effort that goes into building models for an ODSS is aimed at creating small units that perform functions needed by many models. We use the word *module* to describe a building block that needs to be combined with other modules and embedded in a model before it can serve the needs of decisionmakers. For example, one of the key modules in the EFMS predicts the fraction of airmen that will choose to leave the Air Force. This module became part of a number of inventory projection models. A substantial amount of resources was expended understanding this key relationship, but the investment paid off in a module that is widely used throughout the EFMS.

The primary purpose of a decision support model is to study the likely outcomes of decisions. All models involve a substantial abstraction of reality. A model can never predict all of the consequences that a high-level decisionmaker must consider when he or she makes a decision, and a model can never capture the effect of all the factors in the environment that might influence the outcomes from a decision. Thus, the final decision always rests with the decisionmaker. The purpose of a decision support model is to inform the decision—not to make the decision.

4.2   THE PARTS OF A DECISION SUPPORT MODEL

By definition, a decision support model assumes a causal link between the inputs to a system or process and the outputs of the system.[5] In constructing models of this process, it is useful to divide the system's inputs into:

- *Management levers,* which describe the range of actions that are under the decisionmaker's control and how those actions will be implemented

---

[5] The system being modeled is the model's *referent* in the terminology of Rothenberg [1989]

- *Parameters*, which describe the environment in which the decision will be implemented and over which the decisionmaker has no control.

Similarly, it is useful to identify, from among all the system's output, the subset of variables that constitute the:

- *Criteria*, which describe the key characteristics by which the decisionmaker will judge whether or not the decision is a good one.

The relationships in the model are an attempt to describe the way in which some aspect of the real-world system operates. The form of the equation (e.g., whether a relationship is additive or multiplicative) is usually deduced from an understanding of the situation being modeled. The parameters of the model are usually derived by statistical techniques from data describing the situation being modeled. Although careful theoretical and empirical analysis can provide much useful information about the effects of decisions, in the complicated situations where ODSS are used, substantial areas of uncertainty are likely to remain.

4.3 TYPES OF MODELS AND MODULES

Models can be classified according to their purpose. Both models and modules can be classified according to the mathematical and statistical techniques used to build the model. The purpose of a model is either *descriptive* or *prescriptive* [Quade, 1985]. In a descriptive model, the user chooses the value for each management lever (and may choose values for some environmental parameters) and the model describes the outcomes, including the level of each criterion. A descriptive model may be a screening tool that rapidly provides rough indications of the value of a wide variety of alternative decisions, or it may provide detailed projections that are as accurate as possible and may take so long that only a few alternatives can be examined.

In contrast to a descriptive model, in a *prescriptive* model the user chooses a particular criterion function (and may choose values for the environmental parameters) and the model finds the values of the management levers that maximize the function. In prescriptive models the criterion function is usually called the *objective* function.

Both descriptive and prescriptive models frequently incorporate statistical prediction modules. A great variety of statistical techniques can be utilized in developing the predictive equations. The important classes of statistical models, along with the advantages and disadvantages of each class, are presented in Chapter 6. Two techniques, regression analysis and time series analysis, are illustrated in Chapter 7. The module's prediction equations can be evaluated in any computer language, including a spreadsheet. In some cases, however, the entire situation being modeled is too complicated for descriptive equations covering the entire situation to be derived, or the equations that describe the system are too complicated to be solved using available mathematical techniques. In these cases, it may be possible to write procedural rules that express the model's relationships and to program these rules into a *simulation*. The inventory projection model discussed in Chapter 8 is an example of a descriptive simulation model.

Linear programming is the technique most frequently used to find optimum solutions in a prescriptive model. Other techniques include dynamic programming, quadratic programming, and network analysis. See any operations research text (e.g., Hillier and Lieberman [1990]) to learn about these methods. The Year-of-Service Target Generator discussed in Chapter 8 is a prescriptive model.

4.4   THE PROCESS OF BUILDING THE ODSS MODEL BASE

The process of building the model base for an ODSS consists of three logically distinct activities:

- *Conceptual design*, during which the set of models to be included in the ODSS is defined and their interrelationships are specified
- *Model development*, during which each model is specified in detail and is programmed
- *Model test and evaluation*, during which each model is tested for its accuracy and usefulness.

As is by now a cliché in the systems analysis literature, these are not sequential phases of research and development; rather the set of activities is carried out iteratively, with model development sometimes leading to refinements in the conceptual design, and test and evaluation often leading back to further development or even to further refinement of the conceptual design.

As discussed in Chapter 3, the conceptual design phase includes identification of the organizational functions that could use support from decision models. Each function consists of an activity, or a group of activities, that serve some organizational goal. Different models can be built to support different functions, to support different decisions within the same function, and even to support making the same decision under different circumstances. In Chapter 5, we show why we advocate the building of a variety of decision models rather than building a single model that attempts to capture all relevant aspects of the organization's environment.

Chapter 5 also discusses general principles for developing decision support models. Chapter 6 concentrates on the principles unique to the development of statistical prediction modules, since this is one of the most common types of models found in most DSSs. Chapters 7 and 8 provide concrete illustrations of the principles involved in building the model base for an ODSS. Chapter 9 draws together principles of database construction. In Chapter 10, we urge that each ODSS model first be created as a prototype. Prototyping has proven (in several studies and in our experience) to be a most cost-effective endeavor.

In the systems analysis literature, it is usually assumed that the system development process is finished when the test and evaluation activities show the model to be "sufficiently" useful and accurate. In an ODSS environment, the development, test, and evaluation process should never terminate. Rather the ODSS model base should continually evolve to meet changing circumstances and changing management opportunities. Chapter 11 describes what test and evaluation means for an ODSS. It also describes some of the test and evaluation activities carried out for the EFMS, and plans for continuing them throughout the life of the system.

Chapter 5 | Principles for Building ODSS Models

One of the major ways that ODSS models differ from other DSS models and from models built and used outside a DSS environment is that ODSS models are conceptually highly interrelated. This does not mean that the models should be directly connected—indeed we will argue that the only practical way to build a useful ODSS is to include many different models serving different purposes. However, it does mean that substantial effort must be devoted to defining the set of models that the ODSS will contain, to designing these models modularly, and to developing links among the models. After discussing these issues, which cut across all the models in the model base, we deal with issues concerning the design of individual models, including how one fits the model to the organizational decision and the apparent tension between simplicity and realism. Principles concerning individual stages of model building such as the development of predictive relationships, development of prototypes, and test and evaluation are covered in separate subsequent chapters.

5.1 DEFINING THE SET OF MODELS FOR THE ODSS

In principle, a single "organic" model could perform all the functions required by the ODSS and capture all (or at least most) of the major features of the ODSS environment. In practice, however, such a model would (1) execute very slowly; (2) require all users to understand features of the model irrelevant to their own work; and (3) entail a complexity that would stymie development, reduce model utilization, and impede efforts at model updating or modification.

The only practical approach to building an ODSS is to build numerous interrelated models, with most of them intended for specific and limited purposes. We begin by discussing how models can be used to aid decisions and the circumstances under which specific models might be created. These two subsections should help the reader generate a set of useful, potential models for a particular ODSS. The selection among the set of possibilities has to be made based on organizational priorities and cost constraints. In the last subsection, we discuss the advantages and disadvantages of having a system composed of several small models compared to a single global model of how the organization affects the environment.

5.1.1   The Ways Models Can Be Used

Decision support models can be used in a variety of ways. The simplest use of a model is to make a single run to estimate the outcomes of a given set of actions in a given environment and under a given set of assumptions about how the elements in the environment are related. Since alternatives are not considered, seldom can such a single run be used to make a decision. However, the information from such a single run can be used to document the assumptions that underlie a decision and to set up a system for monitoring the results of a decision. The EFMS's disaggregate middle-term inventory projection model (DMI) is frequently used in this way. It projects the number of persons who will be in each occupation and grade at the end of each of the next several years. It is a very complicated model and takes a long time to run. After decisions have been made about policies such as training programs, bonuses, and early release programs, it produces a document called the training plan, which records the amount of training that will be needed in each occupation if these decisions are implemented.

Another simple use of models is to report what actually occurs in the real system, so events can be compared to a model's predictions. An ODSS database may be so complex that it may not be useful to provide a user with direct access to the data. Rather, one might need to provide tools (e.g., a model or other computer program) to organize the data in order to create meaningful statistics or displays. In designing the EFMS and choosing its software, we paid little attention to this reporting function, believing it to be trivial. But it would have been nice to have such tools. (For example, because end-of-term losses and reenlistments from a single cohort of airmen occur over a three-year period, the calculation of useful loss and reenlistment rates from transaction data and status data is not trivial. Substantial effort was involved in creating the data files to enable the test and evaluation of models and the monitoring of actual loss and reenlistment rates.)

A more complicated use of a model is to estimate the outcomes that will follow from each of several alternative actions in order to determine which alternative is better in a given environment and under a given set of assumptions. Having used a model in this way, it would then be possible to use the output from several runs to help make a decision. However, it would be prudent to find out how the choice depends on aspects of the environment that may be uncertain and on assumptions in the model that may be uncertain. This *sensitivity analysis* is usually accomplished by repeated runs of the model varying the parameters of the model that are either most uncertain or likely to have a strong effect on the outcome.[6]

The most complicated use of a model, in the sense that the intellectual process is most difficult to describe, is summarized by Hamming's [1962] adage that "the purpose of computing is insight, not numbers." Frequently, insight into the way that decisions affect outcomes is generated during the process of building the model itself. The process of trying to understand a system at the level of detail necessary to produce a predictive model often generates new knowledge about the system. Also, using the model to help study a problem can help concentrate and focus the mind on the most important factors in the situation, which in turn can lead to the generation of creative alternative solutions to the problem. In addition, using a model can also be a good way for new managers who come without field experience (as is frequently the case in the Pentagon personnel offices of the Air Force) to understand the workings of the system they are managing.

In addition to supporting decisionmaking, models can be used for communication, and this function is likely to be very important in a complex

---

[6] When there are a number of uncertain parameters, sensitivity analyses can entail substantial computational costs because of the need to examine combinations of the uncertain parameters. Rothenberg, Shapiro, and Hefley [1990] offer an approach for greatly reducing the number of computations in this case.

organization. At the simplest level, models document the outcomes to be expected from the chosen decision. The output from models can also be used to explain the rationale for the final decision by showing how the outcomes of the decision compare to those from the set of alternatives that were considered and how sensitive the choice is to the uncertainties in the environment.

The communication function just discussed is most easily accomplished within an organizational community that shares the same assumptions about the real world and that values the criteria in approximately the same way. It requires only that the model accurately reflect the assumptions, accurately model the processes, and accurately measure the criteria. However, since the model makes explicit the causal assumptions about how the world operates and the criteria on which the decision is based, the model can help communicate the reasoning behind the decision to parts of the organization that may not share the same sets of assumptions and values. The model can also help identify the key assumptions on which the organizational units disagree and thereby pave the way for tests of the validity of the assumptions. If well designed, the model will be able predict outcomes of interest to the other organizational units and thus may be able to reduce unwarranted fears about the outcomes that will flow from the decision.

5.1.2   Use Separate Models for Separate Functions, Decisions, and Circumstances

Be prepared to design at least one model for each function. During the conceptual design stage, the model selection process starts by asking what model or models would suffice for each function viewed separately. One should also consider providing separate models for the following:

Separate policies.   For example, in the EFMP we built models to help support decisions about which occupations should receive selective reenlistment bonuses that were separate from the model to support decisions about the training plan. As discussed further in Chapter 8, we did this even though both decisions are part of the same organizational function called skills management, which produces the appropriate number of airmen in each occupation.

Different time horizons.   Even when one is considering a single policy, it may be useful to have separate decision support models to cover predictions over different time horizons. The criteria used to judge the adequacy of a decision may be different in the short run from the long run. For example, consider accessions policy in the Air Force. Congress has legislated that the Air Force must meet a particular end strength (i.e., a particular size for the inventory) at the end of each fiscal year. Thus, as the end of the year approaches, this end strength may become the single criterion against which to judge the decision about the number of persons to access in each of the remaining months of the year. Over a longer time period, when there are more months among which to divide accessions, additional criteria such as the efficient utilization of training resources should be included in the model.

Models to be used to plan for a longer time horizon require a more flexible representation of the environment than models used for short-term decisions. To expand the accession example, the size of the national pool of high school graduates is one of the important environmental factors that affects the feasibility and cost of attaining a given level of accessions. A model designed to examine accessions over a one- or two-year time horizon can assume that the size of the high school pool is fixed. However, a model designed to plan accessions over a longer time period should represent the changing size of this pool.

Prescriptive and descriptive purposes. Even when one has a prescriptive model, it is useful to have a descriptive model that predicts the outcome of decisions chosen by the user. Since models rarely capture all the elements in a decisionmaking environment, there will be circumstances in which the decisionmaker wants to examine the implications of a different decision from that recommended by a prescriptive model. Even if the decisionmaker agrees with the model, he may wish to demonstrate why the selected alternative is superior to one suggested by another person or group.

5.1.3   Advantages and Disadvantages of Multiple Models

The primary advantage of designing an ODSS with multiple models that can be used independently is the simplicity of each of the resulting models. Each model need represent only the parts of the environment that are most important to the purpose at hand. This simplicity has many advantages:

Inspires user confidence.   Simplicity allows the user to understand exactly how the model works and what its assumptions are. This makes it much easier for a user to feel confident about the model.

Easier to use the model.   It is much easier to use a model that is tailored to a single decision. The user will need to determine appropriate values for a smaller number of inputs. The model will provide faster response time. Thus, the user can try more alternatives and is more likely to test model results for sensitivity to assumptions about the environment and for sensitivity to the values of other policies. The importance of sensitivity analysis to good decisionmaking and the increased ease of performing sensitivity analyses with a model that is easy to use constitute a strong argument for simple models.

Better communication.   Because the model is simpler, it is easier for the user to communicate the reasons for his or her decisions and it will be easier for others to understand those reasons. When others disagree with the decision, it will be easier for all parties to identify and debate the key assumptions on which the decision is based.

Easier to build the models.   In most cases, simpler models are easier to build, test, and evaluate. Fewer relationships are being captured in each model and therefore it is easier to write programs and to debug them; also there may be fewer aspects of each model that need to be validated. In some cases, however, a substantial investment of analytic resources may be needed to separate the effects of the different policies in order to design independent models.

Easier to change the model base.   When the model base consists of many small models connected primarily through the database, it is relatively easy to add, delete, or change elements in the model base. Thus, one of the defining attributes of a DSS—that it be *adaptable* [Turban, 1988] or *extensible* [Moore and Chang, 1983]—is greatly enhanced by using multiple, small, simple models rather than fewer more global models.

These advantages do not come without a heavy price, including:

Suboptimal decisionmaking.   Because each model will omit the parts of the environment that are least important to the purposes of that model, each one may be less accurate than one could attain by using all the data in the ODSS database. Also, since the user of each model focuses on only a single policy (or a small group of interrelated policies), he or she must make assumptions about the decisions made with respect to the other policies. It is almost always the case in theory that "better" decisions are possible when all policies may be varied simultaneously.

Complex links among models. When several models serve the same function (or even closely related functions), exhausting attention must be given to ensuring that their assumptions, inputs, and outputs are consistent and that vehicles for linking the models are in place.

High maintenance costs. The number of models may grow so large that updating and maintaining them all becomes more than any organization might manage, and thus the performance of the ODSS may degrade over time.

Educational costs. When two or more models can produce comparable information, users must be taught which model they should be using for which applications, and they must be educated to understand that sometimes different models may legitimately produce different predictions of the same thing.

Development costs. Building multiple models risks introducing a variety of modeling methods and computer languages, burdening the implementers of the system with an unmanageable array of technical requirements.

Except for suboptimality, these costs of using multiple models can be overcome by careful planning in the conceptual design and development stages, by vigilant oversight of the several modelers assigned to each model throughout the development phase, and by teaching users well (especially, but not exclusively, during the implementation stage). These requirements will impose constraints on modelers that add to the usual burdens of good modeling practice.

On balance, we feel that an ODSS consisting of many smaller models, each tailored to a particular decision situation, provides so many advantages in terms of ease of construction, test and evaluation, use, and maintenance that it will be superior to an ODSS based on one or two large models that would capture all the major features of the environment, despite the disadvantages of reduced optimality. Perhaps in an ideal world, an ODSS would contain both—a single major "organic" model with the most accurate possible representation of all major elements of the environment and all major policies, and many simpler, easy to use models to explore the effects of individual decisions. This is rarely possible because of resource constraints. A single organic model seems to us to be an unacceptable choice.

5.2   MODULAR CONSTRUCTION OF THE MODEL BASE

The partition of a model into modular components is absolutely necessary when building a complex model. It facilitates development, testing,
updating, and maintenance. In an ODSS, the conceptual design of each
module must consider the entire ODSS model base, not just a single individual model.

Modular modeling permits specialists to carve up a model so that each
works exclusively on the problems for which he or she is best trained. This
allows more than one modeling problem to be tackled at a time. For example, in the EFMS, the DMI required development of statistical predictions
of how many airmen would leave the Air Force each year and of how
many airmen would choose to retrain into new occupations during a year.
The development of forecasting rates for each of these modules was done
simultaneously by different researchers with statistical skills. An operations researcher wrote the equations that describe how the rates should be
combined with the composition of the current force to determine the characteristics of the future force.

It is usually wise to identify the statistical prediction modules of a
model before specifying the rest of the internal structure of the model.
One reason is that, in order to improve accuracy, the statistical module
may not directly predict the variables needed in the decision support
model. In our case, it was clear that statistical and time series analysis
could produce good predictions of loss rates but not of losses. Loss rates
vary substantially across categories of airmen, but are relatively stable
across time periods within a category. Thus one can predict the loss rates
within each category with reasonable statistical precision. The number of
airmen in each category varies widely across time periods due to a complex set of flows in and out of the category (as will be explained in Chapter 8). Thus, losses could not accurately be predicted by straightforward
statistical techniques. Consequently, the loss module predicts loss rates,
and each decision support model applies these loss rates to an inventory
derived by modeling other flows.

Allowing the statistical prediction module to predict an intermediate
result (e.g., loss rates) rather than the desired variable (losses) may also
mean that the statistical module can be used in more decision support
models. For example, the same loss rate equation will predict the loss rates
for all the airmen in a particular category, or just for the airmen in that

category who are in a particular occupation. The increase in model building efficiency can be substantial because the developmental effort for the forecasting elements is often quite large—greatly exceeding the work of development of other model elements.

Another advantage of modular modeling is that it facilitates updating the model when an improved version of one of its components becomes available. This feature also means that it may be possible to implement a model using preliminary versions of some of its parts. For example, in the EFMS, the Bonus Effects Model (BEM), which predicts the effect of bonuses on reenlistment counts, budget, and inventory, was ready several years before the DMI, even though the design of the BEM specified that some of its inputs would come from the DMI! In the first few years of its use, an inventory projection model that used a greatly simplified model of occupational migration was used instead of the DMI. Thus, the early model user had the model's predictions about the effect of bonuses on reenlistment counts and budget, and an approximation to its effect on inventory, long before the DMI was available. As will be discussed further in Part V, early implementation of some parts of the ODSS can have important implications for organizational support throughout the necessarily long system development time.

A related advantage of modular modeling is that it provides some protection against the risks inherent in the long system development time. The scale and complexity of ODSS development mean that there are many uncertainties about the feasibility, cost, and schedule of system parts. With modular development, parts of the system can be implemented as they become available. This increases the likelihood that the project will succeed in at least some of its aims. Also, because early partial implementation may increase organizational support for the project, it can increase the likelihood that the project will succeed in *all* of its aims.

Toward the end of the conceptual design phase, the proposed collection of ODSS models should be examined, looking for redundancy in the need to predict the same aspect of the environment as a function of the same parameters and decision variables. Even if the models do not need to contain exactly the same set of parameters, it will be more efficient to build a single prediction module whenever the resultant module is only slightly more complex than the distinct modules would be. For example, the DMI and BEM both use exactly the same loss prediction modules.

In some cases, similar sounding prediction problems will require developing separate modules. Monitoring short-term changes in the force size also requires loss projections, but the predictive models that would perform best in that function are quite different from those to be built for the skills management and bonus activities. Rather than force one function to accept the model suitable for another function and rather than attempt to build a single hybrid loss prediction module for all purposes, we chose to design two distinct loss prediction modules.

5.3 LINKS AMONG MODELS AND MODULES

We have already mentioned the building of links among models as one of the costs of developing many models within an ODSS. Defining these links is an important activity of the conceptual design phase (see Chapter 3).

If modules and models are not made properly conformable, havoc can result. If the parts of a model do not fit together, enormous effort is frequently required to develop an ad-hoc solution. Users may find that the results from two models cannot be compared at any useful level of detail, testers of the models may struggle to reconcile inconsistencies in assumptions, or updaters and maintainers may be overwhelmed by diversities in analytical technique.

Careful attention must be paid during the conceptual design phase to identifying the interfaces among modules and models. Once development is under way, it becomes extremely costly to backtrack in the development process to reconcile inconsistencies among models. For example, during the development phase of the EFMP it was decided that the short-term loss models designed for monitoring the total force in the near term could improve the performance of the loss models being designed for skills management and bonuses.[7] Unfortunately, the two models categorized airmen and their reenlistment decisions so differently that combining the two models became a time-consuming exercise that necessitated several *ad hoc* adaptations.

Each analyst must know from the start of the development stage with which other models his own model must conform. As the development stage is organized, analysts can be brought together to struggle with how

---

[7] Section 6.4.4 provides more information about this example.

their models will be made conformable. Managers of the development phase can monitor the success analysts are having in striking compromises. Indeed, two important tasks of the project leader during the development stage are (1) to ensure that individual analysts do not proceed far with their development activities until they have struck bargains with others whose models are related and (2) to adjudicate conflicts between analysts when they have trouble arriving at a consensus that will result in conformable models.

Sometimes, the requirement for conformity is obvious. If one module's output is another module's input, then the units of measure must be made conformable. Other times, the requirement is less obvious. For example, the loss models used for monitoring the likely force size at the end of the current fiscal year use different categories of airmen than do the loss models that feed the skills management activity. If a single Air Force user were responsible for both of these activities, there would have been a strong *a priori* argument for matching the two categorizations more closely. Burdening one user with two accounting systems for the same thing is costly and should be avoided if possible.

A fundamental principle for achieving consistency is that models that will talk to one another should be designed by analysts who talk to one another. A corollary is that the ideal arrangement is one in which models that talk to one another are developed by one analyst or by one team of analysts. In the EFMP, the BEM and the Year-of-Service Target Generator were both designed by the same analyst. Communication was nearly constant, and the two models are especially well tuned to one another. (But project managers should not assume that the single analyst will necessarily build two models so that they conform with each other. The temptation is great to build one model first and not think about the other until later. Project managers should monitor individuals with interrelated models just as closely as they monitor other analysts who work disjointly on interrelated models.)

A difficult goal to accomplish, but one that can greatly enhance the coherence of an ODSS, is to require all analysts to adopt a common set of definitions. This can be a picky, time-consuming task that no one appreciates, but it improves communications considerably across analysis activities and within the user community. The problem is especially difficult when different users have incompatible definitions. If the user organizations have no reason to speak to one another, then they have little motivation to change their jargon. For example, airmen counted as retirement eligible for the purposes of end-strength monitoring include only those who have already completed a full 20 years of service. Those counted as retirement eligible for the purposes of skills management include in addition those who are in their twentieth year of service at the beginning of the fiscal year under consideration, because they could retire sometime during the year. We squandered a lot of time in project meetings trying to clarify what a speaker meant by "retirement eligible." In such cases, the ODSS community may have to settle for some degree of confusion and overcome it by adding clarifying modifiers.

5.4   FITTING THE MODEL TO THE FUNCTION

The design of an ODSS model should be based on the decision to be supported. The process of design requires all the stages of problem definition required for any model. We have organized our discussion according to each of the parts of a model.

5.4.1   Decision Variables and Other Input

The management levers in a descriptive model must cover all dimensions of the decision. The range of choices available to the user should cover all reasonable alternatives. For example, in the EFMP, the levers for analysis of the Selective Reenlistment Bonus (SRB) plan were the bonus multiples to be offered in each occupation, zone, and model time period.

The management levers should be designed to be easy to use. When a decision involves the values of many variables, such as the bonus plan just discussed, the user should be able to specify simple global rules to assign tentative values to all variables, and then review the assignments and modify individual values. For example, the user might start by checking a single box on a menu that says that each occupation and zone should be given the same bonus multiple as it was given last year. Or, the user might check another box that says all occupations that are not on a list of combat critical skills (maintained as part of the ODSS database) should be assigned a value of zero.

The other model inputs give parameters of environmental relationships and describe other policy decisions. Default values of environmental parameters should be retrieved from the ODSS database.[8] For example, counts of the inventory of airmen at the beginning of the current fiscal year with each grade and occupation (and other characteristics) are maintained in the EFMS database. This makes preparing the input data for the models easy and ensures that all model runs use the latest available information.

Whenever possible, the user should be able to retrieve current plans for other policies from the database. For example, the number of persons who will earn an SRB by retraining into a bonus occupation depends on the number of persons who will be prevented from reenlisting in their current occupation through the Career Job Reservation (CJR) program. Thus the bonus manager needs to know the size of the CJR program in order to estimate the cost of the bonus program. During the planning stages of the bonus program, the exact size of the CJR program will not be known. However, like most decisions in large organizations, changes tend to be incremental. Therefore, the models use last year's program as the default value.

5.4.2   Criteria and Other Output

The criteria for a decision should consist of all the benefits and costs that occur because of the decision. It is critical to understand what all the criteria for a decision are before designing a model to support it. The criteria determine what the model must try to predict, which in turn determines the form of the model.

One way to construct the list of criteria for a decision is to begin by listing all the impacts of the decision—i.e., all the things that might change because of the decision. Then reduce this list to outcomes that satisfy two requirements: (1) The outcome is valued (positively or negatively) by the decisionmaker or by others in the organization and (2) it is plausible that the decision affects the outcome by a large enough amount to be measurable and to have a substantive effect on the decision.

---

[8] This is harder to do when models are used on personal computers. When data transfer times are long, the user will frequently prefer an older version of the data to spending time updating his personal database. When the model run is for personal increased understanding, exercising this preference is probably in the interest of the total organization. On the other hand, when the findings are shared with others, an unnoticed difference in the input values may introduce confusion that is costly to dispel.

The primary resource for determining the appropriate criteria will be the person (or persons) who is (are) currently serving as the decisionmakers. However, if the information that he or she is currently using for the decision is limited compared to the planned ODSS database, it is important to explore the value of using some of the additional information. It is human nature to view the way one does one's job as satisfactory and sometimes hard to see the value of additional information. It is also important to discuss the criteria for a decision with the decisionmaker's manager and usually also with managers one or two steps higher in the hierarchy. These managers may have additional insights into the way the decision fits into corporate strategy and long-range plans and/or into how other parts of the organization use the outcomes of the decision.

For almost all interesting decisions, there are multiple and conflicting criteria; for example, (1) increase retention but reduce the amount of money given to airmen who stay in the service or (2) produce more experienced persons in the future without hiring more inexperienced persons now. In a descriptive model, it is rarely necessary to develop a single number that can be used to rank the alternatives. Rather, the decisionmaker is usually satisfied to know what tradeoffs are possible. How much retention can be bought for a fixed budget? How many inexperienced persons must be trained today to retain 10 experienced people five years from now? The actual tradeoffs are usually made more easily outside the model. (Plus, the decisionmaker can then factor in criteria could not be included in the model.)

A prescriptive model, on the other hand, must have a single criterion.[9] When all costs and benefits can appropriately be expressed in terms of dollars (a rare case in complex policy problems), one has essentially three choices: (1) maximize benefits for a fixed level of costs, (2) minimize costs to attain a fixed level of benefits, or (3) maximize benefits minus costs. Even if one cannot measure the exact dollar value to assign to the benefits (e.g., it is difficult to decide the dollar value of a reenlistment because of the difficulty in measuring exactly how much more is produced by an experienced airman than by a neophyte), if one can produce a single measure of benefits then either of the first two kinds of criteria can be used. For example, one could distribute a fixed bonus budget among

---

[9] See Quade [1989] (especially Chapters 6 and 7) for a good discussion of ways to determine and measure objectives in public policy problems. Many of these same issues arise in large corporations whenever internal transactions constitute a substantial part of organizational activity.

AFSCs to attain the best match between the reenlistments and their target, or one could determine the cost required to attain the reenlistment target.

Choosing a single criterion can be a difficult problem in situations with multiple conflicting objectives, costs that cannot easily be translated into dollars, and benefits that are difficult to quantify. For example, in some skills the Air Force wants to have more airmen with substantial levels of experience because they perform better at these jobs. It also wants to treat each occupation equally because all airmen are potentially subject to the dangers of war. Yet to produce the experienced force it needs in certain skills, it is necessary to offer reenlistment bonuses and faster promotions. Thus, there is an inherent tradeoff between the criteria of producing the correct skill-specific force and being "fair" to all persons in the Air Force family. Such inherent conflicts appear in many complicated decision situations.

Various ways have been developed to handle multiple objectives in a prescriptive model:

- Define the objective function to be a weighted sum of each of the individual criteria. It is difficult to determine what the appropriate weights are—especially since they will change with changes in the environment. On the other hand, this can be a useful technique when the user is free to vary the weights. Then the user can try out different weights and see how far he can go in accomplishing each goal or each combination of goals.
- Order the criteria according to organizational preferences, then optimize in sequence. This is known as *preemptive goal programming* [Hillier and Lieberman, 1990, Chapter 8].
- Establish a specific numeric goal for each criterion, formulate an objective function for each criterion, and then seek a solution that minimizes the sum of deviations of these objective functions from their respective goals. This is known as nonpreemptive goal programming [Hillier and Lieberman, 1990, Chapter 8].
- Obtain agreement about the minimum acceptable level of attainment of all except the most important of the criteria and then use these minimum levels as constraints while optimizing the remaining most important criterion.

In addition to the resulting values of the criteria, the model should output its other predictions about outcomes and key intermediate values in the model. These outputs may be useful for documentation, for explaining the predictions of the criteria, for informing stakeholders with different criteria, and for monitoring the outcomes of the decisions.

5.4.3   Relationships in the Model

The hypothesized relationships in the model predict how the model's outputs and intermediate variables change as the model's inputs are varied. The relationships are built from a combination of deductive reasoning and statistical analysis of data describing the system. In building the EFMP, much of our effort was devoted to developing accurate statistical forecasts of loss rates and we expect that most organizations complicated enough to need an ODSS will have a similarly large forecasting problem. We have devoted Chapter 6 to the principles of building good statistical prediction modules, and provide examples in Chapter 7.

5.5   SIMPLICITY VERSUS REALISM

Increased realism in the structure of a model does not guarantee increased accuracy in the results from the model. In statistical models, adding too much detail can dissipate one's information so that no relationships are determined with statistical accuracy. For example, in the loss models used for skills management activities, occupational categories that have had few airmen in them over time are lumped together into larger clusters, and loss rates are assumed to be the same for all occupations within a cluster. Statistical theory demonstrates that this less realistic assumption can produce more accurate forecasts for each occupational group and for all of them taken together than would a more realistic model that allowed a different loss rate for each occupation.

Statistical models are not the only instances in which simpler models can outperform more realistic models. Adding realism adds complexity. Adding complexity increases the likelihood of programming errors. Thus, adding detail can lead to less reliable computer code and therefore to less reliable outputs. Also, more detailed models often require more assumptions—assumptions that can, if wrong, undermine the reliability of the model's output.

But complexity can improve the performance of a model. The loss models used for skills management outperform those used in the Air Force's previous system in large part because the new models incorporate the realistic, but complicating, assumptions that loss and reenlistment decisions depend on economic factors, and that those factors may be different in the future from the way they have been in the recent past.

The question then is this: If making a model more complex will improve the performance of a model, is the loss of simplicity worthwhile? The answer will depend heavily on how often the model is used and how quickly results from the model are needed after a query is initiated. The answer will also depend on how important it is to have the model be more accurate. More complex models take longer to run. The DMI takes several hours to run. This is a very complex model, but it is typically only run a few times a year. Moreover, the run time is known well in advance, so the runs can be scheduled at convenient times. To develop the training program, accurate forecasts at an extended level of detail are required. Only a very complex model could provide such detailed forecasts with the desired level of accuracy.

Very complex models should only be designed for very important, but infrequent applications. More regular applications require models that are no more than moderately complex. But one more class of applications remains to be noted. Analysts within an organization may wish to cull options for detailed analysis from a very large set of alternatives, or they may wish to offer informed guesses to decisionmakers on what is sometimes very short notice. Both of these types of applications require models that can be run very quickly, and hence require especially simple models. Culling options from a broad set requires winnowing the outliers—setting aside those that are by far the worst or selecting those that are by far the best. Such a process does not require great accuracy. It would be nice if the predictions from these models were also very accurate, but if immediate feedback is needed by a decisionmaker, one must settle for the most accurate estimates that can be made quickly.

5.6   DOCUMENTATION

Although documentation is important for any model development exercise, it is even more important for an ODSS because of the large number of people involved in system use, maintenance, and development. Also, because of the large turnover in organizations, it is necessary that information be conveyed in a permanent form rather than predominantly through verbal education.

The models in an ODSS require four different types of documentation. First, an *executive summary* that describes the model's capabilities and why one might want to use it. It is intended for managers throughout the organization who are involved in reviewing model decisions, in supervising decisionmakers, or in managing areas that are affected in some way by the decision.

The second type of documentation is written for the *user*. It provides detailed examples of how to use the model and examples of model input, output, and the use of the output.

The third type of documentation is more akin to *model documentation* in a more traditional environment. It describes the mathematical, algorithmic, and/or statistical foundations of the model, and the computer code used to implement the model.

The fourth type of document should describe the *procedures for updating and maintaining* the model. It should also describe the circumstances in which one should reevaluate the model's algorithms. It should describe how frequently statistical parameters should be updated and provide code and documentation for recomputing them with new data.

Chapter 6 | How Statistical Concerns Influence Modeling

6.1 INTRODUCTION

"The best qualification of a prophet is to have a good memory."[10] For ancient prophets, "good memory" meant being familiar with a wealth of stories handed down from generation to generation. For modern prophets, "good memory" has become statistical acumen plus a thorough knowledge of what data can be assembled about the past.

Modern prophets apply statistical techniques to historical data to choose a model that will forecast the future most accurately. Both the statistical tools and the historical data that these analysts use to build their models can markedly influence the structure of those models—much as the equipment and materials of engineers influence the architecture of buildings.

A building's functions dictate its design, but the design must also accommodate available technology and materials. The arches of medieval cathedrals accommodated the building technologies of their day; early American skyscrapers were limited by the steel then available. It is the same with models. A model's form will be dictated by its functions, but

---

[10] The Marquis of Halifax quoted in Granger [1989].

the model must be bent and twisted to accord with current statistical technology and the model that can actually be built will be constrained by the data available.

Though technology and data must always be considered, first and foremost, model designers, like builders, must attend to function. Medieval architects heard the call for buildings that reached to heaven, so they strived to discover the principles for building tall structures; modern model builders must know what their models will be used for, and then look for suitable statistical principles.

6.2   HOW THE USES OF MODELS INFLUENCE THE STATISTICAL METHODS

Several dimensions of a model's use critically influence the statistical methods needed to build them: (1) Does the user need results from the model quickly, say in a matter of minutes, or can the user wait a longer time to get results? (2) Does the user need detailed results, or are summary results sufficient? (3) Does the user place a high value on very accurate results, or will less accurate answers suffice? (4) Is the model intended to guess the consequences of the organization's actions, or is the model intended to guess what the future will look like independently of the organization's actions?

6.2.1   Speed, Detail, and Accuracy

Demands for speed, detail, and accuracy will condition the building of every model in an ODSS, but the weight given to each of these demands will depend on the organizational activity that the model supports. An ODSS must be ready to balance speed, detail, and accuracy. This balance can sometimes be achieved by compromising within a model; sometimes it requires building multiple models.

Users needing answers in a hurry will judge models as much on their speed as on their more traditional statistical properties (like "mean square error of forecast"). In the design of such "quick" models one must be ready to compromise statistical performance to enhance operational performance. A decisionmaker cannot afford the luxury of slow models if the decision must be made immediately after the need for a decision is recognized. Indeed, even models quick to execute may not serve well in such circumstances if the data needed for the model are not available in a timely way. (For example, to examine the Air Force's Trained Personnel Requirements [TPR] and determine an appropriate training program, conferences occur at six-month intervals. But the relevant data needed for the Fall TPR conference are not available until the end of the fiscal year, leaving barely enough time to run the relevant models.)

Notice that the "quickness" of a model refers to the time it takes to run it, not to how long it takes to develop it. The analytical effort required to build a fast, easy to use model that is sufficiently accurate for, say, winnowing a large number of alternative policy options to just a few, may be greater than that required to build a model that yields still more accurate results but is cumbersome and slow.

The chief impediments to speed in the use of a model are large input files, a large number of computations to arrive at a prediction, and a large number of intermediate input and output steps on the way from initial inputs to final results. A quest for detail or accuracy can press one to introduce all these impediments. Detailed output often requires both detailed input and time-consuming computations for each item of detail. Accuracy can often be achieved only by estimating more disaggregated entities and combining the several estimates into an aggregated whole. This requires increased computations (as the many estimates are formed) and may call for intermediate input and output procedures (if the disaggregated estimates must be produced separately from the aggregation process).

For what kinds of applications might users be willing to sacrifice speed? When decisions have very costly consequences, decisionmakers are likely to value highly predictions free of bias and forecasts with low mean square error; accuracy will be the order of the day. Moreover, the decisionmakers will often want detailed information in such situations. An ODSS should eschew speed in these high-cost circumstances and trade time of execution for accuracy and detail.

While adding detail may improve accuracy, it may not. Try the following exercise. Guess how long your next door neighbor is (1) from ground to knee, (2) from knee to waist, (3) from waist to shoulder, (4) from shoulder to top of head. Now, without reference to those guesses, guess (5) how tall your neighbor is. Compare the sum of (1)-(4) with (5). Which guess do you think is better? (How might you reconcile the two? We address this question in Section 6.4 below.)

This exercise highlights the two approaches one can take to developing forecasts. One could forecast disaggregates and sum them, or one could forecast an aggregate and break it up into disaggregate parts. In the example above, most people do better by starting with an aggregate estimate and then breaking it up. But if one is forecasting household income, one can often do better by first forecasting earned income and unearned income and then summing the two. Which approach to take is a matter for empirical investigation. In the EFMS we have examples of each approach.

It is also possible (e.g., because of the complexity of the model) that an accurate forecasting model will run slowly but not provide much detail. Important decisions whose consequences are especially difficult to forecast may warrant slow models lacking in detail. For example, because changes in military retirement policy can have important consequences for the military's readiness and for its budget, we found it worthwhile to build for the EFMS a very complicated model that predicts the consequences of alternative retirement policies. This model does not provide very detailed estimates of loss rates (for example, it does not distinguish among occupations), but the estimates it does produce are much more reliable than we could obtain from a simpler model. This complicated model cannot be used quickly, nor does it offer much detail, but the importance of the decision it supports warrants the time it takes to use the model.

When building a model for a single user, as in traditional decision support systems, the trade-offs among speed, detail, and accuracy are often made within a single model. The user's chores are often narrowly enough defined that a single model can meet all of his or her needs. Sometimes in an ODSS a single model can be built that serves the needs of all of its potential users in terms of speed, detail, and accuracy; but often there will need to be several models that seemingly perform the same task. Because an ODSS spans several functions of an organization, the demands for speed, detail, and accuracy may be irreconcilable. The solution is to build several models, each making the trade-offs differently. For example, the EFMS contains five different models for forecasting how many airmen would leave the service in a given time period. Two of these models were made to run faster than the others by sacrificing elements of detail. Two of the slower models provide extensive detail, but differ in when they provide increased accuracy; together they are more accurate than either alone. The fifth model, the retirement policy analysis model, offers very little detail, but allows accurate forecasting in particularly important circumstances. Reconciling the results from several models within an ODSS that offer different answers to the same question is a task we discuss in Section 6.4.3.

6.2.2 Predicting Consequences and Making Forecasts

Almost all models in an ODSS provide guesses about what will happen in the future. Sometimes these guesses are about the potential consequences of an action the organization is considering. For example, the Air Force frequently wants to guess what the effect of higher or lower reenlistment bonuses will be on future loss rates. Other times, the organization has no interest in such causal matters; it simply wants to guess the future state of the world. For example, to guide their early release and accessions plans, the Air Force wants to predict what losses would be in the near term if there were no early releases; there is no concern here about what will influence those numbers, there is simply a need for the guess itself. It is convenient to distinguish these two kinds of guesses by referring to the former as predicting consequences and the latter as making forecasts. (Alternatively, one could distinguish forecasting consequences and forecasting states of the world, but the former depiction we find more convenient.)

Predicting consequences of actions is more demanding than making forecasts. During a late nineteenth century cholera epidemic, Russian peasants noted that the appearance of doctors from Moscow heralded a sudden rise in deaths from cholera. During the early nineteenth century, women learned that babies born at home were less likely to die than those born in hospitals. (Indeed, babies born in taxis on the way to the hospital were less likely to die than those born in hospitals.)

Both peasants and pregnant women could correctly forecast disasters when doctors appeared. But predicting consequences was more difficult. In hopes of forestalling cholera deaths, the Russian peasants rose up and killed the doctors who appeared. The consequence of the killing was to increase both suffering and deaths. The doctors did not cause the cholera deaths; their arrival stemmed from a government policy of sending doctors to a town at the first sign of a cholera outbreak. In contrast, the pregnant women kept going to hospitals, trusting in their fashionable physicians. The consequence of this trust was that doctors kept killing newborn babies—until scientists discovered both antiseptics and the germs the doctors had been carrying from cadavers to birthing rooms.

A model used for predicting consequences must distill spurious correlations, like the one observed by the peasants, from causal relationships, like the one observed by the nineteenth century women. This distillation can greatly complicate both the model used and the process required to build the model. The Russian peasants believed that the arrival of doctors increased the number of deaths when in fact it decreased them; the peasants' estimate of the effect of doctors on deaths was statistically biased. The statistical methods for obtaining unbiased estimates of consequences are more complicated than the methods required to obtain an accurate forecasting model.

To study consequences, one must use "conditional models." We call these "conditional models" because their predictions should be reported in the form: "If unemployment is 4% next year, we expect the loss rate to be $x\%$." Conditional models can be used for both causal predictions and forecasts. But if one is simply forecasting, conditional models need not be used. Instead one can use "time series models." These models forecast the future value of a variable not by looking at what other variables are expected to be in the future, as in conditional models, but simply by extrapolating from the past values of the variable in question.

Conditions in the immediate future are often very much like conditions in the recent past. Consequently, time series models' extrapolations can frequently forecast the immediate future extremely well. A corollary to this is that modest errors in analysts' expectations about future circumstances can easily, when forecasting the immediate future, lead conditional models to forecast less well than time series models. As we look further into the future, conditions are more likely to change markedly. Consequently, time series forecasts frequently forecast the more distant future poorly. If, when forecasting the more distant future, analysts have reasonably accurate expectations about what future circumstances will be, conditional models are likely to outperform time series models.

These contrasting strengths of time series and conditional models suggest that an ODSS may want to develop both types of models for some forecasting activities, relying on the time series models for the short term and the conditional models for the long term. Where the short term ends and the long term begins is an empirical matter; the long term begins when conditional models begin to forecast better than time series models. If the short term proves long enough, one might need only a short-term model. If the short term is short enough, one might ignore it, and need only a long-term model. The design of the EFMS assumed that the differences in forecasting performance between time series and conditional models would justify building two sets of models: one for the short term, which we expected to be three months to a year, and one for the longer term. The assumption was proven to be a valid one. The need to distinguish between the short run and the longer run is likely to be a common one in ODSS development.

Conditional models will perform better when the analysts' expectations about the future are accurate. The further into the future we look, the less confident we can be about our expectations, and the less reliable our forecasts will be. In the EFMP we referred to "the middle term" as the part of the long run across which we were prepared to overlook the uncertainty in our expectations. For example, in the EFMS one knows the race, sex, and education of the airmen currently in the service, but is uncertain about the traits of future entrants. Since one or two years in the future the force would be composed primarily of airmen whose traits we know, with relatively few new entrants, we were willing to ignore our uncertainty about the force's demographic makeup when making forecasts one or two years ahead. In the EFMS we rely on our nonshort-term models primarily over the next fiscal year or two; consequently, we refer to our models beyond the short term as middle-term models. If we used the models to forecast further into the future (say 7 to 10 years), the bulk of the force would be airmen whose traits are guessed; in such cases we would refer to the models as long-term models.

Having models for several time horizons can introduce a problem of coordinating results. Since the models are frequently quite distinct, there is little or no assurance that their results will blend smoothly together. Users who see abrupt discontinuities in forecasts can be troubled. Integrating models across time horizons is a problem akin to that of reconciling conflicting answers to a single question from several models in an ODSS. We discuss the reconciliation of conflicting answers in Section 6.4.3.

An ODSS will need models for predicting consequences and models for making forecasts. The structures of the models and the statistical methods used to build them will vary between the two uses. However, only occasionally will a model suitable for predicting consequences not fill the bill as a model for making forecasts.

Although in the EFMS we needed separate models for short-term and middle-term forecasting, we did not need separate models for forecasting and predicting consequences. The conditional model we designed for predicting the loss rate consequences of Air Force policies in the next one to seven years was also suitable for making forecasts over that period. However, this double duty complicated the building and evaluation of the model, as we describe in detail below.

6.3   TIME SERIES MODELS AND CONDITIONAL MODELS

6.3.1   Time Series Models

Time series models can be extremely simple. For example, loss rates next year might be modeled as being the same as loss rates this year, as was done in some loss models used in the Air Force's TOPCAP system (the system that the EFMS was designed to replace). Alternatively, a time series model may produce its forecast by describing the future value of a variable in terms of a complex function of its past values. For example, the EFMS uses a time series model to forecast loss rates over the next several months based on a complex manipulation of loss rates from the past several years.

There are two general approaches to time series modeling. First, Box and Jenkins [1976] developed methods for estimating models that forecast future values of a variable from a mixture of moving averages and autoregressions.[11] Second, Cleveland, Dunn, and Terpenning [1976] developed methods for building forecasting models that use statistically robust techniques such as medians and trimmed means.

Box-Jenkins time series models are especially useful when one has a long record of historical data from a system whose inner workings have remained stable. Many physical processes meet these conditions. Robust time series models are especially useful when a shorter record of data is available, or when the system in question tends to undergo relatively frequent structural changes, or when measurement errors in the data tend to be relatively large from time to time. In the development of the EFMP we experimented extensively with Box-Jenkins models but found their forecasts to be too sensitive to the measurement errors common in the available data. Instead, we built robust time series models and simple moving average models for forecasting losses several months into the future. (Simple moving average models are, in fact, special cases of Box-Jenkins models, but we did not use the Box-Jenkins methodology to arrive at them or to assess them.)

Time series models are well suited for making "quick" forecasts as long as they eschew excessive detail. For a single variable, the models require only the variable's past values and the parameters of the model as

---

[11] An autoregression expresses the current value of a variable as influenced by all of its past values and by an unpredictable current element; a moving average expresses the current value as influenced by the recent unpredictable elements and a current unpredictable element.

inputs; the computation of predictions is relatively quick. If the input data can be produced quickly, as is usually the case, these models are well suited to quick analysis. Box-Jenkins models, which can be tedious to build, are especially quick in application. Robust time series models rely on more computations at time of use than do Box-Jenkins models and may therefore be slower in use.

In the short term, time series forecasts may do much better than conditional forecasts. The airmen who made decisions about leaving the service last month may have much better information about current employment prospects than an analyst can gather quickly, hence the airmen's decisions may contain more information about loss rates over the next few months than is contained in available "conditioning variables," namely the analysts' best guesses about what economic conditions will be in those months.

The longer the term of the forecast, the more likely that the use of conditional models will be appropriate. Airmen who considered leaving the Air Force last month faced circumstances very much like the circumstances facing airmen next month, but by next year the conditions may well change markedly. Hence, last month's loss rates forecast next month's loss rates much better than they forecast next year's loss rates. If I wish to forecast next year's loss rates, I would do well first to make a guess about how unemployment, pay, and bonuses are likely to change over the year and use these guesses in a conditional prediction model.

6.3.2 Conditional Models

Conditional models can be as simple as a single linear model that predicts the future value of one variable from the value of another variable. (We refer to the variable from which the prediction is made as a "conditioning variable.") But conditional models can also be very complex, embedding the variable to be predicted in a system of nonlinear equations that must be solved simultaneously to yield a prediction for the variable of interest.

We categorize conditional models in two ways. First, we focus on the model's relationship to causality. Second, we focus on the mathematical form of the model.

If one has no need to trace causality, one may build a correlation model. The variable to be predicted is expressed as a function of other variables whose values are given and with which the variable of interest is expected to be highly correlated. The peasants' model was a correlation model. Actually, all prediction models rely on correlation. But in the models we dub "correlation models," variables are included in the model for no other reason than that they are contemporaneously correlated with the variable to be predicted; or, conversely, variables are excluded from the model only because they do not add noticeably to the correlation between the predicted variable and the conditioning variables.

If one is interested in causality, one must build either a "structural model" or a "reduced form" model. A structural model offers the most complete depiction of a causal process, but demands more information than a reduced form model. (See any introductory econometrics text for more details than provided below.)

A structural model purports to represent the behavior of actors within a system and the institutions within which they act. The classic economic application of a structural model is the model of supply and demand. One equation in the model depicts the quantities of a good, say, gasoline, that buyers will want to buy, given the price of gasoline and income. A second equation in the model depicts the quantities of gasoline sellers will wish to sell, given the price of gasoline and the prices the firm pays workers, raw materials, etc. A third equation in the model expresses the market clearing condition that buyers and sellers must agree how much to exchange for a trade to occur. (This model is depicted in equations later in this chapter.)

In a structural model, some variables are determined within the system (in the economic example, the quantity of gasoline that will change hands and the price at which it will change hands); these are termed "endogenous variables." Other variables in such a model are determined outside the system (in the economic example, the incomes of buyers and the prices paid by the firm for workers, etc.); these are termed "exogenous variables." A structural model can be used to predict how changes in an exogenous variable will influence an endogenous variable. Thus the supply and demand model could be used to predict how a law that raised the price of crude oil (the raw material) will change the price of gasoline.

To write down the structural form of a model requires extensive information about both institutions and behavior. That information must allow one to say not only what the consequences of an action are, but how those consequences unfold. When a model is needed only to predict the consequences of an action and not to detail how those consequences unfold, one can use a reduced form model. A reduced form model expresses each endogenous variable in a system as a function of all the exogenous variables in the system. To predict how a change in an exogenous variable will influence a single endogenous variable, one need only look at the equation for that endogenous variable.

Reduced form models are generally much easier to build than are structural models (see the discussion of estimation techniques below). However, an ODSS frequently requires some structural models. For example, the Air Force needs to know loss rates by grade, but both loss rates and grade are endogenous variables. In essence, one is asking how policy will affect two endogenous variables, loss rates and grades. Therefore, to forecast what loss rates will be by grade requires a conditional model of loss rates that includes grade as a conditioning variable. The endogeneity of grades implies that this cannot be a reduced form model, but must be a structural model. (Any model that includes endogenous variables among its conditioning variables is a structural model.)

The second categorization of conditional statistical models is by their mathematical form. Conditional models are either linear or nonlinear. Here the focus is on the parameters of the model, not on the variables. If the parameters of the model that are to be estimated when one builds the model appear linearly in the model, estimation is generally much easier than if the parameters appear nonlinearly. An example of a linear model would be:

$$Q^s = aP + bY^2$$
$$Q^d = cP + gW + hR$$
$$Q^s = Q^d$$

where the parameters to be estimated are a, b, c, g, and h. The appearance of Y squared does not upset the linearity because Y is a variable in the model, not a parameter to be estimated. An example of a nonlinear model would be:

$$Q^s = aP + bY$$
$$Q^d = abP + gW + hR$$
$$Q^s = Q^d$$

where the parameters to be estimated are a, b, g, and h. The appearance of the term ab in the second equation is the nonlinearity. The fact that Q, P, Y, W, and R all appear in linear form does not matter because they are not the parameters to be estimated; they are the variables in the system.

Nonlinear models impose additional computational burdens on the model builders. Nonlinearities should be avoided whenever such avoidance does not undermine the accuracy of the model's predictions. When nonlinearities cannot be avoided, the computational burdens they entail sometimes sharply circumscribe the numbers of variables that can be included in the model. For example, in the EFMS, to model the effects of changes in retirement policies on loss rates, we had to build a highly nonlinear dynamic programming model. The model could not be estimated unless we excluded from the model many of the conditioning variables that one knows are correlated with loss rates.

In estimating linear models, adding more explanatory variables is hardly ever an undue computational burden. One can always add an additional variable if it promises to add explanatory power to the model. This feature of linear models can give them a striking advantage over nonlinear models, which often cannot be estimated if the number of explanatory variables is not small. If highly nonlinear models are needed for some special conditions, it may be worthwhile to build two models, the nonlinear model with few explanatory variables for the special-purpose applications, and a linear (or less nonlinear) model with many more explanatory variables for use in ordinary conditions.

For example, in the EFMS, we built two loss models for making long-term forecasts: one linear and the other a nonlinear dynamic programming model. Our linear loss rate models provide more accurate forecasts of loss rates as long as the retirement system does not change; the dynamic programming model performs better only in the special condition of a retirement system change.[12] Having the two models allows us to get better forecasts than we could manage with either model alone.

Time series models and conditional models can be combined to form a class of models called "multivariate time series models." These models posit that the future values of each of a set of variables can depend on both the past and future values of other variables and the past values of itself. For detailed discussions of this class of models, see Harvey [1989, 1990].

---

[12] Actually, the dynamic programming model is designed to examine a broader class of compensation changes that includes retirement system changes, but retirement changes are the most important special condition for which the model is useful. One benefit of building the nonlinear model was that we were able to use it to study, by simulation, just which kinds of compensation changes should not be studied using linear models.

6.3.3 A Base Policy for Forecasts

All forecasting techniques are based at least in part on an historical record of the past. What actually happened in the past was the result of a combination of policy decisions and environmental factors. Some of the decisions may have caused sharp discontinuities in the data, which makes modeling efforts difficult.

One approach to this problem is to remove the effects of the decisions from the data series in an analysis file so that the entire analysis file describes one's best estimate of what would have happened had a single policy been in effect. This allows one to build simpler, more accurate forecasting models. The major price paid for this advantage is in the complexity of the data processing required to build the analysis file.

An example should help illustrate what we mean. The Air Force has sometimes found itself in the situation of being over end-strength amounts as the end of a fiscal year approached. In these years, it instituted a policy of early release, which allowed persons whose contract was due to expire during an interval from the end of the fiscal year until a fixed date to leave the service early. Statistical analysis showed that the early release program affected only the timing of losses not the total number of losses—i.e., persons who were planning to leave the Air Force at the end of their contract were allowed to leave early. The early release program has a dramatic effect on calculated loss rates and, since the size of the program varied tremendously from year to year, the raw data exhibited substantial swings in loss rates.

In developing statistical prediction modules for loss rates, we created an analysis file in which it appeared that none of these early releases occurred. The persons who left the Air Force under the early release program appeared in the analysis file to have stayed in the Air Force until the day their contract expired and then to have left. Our loss prediction modules provide forecasts of what will happen in the absence of an early release program. We call these forecasts *policy-free* forecasts, but they actually reflect the policy of no early release program. The loss prediction modules were much easier to construct because the underlying data were much more coherent.

The decision support models are able to simulate whatever early release program the user wishes to implement. Indeed, one of the models uses the output of a single forecasting run as the input to many runs in which the user varies the early release program and accession timing to obtain the desired end strength. Because the forecasting is done outside the model, the user receives a very quick response time from the model.

6.4   STATISTICAL CRITERIA AND STATISTICAL METHODS

Forecasting models and prediction models are assessed by somewhat different statistical criteria. Take the example of loss rate models. In forecasting loss rates, one asks how close to true loss rates, on average, one's guesses of loss rates will be. In a prediction model, one asks how close to truth, on average, will one's guesses be about the *changes* in loss rates that will result when, say, bonuses are *changed*. The focus on changes in prediction models introduces a concern for the individual parameters in the model, whereas forecasting requires attention only to the overall results from the model.

Forecast models will be judged by the mean square error or the mean absolute error of their forecasts. Prediction models will be judged by the unbiasedness of their parameter estimates. If prediction models serve double duty (generating forecasts as well as predictions of consequences), then the model must be built with an eye to both criteria.

6.4.1   Statistical Methods and Time Series Models

Box-Jenkins time series models are built using formal and informal procedures for determining which model, drawn from a wide class of models, will use all the information contained in past observations on a variable. The heart of these procedures is to apply a proposed model to past data and ask if the errors in these artificial forecasts could themselves be predicted by another model. If the errors appear unpredictable, the proposed model has passed the statistical test. Considerations of simplicity are used to choose from the candidates that pass the test. The underlying premise of the Box-Jenkins approach is that a model that has used information efficiently in the past will do so in the future.

Robust time series models are based on a different premise. The premise for these models is that good forecasts can be best made by avoiding especially large errors. Two strategies can help: First, when data are contaminated by periodic large measurement errors, the mismeasured data often appear extreme. Thus, by precluding extreme data ("outliers") from having much of an influence on forecasts, a serious source of error can be avoided. Second, when the data indicate a persistent string of forecasting errors, allowing the structure of the model to change relatively quickly can reduce errors arising from applying an outdated model. Such rapid updating will avoid large forecasting errors when the underlying system is subject to abrupt changes. The class of models that can accommodate both downplaying outliers and rapidly updating one's model is less rich than that spanned by the Box-Jenkins techniques; but which approach will produce the better forecasts is a matter for empirical investigation when developing an ODSS.

6.4.2   Statistical Methods and Conditional Models

The most common procedure for estimating linear conditional models is ordinary least squares (OLS). OLS will generally suffice for estimating correlation models and reduced form models,[13] but structural models will require more sophisticated methods because OLS yields biased estimates of the parameters of equations with endogenous conditioning variables.

The most important exception to the appropriateness of OLS when the conditioning variables are exogenous is when variables are omitted from the model. If the omitted variables are correlated with the included variables, the OLS will confound the effects of the omitted and included variables, yielding biased estimates of the parameters on the included variables. For example, the Air Force offers bonuses only to occupations that have unusually high loss rates. If one uses OLS to estimate the relationship between loss rates and bonuses, but omits occupation from the model, increases in bonuses will be estimated to raise loss rates; inclusion of occupation in the model eliminates this bias and permits the use of OLS.

Nonlinear models are candidates for use when there are theoretical reasons for believing that a linear model would seriously misrepresent the phenomenon being studied. In these cases there is a compelling case to use the nonlinear model if the suggested nonlinearity does not overly complicate estimation. However, if estimating the nonlinear model is so difficult that the model cannot include covariates that would much improve the forecasting power of the linear specification, then one must weigh the biases introduced by the linear model against the efficiency lost by exclud-

---

[13]OLS is a special case of the method called generalized least squares (GLS); GLS may yield more accurate forecasts than OLS, but whenever OLS yields biased predictions of consequences, GLS would also.

ing covariates from the nonlinear model. If one does decide to use a non-linear specification, the questions of bias and accuracy continue to dictate estimation technique.

Models used to predict consequences must be built with considerable attention to potential sources of bias. Careful thought must be given to whether variables are being omitted that might introduce biases. If there are endogenous variables among the conditioning variables, estimators drawn from the family called "instrumental variables estimators" should be used. (These estimators are designed to purge biases arising from endogeneity.) Another source of bias to guard against is measurement errors in the conditioning variables. While instrumental variables estima-tors can be used if measurement errors are a serious problem, the best way to avoid biases due to measurement errors is to clean one's data so that measurement errors are relatively unimportant.

6.4.3   How to Combine Competing Forecasts

In an ODSS, one will frequently obtain different forecasts of the same event. In some cases, as discussed in Section 6.2.2 above, the multiple forecasts will arise because different model users have different needs. In these cases, the choice of forecast is made according to the needs of the users. In this section, we consider what should be done when it is not obvi-ous which forecast should be preferred.

By summing the detailed estimates for each occupation, the Disaggreg-ate Middle-term Inventory Projection Model (DMI) produces an estimate of total end strength at the end of the next fiscal year. The Short-term Aggregate Inventory Projection Model (SAM) provides a second estimate of the same quantity. It is possible to combine these predictions to produce a better estimate than either one produces individually.

The middle-term loss rate module of the DMI uses regression analysis to predict loss rates under the assumption that the errors in the equation (i.e., the difference between the prediction and the actual) are independent of one another (see Section 7.3). Loss predictions for the current fiscal year are generated by applying these loss rates to the inventory present at the beginning of the fiscal year.

The short-term loss model used by SAM predicts loss rates based on a time series. (see Section 7.4). Under the assumption that the errors in suc-cessive months' forecasts are correlated, this short-term model should pro-duce better forecasts in the short run than the middle-term models.

When appropriate actions are directly tied to forecasts, it is necessary to choose a single forecast value. In our case, the number of accessions for the rest of the year (which is under Air Force control) had to be set equal to the legislated end strength minus current inventory plus forecast losses. Clearly, one month before the end of the fiscal year, the short-term model will be most accurate. Which model should one use at 6 months? at 12 months?

Forcing forecasts to the values from either model (in our case, the middle-term or the short-term model) are just two extremes of a much wider spectrum of choices, some of which will be superior to either forecast individually. It is useful to think of all the alternative aggregate forecasts that might be formed from weighted averages of two forecasts (waf), waf = w1*f1 + w2*f2, where f1 is the forecast from model 1 and f2 is the forecast from model 2, and the w1 and w2 are positive weights that sum to one. Choosing the first forecast is equivalent to using the average forecast with w1 = 1 and w2 = 0. Choosing the second forecast is equivalent to the average forecast with w1 = 0 and w2 = 1. Statistical theory shows that better forecasts might be obtained from using weights not equal to one or zero.

The mean square error of waf (mse(waf)) is:

$$mse(waf) = (w1**2)*mse(f1) + (w2**2)*mse(f2) + 2*w1*w2*cov(f1,f2).$$

The weights w1 and w2 that minimize the mean square error of waf are:

$$w1! = \frac{mse(f2) - cov(f1,f2)}{mse(f1) + mse(f2) - 2*cov(f1,f2)}$$

$$w2! = 1 - w1$$

These weights can be estimated from a series of forecasts and the actual outcomes. The mean squared errors of a forecast over the sample period give the maximum likelihood estimates of mse for that forecast. The observed mean covariance between deviations of f1 and f2 each measured about the observed actual mean is an estimate of cov(f1,f2). Replacing the actual mean square errors and covariance in the formula for ws! with their estimates is an appropriate estimator for the optimal weights.

Unfortunately, in small samples it is difficult to estimate cov(f1,f2) precisely. In standard practice, analysts assume the covariance is small and use estimates of the mean square errors to form quasi-optimal weights.

The formal statistical analysis above is useful to emphasize an important point: Apart from the costliness of generating several different forecasts, the best practice is *not* to choose one forecast to use in favor of others, but rather to *combine* several forecasts so as to benefit from the informational content of each. Only in the special case in which the mse of one forecast is equal to the covariance between the two forecasts can we say that one forecast is redundant and should be dismissed. (Of course, if one can afford only a single forecast, choose the one with the smaller mse, but remember that this choice is made on economic grounds more than on statistical grounds.)

However, with the important point made that forecasts are better combined than discarded, the question remains open as how best to combine them when the mean square errors and covariance are unknown and little data are on hand to estimate them. Granger and Ramanathan [1984] offer a good procedure that is quite simple to apply. They show that an ordinary least-squares regression of actual outcomes against alternative forecasts and a constant term is superior to the standard practice. The optimal waf would then be formed by taking the alternative forecasts, weighing them by their estimated coefficients from the historical regression, and adding to them the estimated constant from the regression.

In the EFMP, it is extremely difficult to generate retrospective data with which to run the DMI[14] to generate the time series needed to determine the weights to be used in combining the short-term and middle-term forecasts. Because of this situation, a decision was made to gather the data on a prospective basis. After the system has been operating for several years, the regression analysis will be performed and improved forecasts generated. This is just one example of how we expect the EFMP to improve continually.

6.4.4 Data

"Data! data! data!" he cried impatiently. "I can't make bricks without clay!"[15] Like Sherlock Holmes, we cannot expect to build sound edifices from poor quality data. If the first qualification of a good prophet is a good

---

[14] Among the problems are continual changes in the definitions of occupations and the amount of effort required to fit the loss models and blend them into fiscal year loss rates.

[15] Sherlock Holmes in *The Adventures of the Copper Beeches*, by Sir Arthur Conan Doyle.

memory, then the first thing for a prophet to remember is to attend as carefully to gathering data as to playing with it. In building the EFMS, designing and estimating models absorbed no more time than did designing and cleaning and cleaning and cleaning the databases used to build the models.

Data limit statistical analyses in several ways. First, a model cannot include a variable for which we have no data. Second, a small number of observations can limit the accuracy of forecasts and parameter estimates. Third, badly measured variables can introduce substantial biases into parameter estimates and reduce the accuracy of forecasts.

Early in the design stage it is important to determine what data might be required by the ODSS and whether those data are available. The data fall into five categories: (1) the performance measures that matter to the organization; (2) the policy levers that are available to the organization; (3) outside conditions that influence the organization, its clients, and its agents; (4) inside conditions that influence the organization, its clients, and its agents; and (5) variables the organization must report on to clients, to a parent organization, or to government.

One must ask several questions about each category of data: Are historical records available? How long is the historical record? If they are not available for a long enough time to support model building, how long will it be before we have enough data? Sophisticated estimation procedures generally require more data than do simpler methods, so structural models will generally require more data than correlation models or reduced form models. Box-Jenkins models will generally require more data than robust time series models.

Good data are a prime element in good forecasting and good predicting. Measurement errors are like static on the radio: They can disrupt the message, sometimes to the point that you cannot tell what is being said. Turning up the volume may do little to make a static-ridden radio voice intelligible; tuning the station in better may be a far more helpful move. Similarly, getting more data may be less useful than getting cleaner data. Also, if the static originates in the microphone in the studio, even the fanciest receiver will not make the signal clear; only solving the problem at its source will really help.

The key insight needed for thinking about clean data is that which we draw from least-squares theory. If the measurement error in a variable is a small part of the total variation in the variable, the biases introduced by the measurement error will be comparably small; if the measurement error in a variable is a large part of the total variation in the variable, the biases introduced by the measurement error will be comparably large. If the data are "dirty," data cleaning may do more for one's forecasting ability than either fancier techniques or more observations.

Chapter 7 | Loss Modules in the EFMS

7.1 INTRODUCTION

From the very beginning of the EFMP we understood that forecasting rates at which airmen would leave the service and predicting the consequences of Air Force policies for those loss rates would be a central feature of many of the EFMS models. The conceptual design document contained one chapter devoted entirely to inventory projection and loss modules. In this chapter we discuss the design and estimation of the loss modules that are used in the EFMS. Our purpose is to solidify the principles and concepts discussed in Chapter 6.[16] But, as noted in that chapter, function precedes form in building models, so we begin by discussing the functions of loss modules in the EFMS. Later we detail the design and estimation issues that arose in our loss modeling research.

---

[16] Building the EFMS required many statistical exercises besides loss rate modeling, each of which was guided by statistical concerns. We chose to use loss rate modeling to illustrate the statistical issues because those exercises absorbed a substantial portion of the EFMP's resources and because they span almost all of the statistical issues.

7.2 THE FUNCTIONS OF LOSS RATE MODULES IN THE EFMS

Many planning and programming activities in the Air Force require loss rate modules, but the specific module requirements vary widely in their need for speed, accuracy, and detail. The following four examples highlight these differences.

First, every six months the personnel programmers must establish the Trained Personnel Requirements (TPR). The TPR exercise requires projections of the number of airmen in each AFSC (by grade and year of service) over the next three fiscal years. These are the most detailed forecasts required by the Air Force.

Second, every six months the bonus managers must determine what bonuses, if any, will be offered to each AFSC. The bonus managers must be able to examine numerous alternative budget policies and estimate the effect of each on the structure of the force. An unbiased and efficient estimate of the effect of bonuses on loss rates is essential to good bonus management. This estimate must be embedded in a model that allows relatively quick computation of bonus effects on personnel levels.

Third, throughout the fiscal year, personnel programmers must monitor their programs so that fiscal year limits such as budget and end strength are met without unduly disrupting the force. As losses and reenlistments occur during the year, these programmers must adjust enlistment targets, early releases, and other programs so as to adjust the force smoothly to meet the Air Force's constraints. Such short-term programming activities require forecasts of the number of airmen in the force (by grade and year of service) from any given month in the fiscal year to the end of the fiscal year. These forecasts must be made relatively quickly.

Fourth, personnel planners must consider the consequences of possible changes in economic conditions and Air Force policies for the number of airmen in the service (by grade and year of service) over the following several years. Some of the policy changes these planners must consider are adjustments in policy that have occurred before, as in changing bonus levels. But occasionally the planners must examine fundamental adjustments in military compensation, such as when extensive changes in the retirement system are considered. How ordinary and extraordinary policy changes affect loss rates must be estimated to serve these policy planners. For ordinary policy changes, the effects must be quickly calculable. By contrast, extraordinary policy changes are not made without extensive deliberation, so calculating the effects of such changes is allowed to take a relatively long time.

These examples mirror concerns raised in Chapter 6. The first and third examples above call for forecasts of loss rates. The second and fourth examples call for predicting the consequences of Air Force actions. The first, third, and fourth examples all look to the intermediate term; the second example focuses on the short-term. No one loss model could accommodate all these needs.

Early in the project we decided that three empirical research programs were required to provide the loss rate forecasts and predictions needed by the EFMS. First, we needed to build a middle-term loss rate module that could be used to forecast loss rates for each AFSC (by grade and years of service) in years beyond the current fiscal year. We shall refer to this empirical research as the "middle-term loss module research." Second, we needed to build a short-term forecasting module that could forecast losses by grade and years of service. We shall refer to this empirical research as the "short-term loss module research." Third, we needed to build a model that could predict the consequences for loss rates of extraordinary changes in military compensation such as major changes in the military retirement system. We shall refer to this empirical research as the "retirement loss module research." We now describe each of these research projects in turn, with an eye to the lessons they offer for builders of an ODSS.

7.3 MIDDLE-TERM LOSS MODULE RESEARCH

7.3.1 Purposes of the Research

The middle-term loss module research was designed to produce three products: (1) a capacity to forecast loss rates for each AFSC by grade and year of service (called "disaggregate loss rates"); (2) a capacity to forecast loss rates by grade and year of service (called "aggregate loss rates"); and (3) parameter estimates to predict the effects on loss rates of changes in Air Force bonus and promotion policies and in civilian economic opportunities.

The decision to build aggregate and disaggregate forecasting capacities together rested on our observations that most AFSCs had substantial numbers of airmen when data from 5 to 10 years were pooled together and that the occupational mix of the Air Force from one year to the next was relatively stable. This suggested that a suitable aggregate forecasting module could be constructed from a disaggregate module by constructing a weighted average of the disaggregate loss rate forecasting formulas in which the weights reflected the relative frequencies of the various AFSCs.

The decision to combine the estimation of policy parameters and the estimation of forecasting modules in the middle-term exercise rested on their common reliance on occupation variables. The key step in estimating without bias the most important policy parameter, namely, the coefficient for bonuses, would be to include occupation as a covariate in the model. But including occupation as a conditioning variable was also a step necessary to forecast accurately AFSC-specific loss rates. Since the more than 300 occupation indicators were the largest part of both models, combining the two estimations markedly reduced the cost of building the two models.

Combining three functions under one umbrella markedly reduced the complexity of the empirical research required to build and maintain the EFMS. Considerable time was saved by eschewing the building and maintaining of three separate models for these three separate purposes. However, combining the three functions was not without cost. The demand for unbiased policy parameter estimates dictated the unit of observation used in the analysis, a unit of analysis poorly suited to the forecasting functions. As we discuss below, coping with the chosen unit of analysis when forecasting proved a formidable chore.

7.3.2 Design Issues for the Middle-Term Loss Module

Six major design issues were faced in building the middle-term loss modules:

1. Time series or conditional model?
2. Correlational or causal model?
3. What level of detail?
4. Linear or nonlinear model?
5. Is speed of application important?
6. What unit of analysis?

We review each of these in turn.

Time Series or Conditional?

The predictive functions of the middle-term loss modules required conditional models: time series models simply do not allow for asking about the effects of policy changes. Had the middle-term forecasting functions required time series models, it would have been inappropriate to combine the predictive and forecasting functions for middle-term loss rates. However, as noted in Chapter 6, time series forecasts generally do less well than conditional forecasts when the time horizon for the forecasts grows long. The one- to three-year horizon most important for the middle-term was likely to be better served by conditional forecasts. Furthermore, time series models are not well suited to forecasting highly disaggregated series because each series requires its own estimated formula, while, by contrast, conditional forecasts for numerous series can often be estimated in a single formula. Finally, since we were also building a short-term time series forecasting model for aggregate losses, we knew we could eventually check whether the conditional forecasts for aggregate loss rates were better in the middle-term than those that could be obtained from a time series model. Thus, the choice was clear: The middle-term loss module would contain conditional formulas.

CORRELATIONAL OR CAUSAL?

The predictive function of the middle-term loss module also dictated that the model be a causal model, not a correlational model. We wished to say "an increase in bonuses would cause loss rates to fall by x percent." To do this, we needed a causal model that avoided causal interpretations of spurious correlations between policy variables and loss rates. In practice, we were quite content with our efforts to purge the middle-term loss module of spurious bonus effects; we were less confident that we had purged the airman's grade of spurious effects.

AFSCs with historically low loss rates are unlikely candidates for receiving bonuses. Therefore, estimation of the causal influence of bonuses on loss rates requires controlling for occupation. By including AFSC among the conditioning variables, we were able to avoid the spurious correlation between bonuses and loss rates and at the same time exploit the forecasting information contained in the occupation variable.

Airmen eager to stay in the service may work harder to earn promotion; and airmen who earn promotion may have greater incentive to stay in the service. The latter causal link is the mechanism by which the Air Force's promotion policies may influence loss rates. The former mechanism can lead to misestimates of the causal effect of promotion policy. We experimented with instrumental variables estimates of the grade coefficient to see if any evidence of spuriousness existed in the ordinary least squares estimates of the grade coefficient. We found no evidence of bias, but we worry that the instruments used may have contained little information, thereby making our check weak.

Our need for a causal model to analyze bonuses made estimation of the middle-term models markedly more complex, but policy alternatives cannot be assessed without such models.

WHAT LEVEL OF DETAIL?

The first dictate of the level of detail in a module is to provide the minimum level required by the policy application of the module. In the case of the middle-term loss module, we needed loss rates broken down by AFSC by grade by year of service. For forecasting models the second dictate of detail is the minimization of mean square error of forecast, while for predictive models the second dictate is the desire for efficient, unbiased estimates of the pertinent coefficients in the model.

The ALPS loss forecasting model that the Air Force was using when we designed the EFMS forecast loss rates by AFSC, by grade, and by (in essence) years of service. The ALPS forecasts simply projected forward the previous year's loss rates in each cell. This specification provided the level of detail required by the policy applications, but we believed it lost forecasting efficiency by ignoring civilian economic opportunities and military bonuses and pay. We also believed that, by looking only at the previous year, ALPS lost all older information about loss rates. To use the older data required that we also control for the longer term changes in the demographic composition of the Air Force. From one year to the next the proportion of airmen who are single, or college educated, or female changes little; but across longer stretches of time, the mix changes more, and the altered mix influences loss rates.

Controlling for variables by including them as conditioning variables when making forecasts is only one way to add detail to a model. One can also add detail by breaking airmen into distinct groups for which distinct forecasting equations are estimated. (These two approaches are computationally distinct, but in principle one can design a set—probably a complex set—of conditioning variables that accomplishes the same end as breaking the airmen into distinct groups.) In the middle-term loss module, we estimated more than a dozen distinct forecasting equations, some containing in excess of 100 conditioning variables (most of them dummy variables indicating AFSC). There were two considerations that led to so many distinct forecasting equations in the middle-term loss module: (1)

the importance of current enlistment status for loss behavior and (2) the importance of extension decisions for subsequent loss behavior.

The enlistment status of an airman markedly affects the airman's sensitivity to changes in both policy and economic conditions. Airmen in the early years of an enlistment contract must break their contract to leave the service; fluctuations in bonuses, pay, or unemployment rates are unlikely to affect these airmen's departure from the service. Similarly, airmen with almost 20 years of service are unlikely to be very responsive to those same economic fluctuations since leaving the service at such a time would cost them mightily in foregone retirement benefits. Thus we thought it important to break down loss rates, using different forecasts for airmen at different stages of their careers.

Airmen who choose to stay in the service at the end of a term of service can do so by either extending or by reenlisting. Which action airmen who stay take markedly influences their subsequent loss behavior. Airmen reenlist for reasons quite different from those for which they extend, and airmen who extend are at much higher risk of leaving the service in the near future. Thus, we thought that we could better forecast losses if we allowed for fluctuations in the mix of reenlisters and extenders. (Extensions are typically for one or two years. Reenlistments are typically for four or six years. Bonuses are not paid for extensions.)

Partitioning airmen into decision groups that behave differently from one another was in fact a key to our improved forecasting over previous models used by the Air Force. The power of the partitioning rests on (1) the stability of loss rates within the decision groups; (2) the instability of the numbers of airmen within each group; and (3) the predictability of the numbers of airmen in each decision group over the next three years. The ten decision groups for which we estimated loss equations were:

1. First-term attrition
2. First-term expiration of term of service (ETS)
3. First-term extension
4. Second-term attrition
5. Second-term ETS
6. Second-term extension
7. Career attrition
8. Career ETS
9. Career extension
10. Retirement.

We estimated 17 equations because (1) the ETS decision has two steps: (a) the decision to stay or leave and (b) the decision to extend or reenlist given that one stays; (2) two-year extenders must make decisions in each of their two extension years; and (3) we found it profitable to break first-term attrition into attrition in the first 2 months, attrition in the following 10 months, and attrition in the rest of a first term of enlistment.

Figure 2.1 depicts the pattern of losses for a representative cohort of four-year enlistees who enter the service together. The ordinate of the figure is the number of airmen from the cohort still in the Air Force. The abscissa of the figure is the number of full years of service (YOS) an airman in the cohort has already completed in the Air Force. Thus, an airman's first year of service is YOS 0, the second year of service is YOS 1, etc. The loss rates used to construct the figure are means from sample data. With each year of service on the abscissa are noted the behavioral equations that might apply during that year of service for a particular airman. The legend briefly describes the 17 equations.

The figure makes obvious the importance of first-term loss models for forecasting the size of the force. Nearly three-quarters of the airmen leave the service before the second term. In relative terms, losses at the end of the second term and at the 20-year point are also especially large, with nearly a third of the airmen that reach these two decision points choosing to leave the service.

As noted above, the need to estimate the causal effect of bonuses reinforced the policy requirement for including AFSC as a conditioning variable. The desire for an unbiased bonus coefficient also influenced our strategy for incorporating AFSCs in the estimation. For the small number of AFSCs with relatively few members, lower mean square error forecasts of loss rates could be obtained by pooling these airmen with airmen in other, similar occupations. However, pooling occupations would risk biasing the estimates of the bonus effects. To avoid the bias, we conducted our estimation in two steps: First, regardless of the number of airmen in the AFSC, we estimated all coefficients, permitting a separate loss rate for each AFSC. This step produced the estimate of the bonus effect that we used in the EFMS. We then pooled small AFSCs with other, similar, AFSCs to reestimate the mean loss rate for the small AFSCs.

As a practical matter, the two-step procedure would change results little over a single step that pooled small AFSCs initially. However, the two-step procedure allowed us to continue to emphasize for the user community that our estimates of the bonus effects were being carefully controlled to avoid spurious contamination. Being able to claim that we had done so much to avoid biases was, we think, useful in building credibility for the predictions obtained from the middle-term loss module research.

LINEAR OR NONLINEAR MODEL?

We chose simple structures for the middle-term loss equations. Most of our equations posit the probabilistic depiction of a single decision outcome to be a linear function of the airman's traits, circumstances, and economic opportunities.

Linear probability models have the undesirable characteristic that calculated probabilities can be greater than one or less than zero. This will rarely be a problem when the middle-term loss equations are used in the models of the EFMS because (1) the independent variables used for forecasts will be similar to those used to fit the model and (2) the EFMS's models will use average forecasts for all airmen in a cell. Thus we decided in applications to simply truncate to 0 or 1 all forecast probabilities that are out of range.[17]

The severest limitation of our linear probability models is that they do not capture interdependencies among airmen's reenlistment decisions over time. For most forecasting and prediction chores, these interdependencies are of second-order importance. We undertook the retirement loss module research to develop a model suitable for use in those identifiable cases in which the interdependencies are of primary importance.

IS SPEED OF APPLICATION IMPORTANT?

Bonus managers need models that will allow them to screen numerous alternative bonus allocations quickly. Planners need to project quickly aggregate losses under various scenarios. But the TPR exercise and several other programming activities have no particular need for speed. Thus, the middle-term loss module research needed to serve two masters. The disaggregate loss forecasting applications could be quite slow, but the

---

[17]We considered an alternative to truncation, but dismissed it because it would change few forecasts noticeably. The alternative was to transform the estimated linear probability models into corresponding logistic probability functions—functions that preclude estimate probabilities outside the 0,1 range. The rationale for the transformation was an adaptation of the argument of Haggrstrom [1983] that shows conditions under which the linear regression estimates are consistent estimates of a transformation of a logistic function's parameters.

aggregate applications and the bonus management applications had to be fast.

The tradeoffs between speed and accuracy were not made within the middle-term loss model research. Instead, those tradeoffs were made in the ways the various models used the middle-term loss model results. The middle-term disaggregate IPM strained to use all the forecasting information the middle-term loss module could offer. The Bonus Effects Model and the middle-term aggregate IPM, on the other hand, made compromises that sacrificed forecasting accuracy to gain speed.

Thus, from the design perspective, the question of speed was reduced to how various applications might use the middle-term loss module output as inputs into subsequent computations. Disaggregate applications would surely face some computational burden because separate loss rates for more than 400 AFSCs and for more than a dozen decision categories would have to be calculated in every forecast. Aggregate applications would be less burdened since they could collapse the 400 AFSCs into one group whose average loss rate reflected a weighted average of the average loss rates of the 400 AFSCs (where the weights reflected the recent mix of AFSCs). Predictive applications could "borrow" the estimated coefficients of perhaps a single variable, such as military bonus, and calculate the change in predicted loss rate that follows from a given change in the chosen variable. Thus serving two masters seemed feasible at first blush.

However, applications of the middle-term loss module results were greatly slowed because the unit of analysis used in the research did not correspond directly to the unit of analysis used in the models to which loss rates were an input. We now turn to the choice of a unit of analysis.

WHAT UNIT OF ANALYSIS?

The purpose of the middle-term loss modules was to predict loss rates for a fiscal year. The most natural unit of analysis for these loss models would be the fiscal year: Airmen present at the beginning of a fiscal year could be categorized by whether or not they were in the service at the end of the fiscal year, and that outcome could be studied as the dependent variable in a loss equation. However, this natural choice for a unit of analysis poses problems for estimating without bias the effect of bonuses on loss rates.

Observed loss rates in any fiscal year depend, in part, on how many airmen reach the end of their contracts during the fiscal year and how many airmen spend the whole year bound by their contracts. Consequently, if the fiscal year is the temporal unit of analysis, one would have to either specify different expected loss rates depending on how many months the airman has until the end of his or her current contract, or one would have to assume that from one fiscal year until the next the mix of airmen by months until the end of contract does not vary. Neither of these approaches appealed to us; the former is cumbersome and the latter is unrealistic.

Instead, we chose a different temporal unit of analysis, one not based on the calendar, but based on the airman's contractual obligations. We broke an airman's service into distinct chunks based on when the airman signed their most recent contract. Each full year beginning from the airman's contract signing is called a "Year at Risk" (YAR). During each such year, the airman is at risk of leaving the service. Airmen in the last year of a contract are eligible to reenlist or extend; airmen in earlier years at risk in a term can only stay or violate their contracts; airmen in years of service beyond their contracts' end are in extension status and they can reenlist or leave the service during such years. From a behavioral point of view, the YAR calendar is much more pertinent than the fiscal year calendar to estimate the effect of bonuses on losses. For example, all first-term four-year enlistees in their fourth year at risk share 12 months of being able to decide whether or not to accept a reenlistment bonus. In contrast, the fraction of first-term, four-year enlistees who have 12 months to consider accepting a bonus differs from one fiscal year to another.

The YAR unit of analysis facilitates obtaining unbiased estimates of bonus effects, but it greatly complicates implementing the loss rates from the loss module in models such as the middle-term disaggregate inventory projection model. The YAR loss rates have to be transformed into fiscal year loss rates. In essence, each airman has to be given an average loss rate based on how much of the fiscal year will be spent in one YAR and how much in another. The computer code that "blends" the YAR loss rates into fiscal year loss rates is both cumbersome and time consuming.

In retrospect, we are unsure whether the statistical benefits from using the YAR unit of analysis were worth the computational and coding burdens they cost. We might have done better to develop loss models with both units of analysis, using the YAR analysis as a check on a fiscal year analysis. A prototype blending program would still have been needed in order to calculate comparable loss rates from the two analyses, but if the biases from the fiscal year analysis appeared negligible, we'd have been able to simplify subsequent model construction and implementation greatly.

7.4   SHORT-TERM LOSS MODULE RESEARCH

7.4.1   Purpose of the Research Dictates Model Design

The short-term loss module research was designed to forecast losses by grade and years of service for the remainder of a fiscal year from any month during the fiscal year. The design issues faced in building the middle-term loss modules also arose in building the short-term modules. However, the uses to which the short-term loss module would be put made settling those design questions relatively straightforward.

Throughout the fiscal year, personnel programmers must monitor their programs so that fiscal year limits such as budget and end strength are met without unduly disrupting the force. As losses and reenlistments occur during the year, the programmers must fiddle with enlistment targets, early releases, and other such programs so as to adjust the force smoothly to meet the Air Force's constraints. Such short-term programming activities require forecasts of the number of airmen in the force (by grade and year of service) from any given month in the fiscal year to the end of the fiscal year. These forecasts must be made relatively quickly.

The very short-term horizon for these forecasts, from 1 to 12 months, argued strongly for using time series models. Recent loss behavior was likely to be a good guide to loss behavior in the near future: Time series models generally outperform conditional models in the very short-term.

The quick turnaround required for these short-term forecasts further suggested that the level of detail should be kept small, with little more detail than that required for practical use of the loss rates, namely grade and years of service. Because some circumstances of airmen contribute substantially to predicting their loss behavior, a few other traits were used to partition the airmen into decision groups. For example, airmen who have already declared their intent to leave the service are much more likely to leave than are others, so keeping track of how many airmen have already made such declarations can markedly improve short-term forecasts.

The short-term loss model research illustrates how data quality can influence the choice of estimation procedures. The short-term loss model research also illustrates how even a relatively brief lapse in managerial attention can harm the construction of an ODSS.

7.4.2 Choosing an Estimation Method

The chief new insights to be gleaned from the story of how the short-term loss models were built lie in the process by which we chose the statistical methods for estimating these models. In the early modeling stages, we attended too little to what level of detail the models would eventually be required to offer. In the later stages we stumbled against the costs of producing extremely clean data sets and against the communications problems that arise when two groups in the development team develop prototype modules that are substitutes for one another. Neither experience was salutary.

Our initial inclination was to use Box-Jenkins [1976] forecasting procedures for the short-term loss models. These methods have been applied to good effect in other settings. We made a poor judgment early on, however, when we decided to develop the models extensively without including grade in the models. When we built the initial Box-Jenkins models, we gave too little attention to what would be required to rebuild the models later on with grade included. Without grade in the initial models, we were unable to determine from that work whether loss rates varied predictably and extensively with grade. Since grade was a dimension of some policy importance, we needed to know if it much affected loss rates in the short-term. We eventually discovered that including grade meant almost starting from scratch, resulting in a duplication of effort that we would have rather avoided. The lesson is clear: Careful attention must be given to determining the correct level of detail before model building is begun.

When we rebuilt the Box-Jenkins models, we also discovered that the Box-Jenkins procedures were not well suited to our data. The Box-Jenkins models, based as they are on assumptions of normal disturbances, are often very sensitive to outliers in the data, propagating past outliers into forecasts in an undesirable fashion. The data at our disposal are prone to two types of outliers that violate assumptions of normality. First, policy interventions by the Air Force introduce spikes in loss behavior. Second, errors in record keeping can introduce substantial spurious deviations in the historical data.

Since the Box-Jenkins models were not providing acceptable forecasts, we undertook to find alternative time series methods that could deliver better forecasts in light of our non-normal fluctuations in reported losses. We undertook to use robust estimation procedures (see Cleveland *et al.* [1979]) to build our forecasting models.

The robust estimation procedures proved better at accounting for the first class of outliers than for the second. "Real" outliers, those induced by policy measures, could be controlled for with the robust procedures. But bad data led to bad forecasts despite the robust estimation procedures. Consequently, the building of the short-term loss models called for tedious and demanding data cleaning—an effort that the Air Force found very expensive. The expense of cleaning the data sent team members in search of less costly alternatives to the robust models.

The tradeoff here is substantive. If one estimation procedure can produce better forecasts than another, but requires much cleaner data than the other to succeed, the costliness of the data cleaning must be traded against the improvement in performance. In the extreme, if preparing the clean data takes longer than the forecast horizon, the seemingly better method is simply infeasible.

A clue that led to the discovery that the original data were dirty were marked fluctuations from month to month in the predicted loss rates obtained from applying the robust forecasting techniques to those data. These fluctuations were unreasonable, and were unacceptable in forecasts of short-term behavior.

The analysts who sought a less expensive approach to forecasting short-term losses overcame the instability in forecasts by choosing a different unit of analysis than was used in the robust work. To see the change in perspective these analysts brought, consider a cohort of airmen who are 12 months from their scheduled date of separation (DOS). The short-term forecasting problem is to predict how these airmen will behave in each of the next 12 months. The analysts pursuing the robust method emphasized that 1 month from now, these airmen will be 11 months from DOS; 2 months from now they will be 10 months from DOS; and so on. This emphasis leads one naturally to ask how people 12 months from DOS last month behaved; how people 11 months from DOS last month behaved; how people 10 months from DOS last month behaved; and so on. Just such recent behaviors were used in the robust model for making the required forecasts. The analysts looking for an alternative approach emphasized a different perspective. They emphasized that one year ago there was another cohort that was then 12 months from DOS. This emphasis leads one to ask how that cohort of one year ago behaved in each of the following 12 months. That year's behavior forms the alternative basis for making the required forecasts.

This shift in the unit of analysis yielded forecasts that did not suffer from the month-to-month fluctuations that plagued the robust forecasts. The smoothness of these new forecasts arose in part from the new unit of analysis and in part from the simplicity of the mathematical model these analysts used. The analysts seeking an inexpensive alternative to the robust models chose a very simple mathematical specification for their loss model. This simplicity was one virtue of their model. (Remember the "guess your neighbor's height" problem from Chapter 6.) There is a lesson here. Analysts will tend toward complex models even when simple models may suffice. (Our first inclination, recall, was to use the rich, but very complicated Box-Jenkins models.) When a phenomenon is complex and the data about that phenomenon are questionable, one may do much better with the simplest models than with complex models.

Moreover, the analysts working with the alternative unit of analysis added an explanatory variable that promised to improve short-term forecasts: an indicator of an airman's declared intention to leave the service. Airmen who have declared their intention to leave are highly likely to separate from the service. Moreover, airmen who near DOS without having declared an intention to leave are particularly likely to stay in the service. Thus, the declaration of intent variable promised a marked improvement in short-term forecasts.

It is no doubt true that adding the intention to leave the service variable improved short-term forecasting. Less clear is whether the alternative unit of analysis improved short-term forecasts. The smoothness of the forecasts was a clear advantage, but the accuracy of the forecasts remained open to question.

One must be cautious when arguing that one model is performing better than another with dirty data. One should ask whether the model is providing better forecasts of what is really happening or is only seeming to do so. The risk is that the model forecasts the bad data, not the actual phenomenon, well. The unstable forecasts of the robust model pointed to errors in the underlying data. The alternative approach suppressed the instability of forecasts but did not guarantee that the errors in the data were not leading to poorer forecasts than were necessary.

The analysts who developed the robust models remained skeptical of the alternative approach. They worried that the alternative method masked but did not overcome the perils of bad data. The analysts who developed the alternative methods remained adamant: The cost of cleaning data was too high to justify using the robust models, and the alternative model appeared to perform well.

Unfortunately, the two sides in the debate hardened in their positions, and communications suffered. Important points were missed by both sides, and the development of reliable models was thereby threatened. On the one hand, the data cleaning costs for the robust models were excessive; a less expensive alternative to the robust models was needed if at all possible. On the other hand, cleaning would only be too expensive if it were required in the actual operational mode; cleaning was not too expensive to be included as a part of building and evaluating the models. In the developmental stage, one should be willing to go to great expense to create clean data even if only to verify that forecasts from less clean data are sufficiently accurate to warrant foregoing such cleaning in the operations. The EFMS ultimately relied on models built using uncleaned data and the alternative unit of analysis. Because the performance of these models using dirty data was not evaluated with clean data, their reliability remained questionable; we did not know which the models predicted well—reality or the dirt in the data.

Fortunately, after some years we can say the alternative models have worked well in practice, but putting them on line without resolving the data quality issue entailed risks. On a brighter side, the good performance of these forecasts draws attention to the profit one may reap from considering alternative perspectives on one's data: The unit of analysis may markedly affect the quality of one's estimates.

7.4.3 Communication, Coordination, and Project Supervision

Why weren't the strengths of the two sides combined? Why didn't a consolidated research program emerge that incorporated the insights of both sides? Largely, the problem was that for a brief period in the later stages of the EFMP, the cohesion of the development team slipped.

The EFMP was a large and long project. Maintaining cohesion among the many analysts working on the project required extraordinary energy from the senior staff. Early in the project, team meetings were frequent, and senior staff spent many hours ensuring that related subprojects communicated with one another and mediating differences of opinion about project work. Sustaining a high level of cooperation across working groups requires leadership in peak condition. In a project that lasts more than seven years, there will inevitably be lapses. In the EFMP, two senior staff members simultaneously went through distracting personal experiences just as another senior staff member was beginning to wind down involvement in the EFMP. When the two short-term loss model research teams most needed to coordinate, the attention from senior staff lapsed, and the two efforts diverged and become increasingly unable to benefit from one another's insights.

We were fortunate that the lapse in managerial support wasn't more costly. Others may not be so lucky. But our good fortune was more than just luck. We had few such lapses for two reasons. First, the senior staff were deeply committed to the project's success and firmly believed that success required close coordination of research efforts by all team members. Second, several senior staff members shared the responsibility for coordinating research and for mediating disputes; the chance that they would all overlook a conflict simultaneously was small.

7.4.4 Lessons

Six lessons can be learned from the short-term loss model research: (1) the detail needed from a model must be determined before one starts estimating the model; (2) data cleaning costs may be high enough to warrant making forecasts from dirty data; (3) if one has only dirty data or data cleaning is prohibitively expensive, a complex phenomenon may be modeled best with a very simple model; (4) forecasts made with dirty data should be tested against cleanly measured outcomes in the developmental stage, even if cleaning the data is quite costly; (5) the unit of analysis one chooses may markedly affect the quality of one's forecasts; and (6) senior staff members must remain vigilant and work constantly to sustain communication among team members so that research efforts remain coordinated.

7.5 RETIREMENT LOSS MODULE RESEARCH

A major attraction of a military career is the generous retirement benefits. Airmen as young as 38 can retire and receive half-pay for the rest of their lives. When we built the EFMS, the services were considering the first major changes in their retirement system in many years. We thought it important that the EFMS have the capacity to inform policymakers, planners, and personnel programmers about the potential effects of retirement plan changes on the career decisions of airmen.

A barrier to building such a model was that we had not observed major retirement plan changes in the post-World War II era, so we could not perform straightforward statistical studies of how previous changes in retirement compensation altered loss behavior in the Air Force. We overcame this barrier by looking at retirement benefits through the glasses of economic theory.

Economists see retirement benefits as part of an individual's lifetime stream of income. Economists predict that people will respond to changes in retirement benefits just as they would respond to other changes in the stream of their incomes. Consequently, by looking at historical fluctuations in airmen's income streams, economists can predict how airmen are likely to respond to changes in retirement plans.

The models required to examine airmen's lifetime earning streams are quite complex. They require looking across all an airman's future enlistment decisions simultaneously. The convenient breakdown into first-term, second-term, career, and retirement decision groups that greatly simplified the middle-term and short-term modeling efforts could not be applied in the retirement loss module. To somewhat simplify the model, the level of detail was restricted to year of service and grade. This simplification resulted in easily calculatable loss rates, but did not make the model's parameters easy to estimate.

The retirement loss module was a boon to the EFMS. It gave the system the capability of modeling infrequent, complex changes in compensation schemes. Further, the availability of the retirement loss module freed the EFMS's workhorse subroutine—the middle-term loss module—to use simpler equations to forecast loss rate changes caused by the more frequent simple alterations in compensation policy, such as pay and bonus increases. Finally, the retirement loss module freed the middle-term loss module to include in its simpler equations a larger number of covariates than could be included in the highly nonlinear retirement loss module.

The chief lessons to be gleaned from the retirement loss module exercise are two. First, do not add large amounts of complexity to your most frequently used models to accommodate infrequent, special-purpose applications. Instead, build special-purpose models for those applications.

Second, social science's theories offer information that can be used to supplement, and sometimes substitute for, historical data. When historical data seem inadequate to your task, ask social scientists if their more arcane theories can serve your needs.

Chapter 8 | Decision Support Models in the EFMS

8.1 INTRODUCTION

The purpose of this chapter is to provide concrete examples of our principles for model base design in an ODSS. We use three of the models that were built in the EFMS in order to illustrate a number of decisions that are necessary when designing an ODSS model base: number of models, division into modules, amount of detail, management levers, accuracy, ease of use, and model integration. The discussion of the models shows how we made these decisions in accord with the following principles for designing ODSS models (see Chapter 5):

- Fit the models to the decisionmaking circumstance by building multiple models, each with management levers and level of detail tailored to the decisionmaker's circumstances.
- Use modular construction for cost-effective model building. Even when the same code cannot be used, try to use the same variable definitions because this simplifies construction and documentation of input data files and enhances the ability of analysts to improve the models to reflect changing circumstances.

147

- Trade accuracy for ease of use within each model to achieve the balance among these competing objectives that is appropriate to the model at hand. (The purpose of describing our decisions in these areas is to emphasize the need for considering the tradeoffs. We do not suggest that we made the optimal decision in all cases, and other circumstances would certainly call for different decisions.)
- Consider integration and links among models at the conceptual design phase and throughout the process of building the models. It greatly enhances the efficiency of model construction and of system maintenance.

This chapter also illustrates a frequent, but unpredictable, outcome from model building activities. The analyses necessary to build good models frequently produce additional insight into the way that policies affect outcomes. This insight can be of enormous value and may occasionally justify the entire cost of building the ODSS.

The three models discussed in this chapter are all designed to support the skills management function—managing the occupational mix of the enlisted Air Force. The policy options available to the skills managers and the constraints on their choices are discussed in the first section that follows. How the conceptual design of these three models addresses the decisionmaking problem is covered next. The remaining sections of the chapter describe some of the tradeoffs made in model design.

8.2 OVERVIEW OF EFMS MODELS FOR SKILLS MANAGEMENT

8.2.1 The Decisionmaking Environment

Authorizations specify the number of personnel in each occupation and grade that are required to meet the Air Force mission. Producing an inventory that will meet this target is called skills management.

A wide variety of management levers is available to the skills management team to help it produce the desired inventory. For example, consider the following:

1. Bonuses are offered to members of selected specialties on the condition that they reenlist. The amount of the bonus offer varies by occupation and year of service (YOS) zones.
2. Airmen entering the force (non-prior service (NPS) accessions) can be assigned to occupational specialties where they are needed.

3. Personnel can be released from their enlistment contract earlier than their scheduled ETS.[18] The total number of persons to be released each year is decided elsewhere, but the skills manager can ensure that AFSCs (i.e. occupations) that would suffer shortages from the program are exempted from participation in the program.
4. Reenlistment at the end of the first term is controlled by occupation through the Career Job Reservation (CJR) System. Quotas are set in specialties where surpluses of career airmen might otherwise develop. Airmen in these specialties are offered the opportunity to retrain into a specialty with personnel shortages.
5. Retraining among specialties is used to balance the mix of more senior personnel.
6. A two-tier promotion system is used, under which designated occupations receive a higher promotion rate than that given to all other occupations.

These decisions are highly interrelated. For example, one can increase the number of skilled personnel who will be in a specialty a year from now by increasing the number of personnel to be retrained, by increasing the bonus, or by placing the specialty in the high promotion tier. One can decrease the number of persons by reducing the rate of input to the skill, by lowering the CJR quota, or by lowering the bonus if the skill has one. One can also decrease personnel in the short run by using an early release program.

Despite the variety of levers available, the choice of a set of desirable policies is constrained by a combination of factors. Many of the jobs performed by enlisted personnel require skills that can be learned only through extensive experience or training and frequently require both. Thus it is not possible to produce instantaneously a force that meets current needs. Rather, the needed personnel must be "grown" over time as they learn occupational skills. Much of the learning occurs on the job and therefore requires the time and attention of those already skilled.

Air Force personnel policy emphasizes the importance of the individual airman; therefore, policies consistent with high morale are preferred. For example, quotas are not set for second term reenlistments, and trans-

---

[18] This is the policy whose effects were removed in developing the loss analysis database discussed in Section 6.3.3.

fers among specialties are determined in a way that maximizes the number of such transfers that are made voluntarily.

Implementation of some programs requires long lead times. Because Congress approves the total amount of funds that may be awarded as bonuses, the Air Force must request bonus funds in advance. Barring changes by DOD or Congress, the maximum amount of bonuses to be awarded in a fiscal year is typically fixed about 30 months before the end of that fiscal year. However, the Air Force can decide on the allocation of the bonus budget among specialties much closer to the time when the bonuses are offered. Decisions about training in a fiscal year are usually made in March of the preceding year so that the training command can acquire and schedule instructors and other resources.

Despite the long lead times necessary for an orderly schedule of resource use, changes are continually being made in the target force in response to decisions by the Air Force leadership, DOD, and the Congress. Thus skills managers must plan for a three-year time horizon and continually modify those plans to meet a moving target in the short run.

8.2.2 Models Needed

Although all the models we discuss support the same large organizational function—managing the occupational mix of the enlisted Air Force—the decisions involved are made in quite different environments and have quite different needs for information. Consequently, we had to build separate models that are quite different in the amount of detail they capture and the kinds of management levers available.

We will discuss three separate models: the Disaggregate Middle-term Inventory Projection Model (DMI), the Bonus Effects Model (BEM), and the Year-of-Service Target Generator (YOSTG). Each of the decisionmakers served by these models needs to know how many experienced airmen will serve in each occupation in each future fiscal year. The future inventory is determined by a variety of factors within and without the control of the skills managers. It depends on the grade and occupational mix of the current inventory, because in the short run the existing inventory is the only large source of experienced airmen. It also depends on the decisions of airmen concerning whether to reenlist in the Air Force or to leave the service. As was discussed in Chapter 7, their decisions are influenced both by economic factors outside the control of the skills managers and by the bonus offer, which is under the control of one of the skills managers. The total number of airmen that will serve in each grade in each future year is determined by DOD and Congress. The skills managers' only control over promotions is through the designation of which occupations will belong to the tier that receives faster promotions. On the other hand, the skills manager has almost complete control over the occupational distribution of the NPS accessions who will join the Air Force in the future.[19]

The information most needed by the skills managers is an estimate of the inventory by occupation and grade that will exist at the end of each of the next three years if a specified collection of policies were to be implemented. Thus, we designed a disaggregate (i.e., the inventory is counted by occupation code or AFSC) inventory projection model to provide as accurate a picture as possible of the number of airmen in each AFSC and grade over the next few years. The design of this model (DMI) is the subject of Section 8.3.

Managing policies such as bonuses and CJRs that are targeted to particular YOS groups or to persons in particular terms of enlistment involves deciding how many persons one would like to have in each year group and how many people one would like to reenlist. The manpower function considers only AFSC and grade[20] when it provides the target for the skills managers. Translating this target into a target by AFSC and YOS and into a target for the number of reenlistments by AFSC is the task of the YOSTG, which is the subject of Section 8.4.2.

The DMI can describe the inventory that would result from any bonus plan. Thus the bonus manager could formulate a particular bonus plan, use this model to project the inventory, and compare each year's outcome to the YOSTG target for that year. However, because of the detail needed to estimate accurately the training plan, the DMI takes a substantial amount of time to run. In addition, a three-year bonus plan involves determining the bonus multiple that will be offered each year to each of hundreds of AFSCs in each of three YOS zones. The number of possible bonus plans is

---

[19] The Air Force appears to be a reasonably attractive employment opportunity to young high school graduates. It is thought that recruiting efforts can produce all the qualified candidates that are likely to be needed for the foreseeable future. In the very short run, the occupational distribution of NPS accessions is constrained by the training schedule and by commitments made to recruits concerning their training.

[20] This statement is somewhat of an oversimplification because much of the manpower effort is based on "skill level" rather than grade. However, in most cases skill level categories are an aggregation of grades, and the distinction is not necessary for understanding the rest of this book.

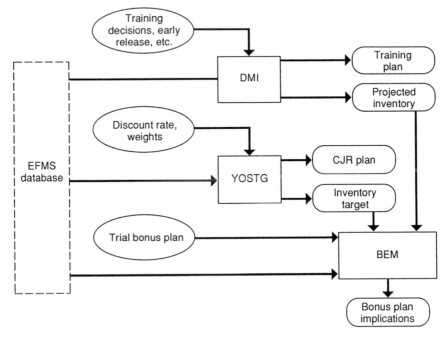

Fig. 8.1 Skills Management Models

enormous, so the skills manager needs to able to evaluate many alternatives quickly. Thus the BEM, described in Section 8.4.3, provides a fast, easy to use, description of the outcomes of alternative bonus plans.

The interrelationships among the three models are shown in Fig. 8.1. All three models draw similar information from the EFMP database and provide information about what the inventory would look like if specified policies were implemented. All employ the ability of the loss models to produce accurate forecasts of loss rates and to predict how the rates depend on bonuses and economic conditions.

The DMI and BEM are descriptive models. The DMI can predict the impact of all currently used skills management policies and is more accurate than the BEM, but takes much longer to run. The BEM predicts only the effects of changes in the bonus plan on budget, reenlistment counts, and future inventory. It can examine bonus plans very rapidly because it uses information about the projected inventory from the DMI as the basis for its calculations. The BEM is run many times with the same DMI input.

The BEM displays a comparison of the inventory predicted to result from the bonus plan and the YOS target generated by the YOSTG. The

YOSTG is a prescriptive model. It produces a suggested plan for the CJR program as well as YOS targets for the BEM.

8.3 THE DISAGGREGATE MIDDLE-TERM INVENTORY PROJECTION MODEL (DMI)

The DMI is a detailed, accurate, but slow model. The primary use of the DMI is to produce the training program for each of the next three years. The training program describes the number of persons to be trained during each fiscal year into each AFSC by category such as NPS accessions or first-term reenlistees.

The DMI takes the existing inventory and ages it to predict the inventory at the end of each of the next several fiscal years. The DMI is typically run to predict three years into the future, because that is what is needed to decide on the training program. However, it is fairly accurate for up to seven years, so it could also be used for longer term occupational planning.

The DMI is an expected value simulation model that estimates the number of airmen in each of a set of disjoint categories called IPM cells. The prediction of each year's inventory is produced by estimating the expected numbers of annual losses, reenlistments, promotions, and flows among AFSCs based on the inventory existing at the start of the fiscal year and various input parameters. The model then describes the inventory at the beginning of the next fiscal year by adjusting the YOS of the inventory that remains after these flows have occurred and adding accessions. The process is repeated in an identical manner for each subsequent year.

8.3.1 Procedures for Running the Model

Although the DMI contains many design features that would enable the model to be used in a "what if" capacity, the substantial amount of time required to run it mitigates against such use of the model.[21] Instead the model is used primarily to compute the consequences for the training plan of the set of rules that have been chosen for the training program and all other skills management programs. Because of its long running time, the

---

[21]The design of the EFMS includes a 'Part of the Force' model to provide more rapid 'what if' analyses of occupational groups. This model has not yet been implemented, but may be in the future.

model is primarily run within the SMO rather than directly by the user. Consequently, it was not necessary to invest the considerable resources required to make the model "user friendly."

Usually the model is run twice. In the first run, few management actions are taken (e.g., all persons who wish to retrain into any skill are allowed to do so; all skills receive 100 percent manning, etc.). The skills managers examine output from this run in order to determine where problems would arise and how they should address them. A second run is then performed that includes the chosen management actions and calculates a realistic training plan.

The output from the model is a file that describes each year's inventory. This file is then input into a spreadsheet for a microcomputer. Many analyses of these data are precoded so that the skills manager can easily retrieve information about the needed training plan and the comparison of the expected inventory with the authorization target. In addition, the skills manager can use the spreadsheet program to summarize data easily in new ways. Having the model create a file rather than particular displays is a form of modular design that enhances the simplicity of the model (and thus its maintainability) and the flexibility of the displays (and hence their adaptability to changing circumstances). The availability and ease of use of spreadsheets have greatly enhanced the cost-effectiveness of this technique.

8.3.2   Management Levers and Other Input

The primary management levers are the rules that have been chosen for the training program, because the primary purpose of the DMI is to calculate and document the plan for training into each occupational specialty (AFSC). However, the effect of the training program depends on many environmental parameters. Therefore, the inputs to the model include (1) the initial inventory, (2) loss and reenlistment rates, (3) promotion rates, (4) early release programs, (5) migration flows across AFSCs, and (6) restrictions on NPS accessions.

To be used in the DMI, flows need to be described for each IPM cell. A variety of techniques was used to make this enormous amount of data manageable. In some cases, a computer program that we call a preprocessor is used to calculate the number corresponding to each cell. In other cases, the user inputs an aggregate number, and the DMI itself spreads that aggregate down to the cell level. In still other cases, there is a method for calculating the number within the DMI and the user merely inputs the numbers that are exceptions to the calculation rules.

Maintaining inputs to the DMI and documenting its output are simplified because it obtains its data directly from the EFMS database whenever possible. For example, the input loss rates are generated by a preprocessor from EFMS data files.[22] As discussed in Chapter 7, these loss rates depend on estimates of the unemployment rate and military pay and on the amount of the bonus offer. Official values of the economic variables are generated by an economic analysis unit in the Air Force. The bonus information lists the amount of the bonus offer in each specialty and zone. Current values of the bonus plan are maintained within the EFMS and thus are easily available for the purpose of generating loss rates. The loss rates output by the preprocessor become part of the EFMS database and can be used as input to other models.

The management levers in the model concern flows of persons entering and leaving each specialty. The design of the levers matches the kind of decision that is made by the skills manager. We give three illustrations of how management actions are modeled, ranging from the least controlled flow to the most controlled flow.

- *Disqualification flows.* One of the least controlled flows are those that occur when airmen become disqualified from their existing skills—usually because of a disability of some kind. These flows are unplanned. The model uses historical rates to estimate the number of airmen who leave each AFSC annually. Only the set of AFSCs that they will join is controlled by the skills manager. The management levers in the model consist of a list of the AFSCs that can receive this flow and the proportion of the flow that each chosen AFSC will receive.

- *CJR retraining flows.* The migration that occurs at the first-term reenlistment point is determined jointly by airmen decisions and the skills manager, who uses the CJR program to direct airmen from overage AFSCs into shortage AFSCs. The management levers in the model consist of the CJR quota for the number of retrainees into each

---

[22] The Year-at-Risk file, which is discussed in Chapter 9.

specialty for each year.[24] The calculations begin by estimating the number of persons who wish to change AFSCs through the CJR program. The rates used for these decisions come from historical data and from a regression model not unlike the one discussed in Chapter 7. These persons are added to a pool of persons who wish to retrain. Relative preferences for each gaining AFSC are calculated from historical data and are used to estimate the number of persons who would wish to enter each specialty. Any who are in excess of the quota are returned to the pool for distribution to different specialties. The user may specify that a fraction of those who exceed the quota are to be lost instead of retraining into a different specialty.

- *Gains from NPS accessions.* The number of non-prior service accessions needed in any year is calculated at the end of that year's simulation, but the calculation depends on the skills manager's input. It is rarely possible to fill all authorizations; because of disconnects in the planning process, authorizations often exceed planned end strength. The skills manager selects AFSCs that are particularly critical and inputs "fill rates" saying what percent of each such AFSC's authorizations will be filled. The fill rates for these AFSCs are usually quite high (100 percent or 95 percent). All AFSCs not given a designated fill rate receive the same fill rate, which is calculated by the DMI so that the simulated inventory meets the input total end strength. The simulation computes the number of NPS accessions who will be trained in each designated AFSC during a year as:

fill rate * authorizations – inventory,

where the inventory is the number of persons who remain from the inventory at the beginning of the year.

8.3.3   Achieving Accuracy

The primary criterion for the design of the DMI was that it produce an accurate count of the inventory by grade and AFSC at the end of each of the next three years. The importance of this criterion led to a decision to design the forecasting modules of the DMI first. We reasoned that we had

---

[24]The YOSTG suggests a quota for each AFSC. The skills manager examines this suggested plan and may modify it to account for factors not included in the model before it is input to the DMI.

to first learn the factors that affected airmen decisions, such as those about leaving the Air Force and about occupational choice. In several cases, we made a further decision to structure the forecasting module based on what data and theory told us would produce the most accurate estimates of air- man behavior. After we had an accurate theoretical model for each import- ant forecasting element, we would develop a way to adapt the forecast to an IPM. In this subsection, we use the loss rate module to illustrate the implications of this decision.

Because of our focus on accuracy and because of the importance of losses to accurate inventory predictions, we allowed the loss rate module to determine the level of inventory detail that would be carried within the DMI. The analysis of losses that was carried out while building the loss rate module showed that a host of factors describing airmen affected the rate at which they leave the Air Force. The most important of these factors defined the level of detail in which the inventory is carried within the DMI.

The DMI needed estimates of the inventory according to the categories of grade and AFSC. Therefore, even if these factors did not affect loss rates, it would be necessary to carry this much detail within the DMI. The DMI includes added dimensions for factors that have all of the following characteristics: (1) substantial effects on loss rates, (2) substantial year-to- year variation in the number of airmen with particular values of these fac- tors who are in a combination of AFSC and grade, and (3) easily and accu- rately predictable. This resulted in adding dimensions for YOS and category of enlistment. A similarly important factor is whether or not an ETS is scheduled during the fiscal year. To be able to predict accurately whether an ETS is scheduled, we added a dimension for the number of years remaining in the current enlistment contract (which we call Years- to-ETS or YETS). The addition of the YETS dimension means the DMI can predict with high certainty the number of persons who will reach the original expiration of their term of service (OETS) in each of the next three years. We did not add dimensions to describe airmen demographics such as sex, race, or education. The demographics of airmen accessions in particular occupations are reasonably stable from year to year and, conse- quently, we lose little in accuracy by assuming that the demographic dis- tribution within an IPM cell is constant from year to year.

Based on this analysis, we decided on an IPM cell structure that distin- guished airmen by AFSC, grade, category of enlistment, YOS, and YETS. Although we eliminated some combinations of factors that were infeasible (e.g., first termers can only take on YOS values of less than eight), the number of cells is enormous and approaches the number of airmen.[25] This is one of the primary reasons why the model takes so long to run. However, it is also the primary reason why the model's predictions are so accurate.

The decision to make the structure of the loss rate module depend only on data and econometric theory and not on ease of use within the DMI led to an important disconnect between the form of predictions produced by the loss module and what was needed by the DMI. The statistical equation for loss rates produced predictions for each year-at-risk in the career of an individual airmen. For example, there is an equation giving the loss rate during an airman's first YOS (i.e. the probability that he will leave) and another equation giving the loss rate during his second YOS.[26] The DMI needs predictions for groups of airmen. Consider an airman who, at the beginning of the fiscal year, has not yet completed his first year of service. His loss rate during the next fiscal year is a weighted average of the two equations just mentioned, with the weights depending on how long it will be until he completes the first YOS. Each IPM cell containing those who have not yet completed their first YOS contains persons who will complete their first YOS at different times and therefore have different estimated loss rates. The same is true for all other YOS.

We were aware of this disconnect very early in the design of the loss rate module. We discussed the problem at length and decided to push ahead with a year-at-risk loss model because such a model would produce the most accurate estimates of the econometric coefficients, such as the bonus effect. We made this decision even though we did not, at the time, have a satisfactory method of going from the year-at-risk rates to fiscal year rates. The solution that we eventually implemented consists of an elaborate computer program (the "blending" program) that has a substantial run time. Thus the accuracy of the econometric coefficients was purchased at a substantial price in implementation cost and ease of use.

In other applications, it may be desirable to begin with the design of the final user model, rather than the forecasting model. Then one can fit the forecasting method's unit of analysis to the level of detail needed in the

---

[25] The computational simplicity of using rectangular arrays led us to retain many infeasible cells. We used four rectangular arrays, one for each category of enlistment, with different ranges of YOS and grade.

[26] Section 7.3 provides more information about years at risk.

using model. Indeed, even in the DMI, we did not always choose small improvements in accuracy when they would have had substantial implementation costs. This strategy is more desirable when accuracy is not paramount and when the forecasting module is to be used only within a single model. It can only be used when the important factors that affect outcomes are known at the start of system design. Otherwise, it is necessary to begin with an analysis of the forecasting problems. After the important factors are identified, one can choose how to handle the interdependencies in the design of forecasting modules and final models.

The point, which we cannot emphasize enough, is the importance of examining the tradeoffs among accuracy, ease of use, and ease of implementation early in the conceptual design of the ODSS. They have enormous implications for how the system will eventually function and the amount of resources that will be required to build it.

8.4   MODELS TO SUPPORT BONUS MANAGEMENT

8.4.1   Preliminary Analysis

After we had defined the need for a Year-of-Service Target Generator (YOSTG) and Bonus Effects Model (BEM) to support the bonus management function, the next step was an empirical analysis of how a bonus offer to a specialty affected the future inventory. Part of this analysis was conducted while building the loss rate module and has been discussed in Chapter 7. This part of the analysis found that, as we had expected, adding a bonus or increasing the bonus to a specialty lowered the fraction of airmen who left at their ETS. It also increased the fraction of persons who reenlisted for another full term rather than extending for a shorter period.

The effects of bonuses are not limited to loss and reenlistment rates, however. Bonuses have substantial effects on the length chosen for the reenlistment contract and on the choice of occupational specialty at the end of the first term. The amount of the bonus that an airman receives can be increased if he signs up for a longer period of time. Table 8.1 demonstrates that airmen respond to this incentive by signing longer contracts. In the early 1980s the Air Force greatly increased the number of specialties in which it offered a zone A bonus. The first two columns of this table show that, as the number of reenlistees receiving a bonus increased, so did the number who chose long (usually six-year) contracts.

Table 8.1

Effect of Bonus on Choice of Length of Reenlistment Contract

		% of all Airmen Who Reenlist for More than Four Years		
Time Period	% Receiving a Bonus	All Airmen	Bonus Specialties	No-Bonus Specialties
7/79–6/80	23	22.0	70.9	7.4
7/80–6/81	51	40.3	71.3	7.7
7/81–6/82	61	44.8	69.0	7.0

The last two columns of the table strongly suggest that it was the bonus that caused this increase. There was no change in the contract length of those in specialties that were never offered a bonus. In specialties that switched from no bonus to some bonus, the percent choosing a long contract typically changed from about 7 percent to 70 percent.

We also found that offering a bonus at the end of the first term to a specialty greatly decreased the proportion of airmen who chose to retrain out of the specialty when they entered the career force, and increased the proportion of retrainees who chose to enter the specialty. We developed regression models to predict the effect of the bonus on the length of the enlistment contract and on specialty choice. These models are used within the DMI, the BEM, and the YOSTG to estimate how the inventory would change in response to a change in the bonus offer.

Although the analysis was aimed at model development for the EFMS, it had substantial implications for Air Force policy. Combining the effects of bonuses on reenlistments, term of enlistment, and career choice in an IPM demonstrated the extent to which bonuses have long-term effects on the occupational distribution of the career enlisted force. Official DOD policy at the time said that bonuses were to be used only to deal with temporary, short-term shortages. However, the real cost-effective use of bonuses is to offer them continually to specialties with high training costs and a reenlistment rate that is too low to meet the long-term need for skilled personnel. Using bonuses for short-term shortages in low training cost skills is never cost effective and can introduce manning problems in subsequent years.

Furthermore, we found that first-term bonuses appeared to have a substantially greater numerical effect than bonuses offered to more senior personnel. Also, since those who have completed two or more terms in the Air Force are very likely to reenlist, almost all of the bonuses offered to them are received by persons who would reenlist anyway. Thus second-term bonuses are rarely a cost-effective long-term management tool and third-term bonuses are almost never cost-effective (see Rydell [1987]).

8.4.2   The YOS Target Generator (YOSTG)

The YOSTG is a prescriptive model that adds a YOS dimension to authorizations (see Carter [1991]). It is needed because some personnel programs act by increasing or decreasing the number of personnel in specific year-groups. To determine how to manage these programs, it is necessary to know how many people one wants in each AFSC and year-group.

For each AFSC, the YOSTG determines the distribution of airmen by YOS that will have a grade distribution as close to the authorization target as possible given personnel policy constraints. The model's objective function measures the goodness of fit of the inventory in an AFSC to its authorizations in each future year. It minimizes:

$$\sum_t (1 - d)^t \sum_j w(j)*(x(j,t) - a(j,t))^2.$$

where $x(j,t)$ = inventory count for grade j in year t,
  $a(j,t)$ = authorization target for grade j in year t,
  $w(j)$ = weight on grade j relative to other grades, and
  d = rate used to discount far future years relative to near future years.

Because authorizations are created without attention to feasibility, it is often impossible to meet both this year's authorizations and future years' authorizations in both grade and AFSC detail. Thus, skills managers must trade today's overages and shortages against future overages and shortages. The YOSTG calculates the optimal tradeoff point given the user's time preference as given by the discount parameter d. This discount rate and the weights on each grade in the objective function are the primary decisions the user must make to run the model. In addition, the user provides lower and upper bounds on acceptable loss and reenlistment rates.

One of the primary criteria used in the design of the YOSTG was to maintain compatibility with the DMI. Exactly the same level of detail and cell structure is used in the YOSTG as in the DMI. Both models use exactly the same input files in many cases. It was judged that the enhance-ment in the simplicity of maintaining the two models would far outweigh the small extra run time of including some unnecessary details in the YOSTG.

The output of the model is a target inventory file that describes all the dimensions of the inventory that are used in the DMI and target reenlist-ment counts. This file is then passed to the BEM, where it is aggregated to the level of AFSC and YOS and used as a target to be reached by the application of bonuses. The target reenlistments are also summarized by AFSC in a spreadsheet program, so that the skills manager in charge of the CJR program may examine the suggested quotas and modify them as needed.

8.4.3   The Bonus Effects Model (BEM)

The BEM [Carter *et al.*, 1988] permits the user to observe easily the effects of alternative bonus plans on projected inventory and bonus expen-ditures during the following three years. Unlike the other two models dis-cussed in this chapter, design of the BEM emphasized creation of a user-friendly model. It is an interactive model and menus were used for all user interfaces. The user can choose a specialty, year, and zone and call up a table that shows the reenlistments predicted to occur at each bonus level. In other tables, the effects of a particular bonus plan are displayed for each user-specified specialty in tables that show the bonus costs that will be incurred each year, a breakdown of inventory by year of service for each planning year, and a comparison of both reenlistments and inventory with targets. These tables permit the user to construct a hypothetical bonus plan and compare that plan with the bonus plan currently in effect or with a previously constructed plan that has been chosen for the base plan.

In constructing the bonus plan for the next three-year period, the user begins with some plan in the computer database. The plan specifies bonus amounts that may differ by AFSC, zone, and year. It may be the current plan or a plan constructed by the computer that produces reenlistments as close to the reenlistment targets provided by the YOSTG as is possible. The user then reviews each specialty by calling up the BEM's tables to examine how this plan and deviations from this plan would affect inven-tory, costs, and reenlistment counts. If he or she decides to change the plan, the computer will keep track of the decision when changing to the next specialty. At any point in the analysis, he or she can call up any of a series of summary tables to review the aggregate effects of the working plan on costs, reenlistments, and inventory.

This model was designed primarily with ease of use in mind. There are 11 possible bonus choices for each of roughly 400 AFSCs, three zones, and three years. The key to allowing examination of the implications of so many possible plans is substantial preprocessing. In fact almost all the information in the BEM's displays is precalculated and stored in tables within the BEM; the BEM itself does little more than retrieve the information requested by the user, keep track of the bonus plan being constructed, and add together elements from different tables to produce summaries across AFSCs. The inventory projection model within the BEM's preprocessor projects only cohorts that will reach OETS during the three years of the bonus plan, using the bonus coefficients of the loss rate module to estimate each cohort's size as a function of the bonus plan. The projections of other cohorts come from the DMI.

The need for speed and ease of use made us compromise the accuracy that could potentially have been available. For example, the BEM's model of occupational choice decision is much simpler than the DMI's in that it does not accurately account for interactions among AFSCs in these decisions. For example, when one AFSC's bonus is increased, the number retraining into other specialties will really decline (because more people will remain in the AFSC with the bonus and because more of those retraining will choose it.) The DMI accurately models these interactions but the BEM does not. We decided to model each AFSC as if it were independent in order to increase the speed of the model so that it could be easily used.

This model was the first operational model in the EFMS. Since the DMI was not yet available, a simplified IPM was written solely to produce the BEM input files. An early prototype version of the YOSTG was used to provide targets. Since the BEM was constructed before several of the forecasting models were complete, the data preprocessing steps contain several awkward and inefficient calculations. Consequently, there are plans to refine and improve the model in the future. However, as discussed in Part V of this book, at a crucial time in the EFMS's development, the availability of the BEM provided proof that the system would eventually be useful. Thus the inefficiency of model development, compared to waiting until all its inputs were well specified was probably a small price to pay for the value of the model to the users and to the system's developers.

8.5 SUMMARY

It may be worth summarizing the many issues in model integration that have been covered in this chapter. We have seen how modular design allowed the same middle-term loss rate module to play a prominent part in three very different models. Using the same variables and algorithms for the DMI and the YOSTG enhances the maintainability of the system and the compatibility of analyses, even though they share no code.[27] Further, an output file created by the DMI is the reason that the BEM can achieve its design goal of providing rapid, complete evaluation of many bonus plans. Finally, the modular design of the BEM allowed it to be implemented before other models were ready.

---

[27]The models do use the same preprocessors to develop input files and, indeed, use some of the same input files.

Chapter 9 | Data for Analysis and Model Building

9.1 INTRODUCTION

Building an ODSS will almost always require creating and using a variety of large input data files. In general, the input data have four primary uses:

* to understand or define the problem being addressed
* to estimate a model
* to test and evaluate a model
* to run a model (input to the model).

Each use requires different types of data, and the data are used in different ways in each case. This chapter deals with data to support the first two uses. We call these types of data files "analysis files," since they are primarily used by analysts engaged in defining and building models. The creation of databases to support the operational ODSS is examined in Chapter 15.

Managers of projects that make extensive use of large data files usually underestimate the amount of effort required to create useful analytical databases. We estimate that about one-third of RAND's total effort on the EFMP was devoted to collecting, examining, cleaning, and structuring data in order to create useful analysis files.

9.2 GENERAL RECOMMENDATIONS FOR CREATING AND USING LARGE DATA FILES

This subsection presents recommendations for creating and using large data files. The recommendations are based on the EFMP and other experiences. Papers by Relles [1986] and Arguden [1988], two of the RAND members of the EFMP, discuss these in more detail.

9.2.1 Challenges of Large Data Sets

Creating and using large data files pose many challenges. Errors are hard to catch, but are very costly if not caught early, and they undermine the scientific quality of the research if they remain undetected. The EFMP devoted a great deal of effort to developing clean data files. A case study of building two of the major analysis files used by the EFMP and the lessons learned from that effort are given in Section 9.3.

Analysis files will normally be created from source data files. The source data are usually collected by others for purposes different from those of the ODSS. One of the major tasks in creating useful analysis files is to understand these data, clean them, and use them to define other variables that are more useful for ODSS purposes.

Typically, however, the data sets are large, and this makes data cleaning much more difficult. Large numbers of observations preclude spotting errors by visual scanning. Large numbers of data items per observation require the analyst to check out more facts about the items and their interrelationships than can initially be absorbed.

As a result, decisions are made about the data that often need to be revised as one proceeds onto the analysis phase of the project. The real trick in data processing is to have all of the necessary information in place so you can smoothly revise those decisions when you discover it is necessary.

9.2.2 Steps in Cleaning Data

Knowledge of the data grows throughout the entire research process. However, it is convenient to divide the research process into two phases: (1) an audit phase, where cleaning the data and increasing the researcher's understanding of the data are the only goals, and (2) an analysis phase—data analysis and model fitting—where incidental discoveries about problems or misunderstandings of the data frequently occur. This chapter deals exclusively with the audit phase: things to do to increase the chances of getting all of the data problems resolved before the analysis phase.

Four particular aspects of the audit phase require attention:

- *Examining the frequencies with which the data items take on each value.* Frequency distributions provide the basic information with which to judge data quality and the data's consistency with its documentation. They disclose undocumented codes and gaps between data values that signal potential outlier problems.
- *Listing a number of complete records from the file.* Listings supplement frequency distributions, enabling analysts to examine relationships among variables.
- *Constructing new variables for analysis from one or more source variables.* Variable construction rules must resolve numerous details, translating codes that may be arbitrary or inconsistent over time into variables about which analytical assumptions will be made. Variable construction rules have to deal with rules of aggregation, including what to do when data items are missing.
- *Defining the units of analysis.* For example, on the EFMP, an early decision to be made was whether the models were going to require data organized by person, person-year of service, or year within term of service.

Three useful techniques for examining data during the audit phase are:

- *Look at the frequencies of the variables.* Not only did this help the analysts to understand the data, it indicated values that rarely appeared, which revealed some miscodings.
- *Look at partial listings of the data.* Partial listings are listings of a small subset of the records in a file. Examination of such listings improved the analysts' understanding of the files by revealing relationships among variables within a given observation. They also contributed to understanding the units of measurement, completeness of the information about a variable, and whether the definitions in the documentation were accurate.
- *Look at totals for key variables* (e.g., numbers that can be checked against official sources). For example, we calculated annual totals for several key variables and compared them to published Air Force data.

The following four principles should prove useful in creating analysis files:

- Do not exclude observations containing missing values from the files in order to avoid selection bias.
- Keep the rules for recoding each constructed variable separate (e.g., in different subroutines).
- Define all constructed variables directly from the source data rather than from other constructed variables.
- Specify the rules for selecting observations from the source files to be included in the analysis files in the code that creates the analysis files.

A great deal of effort should be allocated to the audit phase. Relles [1986] observes that projects involving the creation of large analysis files usually allocate about 60 percent of their file creation resources to the analysis phase and only 40 percent to the audit phase. He suggests that it would be more efficient and effective to allocate about 65 percent of the file creation resources to the audit phase, including more time from the project leader and a senior programmer.

A fundamental concern about secondary source data, such as that used in the EFMP, is how reliable and meaningful the data are. Some questions that we tried to answer before using the data included:

- *Do the data measure objective conditions?* An airman's sex and date of birth are well defined, whereas his reason for separating from the Air Force is less well defined, since the personnel office has a degree of choice, and there are more than 400 codes, some of which are very similar to others.
- *Are all events fully reported?* Changes in an airman's date of separation and category of enlistment are always reported, while changes in marital status and education are not.
- *With what frequency are the events reported?* In the EFMP's analysis files, information on changes in grade is available at only one point during a year, while changes in category of enlistment are available at the time of the enlistment or reenlistment.
- *To what extent are the data artificially affected by changes in policy?* For example, fewer airmen will leave the service in one fiscal year if a large number of them were permitted, encouraged, or even required to leave the service early during the previous fiscal year.

- *Are the reporting categories stable?* Occupational specialties are defined by Air Force Specialty Codes (AFSCs). But the specification of these codes is modified at least twice a year.

We tried to get answers to all of these questions before we even specified the source data files we wanted for the EFMP. However, some questions were only able to be answered after we examined the source data in the audit phase, and others only suggested themselves in the analysis phase.

9.3 BUILDING ANALYSIS FILES FOR THE EFMP

The first task in building analysis files for the EFMP was to define the data to be included in the files. The primary need was for longitudinal data on the service careers of individual airmen, which were needed to build the loss models discussed in Chapter 7. Four types of data were needed: demographic profiles of individual airmen, complete military histories of individual airmen, Air Force personnel policies over time, and economic conditions pertinent to separation/reenlistment decisions. A key requirement was the need to blend frequent, regular observations on an airman's status with inherently infrequent, episodic separation/reenlistment transactions.

The required data were not available from a single source, so data from several sources had to be combined. Most of the files had been compiled routinely over the years by the Air Force, not with analysis in mind, but for reporting purposes. The statistics from these files were usually aggregated to a high-enough level that inaccuracies in the data did not pose serious problems to them.

The first analysis file that we created was called the Enriched Airman Gain/Loss (EAGL) file [Brauner *et al.*, 1989]. It provided the first two types of data that were needed. It was built using a file on new enlistees and data from two monthly files on airmen: the Processing and Classification of Enlistees (PACE) file, which contains background information on airmen collected before, during, or shortly after basic military training; the Uniform Airman Record (UAR) file, which provides a snapshot of the enlisted inventory at the end of each month; and the Promotion, Demotion, Gain, Loss (PDGL) file, which provides monthly transaction information. We used data from the files starting in 1971 (1956 for the PACE file). Each monthly UAR file contains information on 500,000 airmen, while the PDGL contains information on some 30,000 transactions made during the course of each month.

Information from the three files over the period of about 15 years was sorted and merged by airman to produce the EAGL file, which provided snapshot information on airmen at regular points in time, plus information on the types of transactions they made. The EAGL file was then restructured to make it easier to fit the loss models, and data were added on Air Force personnel programs (e.g., bonuses) and economic conditions (e.g., unemployment rates) over time to produce the analysis file that supported the middle-term disaggregate loss modeling activity. This file was called the Year-At-Risk (YAR) file [Murray *et al.,* 1989]. At each step in the creation of the EAGL and YAR files, a considerable amount of time was spent trying to understand the data and all its quirks, doing specialized programming and ultimately mapping the data into a convenient format to enable the loss models to be fit. These steps and the lessons learned in each step are discussed in the following three subsections.

9.3.1   Data Acquisition

Several different files were acquired over the course of the EFMP. Each posed its own special challenges. In this subsection we present five general recommendations for how to proceed with new data files, and motivate each recommendation with an example from the EFMP.

The EAGL file contained three distinct types of records on each airman, strung together in a variable-length format: background demographic information on the airman, annual snapshot information for each year the airman was in the service, and information on transactions (e.g., reenlistments) that took place during a year of service.

Variable-length records are very hard to work with. Programming languages and statistical packages have a much easier time with input logic when data are read from fixed format records. The first thing we did when we received a new EAGL file (once a year) was to split it into three separate rectangular files. Using statistical programs, we could then generate and study listings and frequencies of the variables to begin to understand the data.

- **Recommendation 1.** Transfer data whenever possible in fixed format records, using multiple files in preference to variable-length records.

The importance of this principle is greater today than it was in 1983 when the first EAGL file was built. Data files now are more useful if they are not tied to specific hardware. IBM variable-record formats, which have binary information embedded in them that describes the length of a record, are not easily read by other machines; e.g., UNIX-based desktop workstations. Simple ASCII files are easily transported between IBM and virtually every type of workstation. It would have been much easier then, and now, to transport files in that form.

* **Recommendation 2.** Share programming code.

Everybody should have access to the programming code. Miscommunication between analysts and programmers should be expected, and the chances of detecting it are much greater if the analyst gets to read the code as well as peruse through output. The programming code is the clearest, most accurate way of communicating information about the calculations (e.g., the definition of intermediate va. ables).

* **Recommendation 3.** Work with very small samples initially.

Programming tasks are so complicated and so dependent on the data that it usually takes three or more iterations to get things right. At the beginning, we needed at least ten iterations to produce the EAGL files. The benefits of using very small samples would have been twofold. Each iteration would have been a lot cheaper, simpler, and faster, inasmuch as the problems associated with large files (e.g., the use of tapes, long turnaround times) would have gone away. Also, if small samples had been used, the files could have been cleaned and debugged at RAND instead of in Monterey at the Defense Manpower Data Center (DMDC).

Updating the EAGL file was also a difficult process. The file had to be updated every year, when a new June snapshot was received. Yet, adding another snapshot necessitated enough changes to the data preparation program that additional bugs would get introduced. Initially these bugs were found by dumping some cases and tracing through their listings. In effect, each airman became a case study, and we would ask whether the story told about him was reasonable. We would usually find a couple of aspects of the story that needed to be fixed. After creation of the first file, it became more efficient to focus on what had changed between files. File comparison programs were used to annotate the differences.

The EAGL file was derived from PACE, UAR, and PDGL records. The PACE file provided basic information about a person; the UAR provided his status every June; and the PDGL told about his transactions during each year—reenlistments, extensions, and losses. The EAGL file was developed from about 15 years of monthly records, and was created at

DMDC because of the sheer volume of information and the costs of processing it at RAND.

In retrospect, that decision was shortsighted. Without the source code, it was difficult to know what was being computed. Similarly, the programmer at DMDC was removed from the details of what the data were to be used for, so she did not know to which assumptions to draw our attention. Numerous iterations resulted from this separation of effort. In each iteration, we would receive a 10 percent sample of the EAGL file (e.g., all cases where the seventh digit of the Social Security number was a five), dump and examine the records, notice an anomaly in the output, and suggest modifications to the code that would take care of the problem. Ten percent of the EAGL file consisted of about 150,000 cases. It would have been better to have received about 1500 records (e.g., all cases where digits eight and nine were 50), and developed the data processing programs ourselves. Iterations would have been considerably faster, and we would have been spared the extensive time spent trying to find bugs without having good access to programming code.

- **Recommendation 4.** Hold onto at least one generation of listings in machine-readable form, and use comparison programs to flag the differences between old and new listings.

We never got beyond the point of needing to generate at least some listings. But we did need a more effective means of drawing to our attention the things that had changed between files. A standard approach is to count observations, but we wanted more than that: a shorthand for what variables had taken on new values. To do this, we computed one-significant-digit frequencies, and produced side-by-side counts of old versus new values. File comparison programs enabled us to flag easily differences in certain variables between generations of files.

- **Recommendation 5.** Generate frequencies of all variables to one (or two) significant digits, and use compare programs to identify the differences between old and new listings.

9.3.2 Specialized Programming

Having finally created a good EAGL file, the next task was to use it to build an analysis file to support the middle-term loss modeling. The structure of the analysis file was determined based on the kind of models to be fit and the software that would be used to fit them. This defined the formats needed for the data and implied the kind of transformation program that would have to be written to reformat the EAGL data.

A mistake we made was to set short deadlines and race to meet them. Data preparation seems like it should be a simple, finite task—a nuisance to put up with before the real work (analysis) begins. Unrealistically tight deadlines lead to poorly designed code that cannot be easily debugged or understood, especially when the code is revisited three months later.

- **Recommendation 1.** Do not underestimate the amount of time and effort needed for cleaning and preparing data files. Projects should expect at least 25 percent of their activity to be devoted to data file preparation.

One aspect of the EFMP files that led to requiring such a large effort was the type of data recode operation required. There are common operations on data that are part of relational data management systems: aggregation, sorting, merging, and new variable creation. Those are generally quite easy to do, and there is ample software around to help. But we were well outside the sphere of typical applications for those systems.

First, our data sets were too large, about 500 megabytes of raw data for the 30 percent sample of airmen that we intended to process. Relational data programs seem to work well on files that are about a tenth that size, but do not work well on files of that size. Second, the reasons one often incurs the cost of going to a database management system is flexible selection and reporting; we were primarily interested in sequential access across the entire file. Third, we were interested in accessing the data in several ways: programming languages such as FORTRAN and PL/1 for variable construction, and SAS for flexible summary as part of the process of developing the variable construction rules. No database management system interfaces easily with all of those programs. Finally, the level of aggregation was so nonstandard that the commands of a database management system would not have simplified our task.

To elaborate on the last point, our contemplated models had units of observation that were very difficult to create from the data we had. The desired unit was the *year-at-risk (YAR)*. The models assumed that every year, depending on when he started his service, an airman would decide to leave the service, reenlist, or continue. Thus, a single airman's records could give rise to a variable number of YAR records, each of which contained his characteristics at some point in the year, as well as the outcome of the stay/leave decision. The logic of the program was therefore to step through an airman's history at the three different levels (person, person by year, and person by year by transaction), determine how many years at risk he had and what were the beginning and ending points, then to infer his characteristics and actions for the year. This was not a simple aggregation, and hence should have been recognized at the outset as being particularly difficult.

- **Recommendation 2.** When you have a nonstandard problem of aggregation, your costs will be a lot higher and you will have to devote a lot more resources to reformatting the data.

This is especially true if there are major changes to the units of observation. In our case, time since the term began was one of the units of observation. We needed to describe the attributes of the airman at the beginning of the term and at various points relative to the end of the term. Midstream, the points relative to the end of the term might change. Even if these points were static, however, it would have been quite difficult to impute what was needed.

In any case, we wrote a program to build the kinds of records we wanted, which was a hard job. The process was started before we fully understood the raw data, and the process was highly iterative. There were anomalies in the data—anomalies brought on by having multiple sources for the same piece of information, with the sources being inconsistent. Numerous judgments had to be made about what numbers to use, based on making the information consistent.

- **Recommendation 3.** Do not underestimate the problems caused by using data from multiple sources.

Data from multiple sources tend to be rich in inconsistencies. This complicates data recoding considerably, especially when there is not one source that is clearly best. Here it was not a matter of doing simple aggregations. Numerous choices were available, which introduced numerous possibilities for inconsistency. About 20 percent of the programming code was devoted to fixing up these inconsistencies.

- **Recommendation 4.** Separate the data recoding process into three steps: (1) fixing the data, (2) making them complete, and (3) making them internally consistent. The amount of code to be written is large enough as is. Breaking the problem into smaller parts will reduce the problems.

ODSS models will always require large, complex data sets. It is important to recognize this and to anticipate a highly iterative process.

- **Recommendation 5.** When data are poorly understood *a priori*, expect data recoding to be a highly iterative process. At each stage, more quirks are discovered, some of them rare events. But known errors cannot be allowed to lie within data sets, so the code keeps expanding to cope with them.

By the time a data set has been completed, the recoding and analytical decisions will probably be hopelessly intertwined; it is not a good idea to try to separate the two. Thus, the standard practice to separate the recoding from the analysis will not work. Analysts need to be intimately involved in the data preparation.

- **Recommendation 6.** The best way to ensure analyst participation is to write readable code.

Everybody should read the code and understand what it is trying to do. Code should be shipped around. If everybody reads the code, they all become responsible for its accuracy, and there is a better chance of discovering errors.

9.4   DATABASE MANAGEMENT

General principles described here can lead to more effective processing of large data files.

The goal should be to obtain a series of simple two-dimensional tables with understandable, well-defined rows and columns. Managing data consists of physically moving the information around to obtain these tables, and having enough of an audit trail so that you can later figure out what you did.

One would not seriously consider writing a statistical package when one does regression. Yet too many people rewrite data management programs when they come to a data management problem. People write FORTRAN programs that do incredible amounts of manipulation, often with buried sort or merge sequences thrown in. The trick to data management is to use readily available tools for data management.

- **Recommendation 1.** Map out the data management plan as a series of relational data management steps. That does not mean throwing data into a database management package, but rather viewing the data processing as a series of modular steps.

There are basically four fundamentally different types of operations in managing data. Data arrive as a collection of two-way tables, with various rules for linking them together. Before you get into a data management task, you should scope out the full sequence of steps to be performed. The steps will involve:

1. **Adding variables (columns) to a two-way matrix.** There are several reasons for doing this. First, many variables have difficult construction rules, so it makes sense to put their intermediate values on the file. Second, new variables might be created through aggregation, linking, or sorting (using standard tools) on the value of some constructed variable. You should obtain frequencies of the values of all the variables created in this step.
2. **Linking files.** Very often files must be joined based on identical values of a common variable. For example, it might be desired to add to an airman's 1979 record the unemployment value for that year.
3. **Sorting.** Sorting the data is something that often has to be done in order to link very large tables. While files can be linked without sorting (e.g., in joining file2 to file1, a hashed list of identifiers can be constructed in file2 in order to find quickly the record that corresponds to each file1 record), this is difficult to do if file2 cannot fit in memory. It is a lot easier to link two sorted files than to bring one or both into memory and merge them there.
4. **Aggregating.** The common types of aggregations are average, sum, minimum, and maximum. With these aggregation functions, it is easy to aggregate in one pass through the data set. Each aggregation record is often linked back to its component records.

Regeneration of analysis files from scratch should be expected. We never took fewer than three iterations to go from raw data files to a usable analysis file. It is important to leave instructions behind that will enable easy reconstruction of the analysis files next time (i.e., a script). The raw data may be updated, perhaps by adding another month or another year; there may be an error in processing based on some analysis (e.g., a variable was left off or a mistake was made); or it may be necessary to explain how the data were processed (e.g., when the research is being documented).

- **Recommendation 2. Maintain simple audit trails.** There are several characteristics of a good audit trail. It should be short—if possible, there should be one step between source data and analysis file. Otherwise, intermediate files may need to be maintained and stored, which increases the complexity of redoing it the next time. Also, since each data set is the focus of one program, the existence of intermediate data sets generally implies that the trail for creating certain sets of variables cuts across different programs, which makes it more difficult to figure out what has been done.
- **Recommendation 3. Write modular code.** Try to put the logic for generating a single output variable or group of data in one place. Code should be modular—made up of several tiny, independent steps, each of which can be understood by itself. Such code is a lot more readable than code that is dispersed in different sections of a program.
- **Recommendation 4. Let programs do it the second time.** The computer is great at doing things the second time. It is not good at doing them the first time. Plan for that. As you stumble through the first series of data processing steps, leave behind instructions for doing it the second time. (If you're programming on UNIX, it is relatively easy to set up shell scripts to do the work.)
- **Recommendation 5. Save intermediate data sets only if you have to.** As computing technology developed over the 1970s, the tendency to save intermediate data files grew with the desire to keep costs down: there was a cost-benefit calculation behind it. But the relative costs on which the calculation was based have changed considerably in recent years. Each of the items in the following list is getting relatively cheaper than the item below it:

- computing (CUP),
- electronic memory (RAM),
- magnetic memory (disk storage),

(All are getting absolutely cheaper, but relative costs are what count in system design and configuration.) Therefore, in system designs, one should use items higher on the list whenever possible in preference to items lower down.[27]

---

[27] This observation was made by Robert Anderson and Norman Shapiro of RAND.

- **Recommendation 6. Recognize that managing data requires meticulous attention to detail.** You must carry around record counts and make sure that a programming step has precisely the right number of records (e.g., the wrong tape might get mounted or the system might crash). When counts are off by even 1 in a million, it is usually a tip-of-the-iceberg sign that something serious is wrong.

Chapter 10 | The Use of Prototype Models and Staged Implementation

10.1 STAGED IMPLEMENTATION

An ODSS could be implemented in several ways. One way would be to develop and implement the constituent models one at a time, leaving their integration into a system to be done when all the models are completed. A second would be to implement the system as a whole after all the models are completed. (This is more or less the System Development Life Cycle [SDLC] approach.) We suggest a process that combines the best features of both approaches and avoids their negative features. We call it "staged implementation." Dennis, Burns, and Gallupe [1987] call a similar approach "phased design," and Boehm [1988] describes a related approach that he calls the "spiral model of software development." Figure 10.1 is a simplified flowchart of the general approach.

The SDLC is a highly structured process in which the total system is developed in a specific linear sequence of steps (see Section 1.4.2). While this is a very efficient process for developing stable, well-defined systems, it is not an appropriate way to develop an ODSS, in which the information requirements are uncertain and the system itself is subject to change.

In staged implementation, some models are developed in parallel with others, and some are developed sequentially, in priority order. Use of a model can begin whenever it has reached the point that the builder and

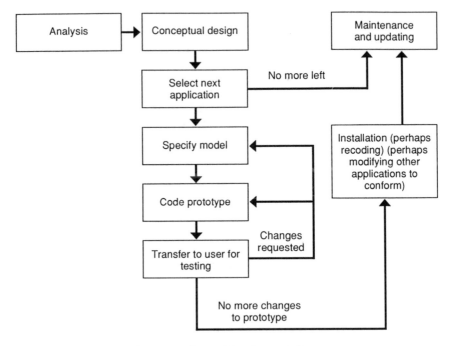

Fig. 10.1 Staged Implementation

user both feel comfortable enough giving it a try (see Chapter 13). In addition to the implementation of models one at a time, the development of each individual ODSS model is an iterative process that applies the middle-out [Hurst *et al.*, 1983], iterative [Sprague and Carlson, 1982] principles for building decision support systems found in the DSS literature. Middle-out development is based on building and using an early prototype of a model to obtain quick feedback on its form and substance. Iterative design involves continual improvements to the model until the users' requirements are satisfied and the model is able to be placed into the overall environment of the ODSS. Boehm [1988] discusses this approach to system development in some detail.

10.2 PROTOTYPING

A prototype is a stand-alone "quick and dirty" version of a model that exhibits some or all of the essential features of a later version of the model in the operational system. It is a tentative model. According to Rothenberg [1990], a prototype can be designed for one of two purposes:

1. to try out a proposed approach to one part of an application (e.g., the user interface) in order to reduce the uncertainty inherent in the development process (he calls this an "evaluative prototype")

2. to provide a surrogate application that can be investigated to improve the design of the eventual system (he calls this "strawman prototyping").

Analysts and modelers are the ones who usually build the evaluative prototypes for an ODSS, while the SMO usually builds the strawmen.

Evaluative prototypes are practically necessary to build for two reasons: (1) No one is smart enough to write the mathematical specifications for complex models without a prototype, and (2) no one is smart enough to write the code for a complex model without passing data through the model and reporting the outcome. (The code that inputs the data, passes it through the model, and reports the outcomes is an evaluative prototype.) On the EFMP, RAND's responsibility was to write the mathematical specifications for the system's models. It was not required to write any code. However, when we started to write the specifications, we found we could not do it without building prototypes (some more detailed than others). This was one of the most important lessons of the project.[28]

Sprague and Carlson [1982] distinguish two types of prototypes—the *throwaway* prototype and the *evolutionary* prototype.

The throwaway prototype is an acknowledged experiment, designed to create user interest, get user feedback, develop builder skills, and reduce risk and investment. It is normally built quickly by modelers (not professional programmers). It may be patched and modified in response to new ideas or user feedback. Once the throwaway prototype proves useful, a cleaner, more efficient version is written and documented by a professional programmer, using standardized procedures previously adopted for the system's models.

An evolutionary prototype is one that is built by professional programmers in a way that facilitates evolution and change. Of course, evolution and adaptation are inherent features of a decision support system. Many such changes do not affect the efficiency of the programs. However, the addition of functions or changes in the user interface almost always leads

---

[28] Because writing mathematical specifications cannot be done without prototyping it is important to include a programmer and data specialist on the project team from the outset (see Section 3.2.2).

to increases in the complexity of the program and decreases in performance. The resulting program is also generally hard to maintain.

In spite of the likely efficiency losses and maintenance difficulties associated with evolutionary prototypes, there are circumstances in which they might be preferred to throwaway prototypes. Their major advantage is that they can reach the fully operational stage much quicker. (A rough throwaway prototype can be developed more quickly, but it has to be reprogrammed before it is considered fully operational.) A quick operational model may be important in helping the ODSS become credible with the user.

The primary advantage of evolutionary prototypes (quicker implementation) becomes more important and the primary disadvantages (lack of maintainability and efficiency) become less important when the application is (1) more urgent and (2) more removed from the user.

Throwaway prototypes become more sensible the closer the model is to users. Proximity to the user will be accompanied by a need to understand the model and explain it to the users, which will be easier once the SMO has built the model after throwing away the prototype. If the SMO needs to understand the inner workings of a model anyway, then the incremental cost of reprogramming it is small; reading the code carefully enough to understand it is a major step toward rewriting it.

Of course, by its very nature, each of the models in an ODSS is likely to have to be rewritten eventually because of changing internal needs or a changing external environment. The major issue is how long to keep a prototype running before reprogramming. If one builds a prototype expecting it to remain part of the system for a substantial time, one risks having devoted too much care to programming, documentation, fine-tuning, and "bells and whistles" if it is thrown away early. On the other hand, if the prototype is built in the expectation that it will be rewritten—cutting corners to save time or research effort—one risks finding that the model is not reprogrammed for a long time. During this time, the system includes a temporary, incomplete model. Thus, effort should be devoted initially to ascertaining which models are likely to be thrown away and which will evolve.

The prototypes will generally include some, but not all, of the features of the final versions of the models. For example, in most throwaway prototypes, the inputs, outputs, and/or user interactions of the prototypes would be different from those planned for the final versions.

The development of an ODSS model using a throwaway prototype includes the following nine steps (see Fig. 10.1):

1. Conceptual design.
2. Mathematical specification (which includes mathematical modeling, estimation of the parameters of the model, and validating the model using historical and hypothetical data).
3. Programming a stand-alone prototype of the model.
4. Testing and using the prototype for some or all of its intended functions.
5. Evaluating the test.
6. Revising and improving the mathematical specification (which includes adding features to the model).
7. Reprogramming the model for inclusion in the system.
8. Preparing and maintaining whatever historical database is needed for updating and reestimating the model.
9. Integrating the model into the ODSS.

All of these steps would not necessarily be carried out for each model, and the development of each model would not necessarily involve carrying out the steps sequentially. There would be a lot of iteration and feedback among the steps. For example, testing of the prototype might reveal problems that would return development of the model to any of the previous three steps (even rethinking the conceptual design).

Development of a model using an evolutionary prototype would proceed in a similar manner. However, step 3 would be followed by a step in which the model would be added to the ODSS. The testing, evaluation, and revision would take place in parallel with its operation by users. The programming in this case would have to include many of the rules for standardization, design of user interfaces, etc., which would be done for a throwaway prototype in step 7. These issues are discussed in Part V of the book.

10.3 BENEFITS AND SHORTCOMINGS OF PROTOTYPING

Prototyping is an alternative to the traditional "life cycle" approach to developing computer systems and models. The major differences between prototyping and the traditional approach are that prototyping does not require tightly written systems design specifications and provides the user with an initial model for actual hands-on experience in a shorter time period. There are many good reasons for building and using prototypes (for additional discussion, see Jenkins [1983] and Alavi [1984]):

- *Timing.* The system can be used to provide support for some applications early in the development process. (For example, one of the EFMS models began to be used for bonus management years before other models were ready to be used.)
- *Quality.* Problems with the models can be identified and corrected early in the development process, and promising ideas can be tried out without incurring large costs.
- *User satisfaction.* Prototyping is an effective way to draw out and clarify user requirements, to obtain user comments on inputs, outputs, and interfaces, and to obtain user commitment to the development of the system. Their involvement in the development and use of a prototype helps them to become more enthusiastic and interested in the system, to feel that they had some real influence in the system's design, to develop a sense of ownership and control, and to conclude that the system is responsive to their needs.
- *User understanding.* Users can gradually become familiar with the concepts, procedures, interfaces, and models of the system. Their early use of prototypes also provides a way for users to gain an understanding of the overall ODSS.
- *Smooth operation.* The system management organization can gradually build up its organization and procedures. It can also develop communications links and a rapport with the users, which can lead to good working relationships.
- *Cost.* Studies have shown (see, for example, Jenkins [1983]) that the prototyping approach leads to lower overall development costs and reduced systems development time.
- *Documentation.* A prototype is a non-narrative form of documentation for the design of a model, which provides an unambiguous description of control parameters, input and output screens, etc.

These hypothesized advantages seem to be borne out in practice. For example, Boehm, Gray, and Seewaldt [1984] compared the development of a model by seven student teams, three of which applied prototyping and the other four a more traditional approach. They found that prototyping resulted in software that had roughly the same performance, was easier to use and learn, had about 40 percent less code, and required 45 percent less effort to develop. Alavi [1984], using a similar approach, obtained similar results. She carried out an experiment that compared the use of prototyping to the use of the traditional life cycle approach to the development of an information system for supporting new plant investment decisions in the chemical industry. She found that prototyping resulted in higher overall user satisfaction with the system, better accuracy and helpfulness in the output reports, and less conflict between users and designers. Also, ease of communication between users and designers, user understanding of the system, and extent of system use were all ranked higher in the case of prototyping.

Prototyping has some associated problems, which must be taken into account before the decision to use prototypes is made. Most of the negative aspects can be avoided by astute project planning and management. Alavi [1984] identifies four drawbacks with prototyping:

1. *It is difficult to prototype large systems.* It is not clear how a large system should be divided for the purpose of prototyping. Moreover, the internal technical arrangements of large prototypes may be haphazard and inefficient and may not perform well in an operational environment.

2. *It is difficult to manage the development of prototypes.* The traditional life cycle approach includes specific phases, milestones, and deliverables, which are established at the start of the project and are used as guidelines for project planning and control. Such control mechanisms have not been established for the prototyping approach.

3. *It is difficult to move beyond the prototype to a finished model.* User involvement and interest can wane after high-priority user requirements are satisfied by a prototype. Users are then not willing to spend time and resources to complete and "clean up" what was intended to be merely a "quick and dirty" early version of the model.

4. *Prototypes can be disappointing to the user.* Prototypes are intended to capture only the essential feel and features of the operational system. If the user is expecting all of the performance characteristics of the operational system, the prototype might result in user expectations not being met and hence disappointment.

These problems pose challenges to ODSS designers and builders. For successful implementation, they must be addressed, but they should be able to be overcome. The problem of breaking large systems into manageable pieces is really a design problem, which was discussed in Chapter 5. The idea is to break the large system into many small models. Each of the small models can be prototyped more easily, and the total system can be built up gradually, piece by piece. Haphazard development of prototypes can be avoided by sticking to the conceptual design, which should serve to provide guidance to the developers of the individual models and coherence to the set of models being developed.

If the difficulty of managing the development of prototypes is recognized before programming is begun, it should be possible to establish the same types of control mechanisms as are used in developing traditional systems. Phases and milestones can be specified. But feedback and model revision must be factored into the process, which might require schedule modifications. Development of the EFMS took considerably longer than expected, which caused difficulties for the project both at RAND and in the Air Force.

Problem 3 may not be a serious problem. If the prototype was designed as an evolutionary prototype and is "good enough," the lack of user pressure might make it easier to shift attention to areas that are now higher priority. If the prototype was intended to be a throwaway and has been integrated into the operational system by building input/output hooks, it is likely to be less efficient than a reprogrammed operational model, but might be satisfactory for some amount of time. If the prototype was intended to be a throwaway and remains a stand-alone program, instead of being integrated into the system and its database, it is likely to interfere with aspects of the overall conceptual design. In this case, the user might not be complaining, but the SMO should press for transformation into an operational model.

The final two problems are harder to deal with. A prototype that is intended to be a throwaway often becomes a permanent part of the system. This is somewhat problematic if the prototype is integrated into the operational system by building input/output hooks (it is still likely to be less efficient than a reprogrammed operational model). But it is likely to interfere with aspects of the overall conceptual design if it remains a stand-alone program, instead of being integrated into the system and its database. The user might not be complaining, but the SMO should press for transformation into an operational model. (The lack of user pressure might permit the development of higher priority models first, a shifting of priorities and lessening of pressures that might be welcome.)

The problem of unmet user expectations is really a problem of deciding at what point the user should be introduced to the prototype. There is a tradeoff between introducing it early (risking the possibility of frustration, disappointment, or disenchantment) or late (delaying the start of feedback, improvement, and usefulness). Actual hands-on use of some of the models can begin to generate enthusiasm among users for the system's potential and, hence, gain political support. But if the models are not ready and/or are oversold, users may become skeptical, political support may be lost, and/or eventual acceptance may be made more difficult.

On the Enlisted Force Management Project, there was often intense pressure to use models that had undergone practically no testing. Most of the time, the SMO resisted this pressure to use untested models. However, the need to "show results" sometimes required concessions. These concessions reaped political benefits because they did illustrate the system's potential power. But the effects were not wholly salutary. The users were quick to dismiss early results if they saw any anomalies whatsoever. We found that one way to shape users' expectations and avoid disappointments was to determine in advance what "errors" (e.g., in precision) would be acceptable and what would be unacceptable. (The issue of when and how to have a user begin experimenting with a model is discussed further in Chapter 13.)

Boehm [1988] shows how the staged implementation/prototyping paradigm described above can be expanded to reduce the element of risk in large system development projects. He presents a "spiral model" (see Fig. 10.2), in which the radial dimension represents the cumulative cost incurred in accomplishing the steps to date, and the angular dimension represents the progress made in completing each cycle of the spiral.

Each cycle of the spiral includes a risk analysis step, in which sources of project risk (e.g., areas of uncertainty) are identified and ways are found for resolving them (which may involve prototyping, simulation, benchmarking, administering user questionnaires, reference checking, analytical modeling, etc.). Among other elements, the process provides a strategy for choosing which portions of the system to prototype, and in which order.

10.4   HOW TO DESIGN AND BUILD A PROTOTYPE

In a decision support system, models must explicitly consider the needs of the user. The user is generally at least as concerned with how he or she

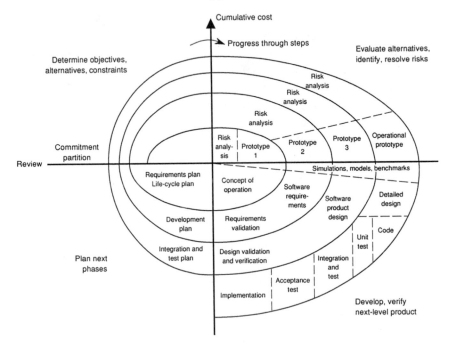

Fig. 10.2 Spiral Model of the Software Process

interacts with the model and how the output screens look as with the specific numbers the model produces. If the model is not easy to use or if the output is not easy to interpret, the model may be ignored. We, therefore, recommend building an ODSS both from the outside in and from the inside out. (Traditional computer models are often built from the inside out. That is, attention is usually focused first on the algorithms and mathematics.) Our suggested approach to programming involves the following four-step process:

Inside Out

1. *Fit the model to the function.* Consult the conceptual design to identify the role the model is supposed to play in the system. Identify the decision variables (e.g., management levers) and other inputs and the criteria for the decision (all of the benefits and costs that occur because of the decision) and other output. (For further discussion of this step, see Section 5.4.)

2. *Specify the model's calculations.* Given the model's desired outputs, management levers, and other inputs, it should be possible to determine an algorithm that will transform the input data into the

desired outputs. (For further discussion of this step, see Chapters 6, 7, and 8.)

Outside In

1. *Design output screens.* Users can usually specify clearly and completely the outputs they would like to obtain from the model, although they may be unable to specify how they might be obtained. Rather than make a list of these outputs, it is a useful exercise for both the user and model designer to have them jointly design the output screens. This enables explicit specification of format and level of detail.

2. *Specify user interface.* This step includes the identification of the data to be input by the user and the manner in which the data will be supplied. In particular, this step will result in agreement on which input data will be read from a data file and which will be supplied by the user at the time the model is run. For the latter, there should also be agreement on how the data will be supplied (e.g., through prompts) and whether to include default options (i.e., values supplied automatically if the user does not choose to supply them).

The inside-out and outside-in processes can be carried on in parallel, once agreement has been reached on the decision variables, the criteria for making the decisions, and the other output that might be desired in step 1 of the inside-out process. Agreement on these is worked out among members of the project team, which includes the analysts, SMO members, and the user.

The two steps of the outside-in process can be facilitated by the use of software packages designed specifically for this purpose. These packages can be used to create shells for models that enable the interactions with the user to be simulated and the output screens to be displayed before the "guts" of the model are defined. One such package is called C-Scape [Cooke *et al.*, 1987]. It allows a model developer to specify input and output screens on-line using a built-in editor. The editor includes such capabilities as block movement, line drawing, and centering. C-Scape also allows computation time to be simulated by building in time delays. By showing different delay times to users, modelers can get an idea of what delays would be acceptable to them and what delays would not. Such information can be invaluable to the model designers and builders in deciding how complex the model can be made.

Using an interface prototyper such as C-Scape has many benefits. Most important is that it makes it more likely that the user will get what he or she actually needs. For example, screens can be designed and revised "on the spot," with the user sitting at the modeler's side. It is also a wonderful device for facilitating communication between the user and modeler. As a result, users feel that they are intimately involved in the modeling process.

C-Scape was used successfully in developing several of the inventory projection models for the EFMS. In one case, interacting with the hollow shell induced potential users to become excited and interested in the model. Even though the same persons had previously been introduced to the proposed model through meetings and briefings, they identified more closely with the specific inputs, outputs, and model capabilities when they were displayed with C-Scape.

Chapter 11 | Test and Evaluation of ODSS Models and Modules

11.1 WHAT IS TEST AND EVALUATION AND HOW SHOULD IT BE DONE?

By "test and evaluation" (T&E), we mean the collection of activities that measures how much credence a decisionmaker can rightly give to the output from an ODSS model. An ODSS contains numerous computerized models of the real world. The output from some of these models is meant to suggest how the real world would respond to given decisions and policy changes. Before a decisionmaker relies on a model's output, he or she will want to know how close the model's estimates are likely to be to the real-world responses. T&E explores this question.

It is important to distinguish test and evaluation from what is often called validation. Thomas [1989, p. 260] defines validation as "testing the 'agreement' of the model with 'reality.'" For a model to pass T&E, the model's output need not strictly conform to actual events. Our definition of T&E is closely related to Miser and Quade's [1988, p. 529] definition of validation as "the process by which the analyst assures himself and others that a model is a representation of the phenomena being modeled that is *adequate for the purposes* of the study of which it is a part."

In the context of an ODSS, to pass its T&E, an ODSS model need only identify the significant consequences of alternative decisions accurately enough for us to distinguish a best decision from others. That is, if one decision is actually better than another, the model must show it. This standard for success in testing and evaluating ODSS models is shaped by decisionmakers' needs to assess alternative actions. The accuracy of a decision model *per se* matters much less than the usefulness of the model's output to a decisionmaker.

Larson and Odoni [1981, p. 543] endorse this principle:

> A model's comparative advantage in decision aiding is, in our opinion, more relevant than its predictive accuracy. In this light—to overstate the case—a model could be a factor of 2 in error on the primary performance measure, but (as long as the factor remains constant) the model would be fine for rank-ordering alternatives and assessing their relative merits. Of course, we do not advocate factor-of-2 errors. But we believe energies directed at concerns for multidecimal accuracy might be better expended in other parts of the implementation process.

In a similar vein, Gerjuoy [1977] wrote:

> A less expensive and less valid forecasting system may be preferable to a more expensive and more accurate one when the greater accuracy does not lead to sufficient improvement in decision benefits or reduction in decision costs to pay for the added expense.

But beware a model that has passed T&E for a single class of decision situations! Do not use such a model in other situations without putting it through additional T&E. (By contrast, if you happen upon a valid model, you can trust it in a very wide variety of situations.) The heart of successful T&E is to assess each model's performance *in the uses for which the model is intended.* If the model performs well when used as I will use it, it does not matter that the model would perform poorly in other uses. (See Hodges [1991] for a lucid discussion of how even "bad" models may be put to good uses.) But beware! Just because a model performs well in my use does not ensure that it will work well in yours. Each planned use of a model should be assessed in the T&E of the model.

It is fortunate that T&E does not require validation. In the complex settings in which ODSS models are normally found, one cannot easily demonstrate strict conformity with reality, or even determine the reality against which it should be measured. Establishing validity often requires both a controlled experimental situation and an expenditure of resources not available in building an ODSS.

How should one test and evaluate an ODSS model? We have no all-encompassing answer to this question. For each ODSS model the answer will differ according to the uses of the model. Nevertheless, we do recommend eight general rules, all of which derive from a single fundamental principle: a well-designed T&E must reveal how well a model will serve decisionmakers.

Our eight rules for conducting a T&E are that a T&E should (1) be conducted with real-world data; (2) not rely only on the data used to fit the model; (3) focus on how a model will be used, and hence check not just how well the parts of a model work, but how well the model as a whole works; (4) simplify the problem, for example, by varying one dimension at a time in a multidimensional problem; (5) drive competing models from the field—a model is "good enough" only if it is at least as good as available alternatives; (6) check both the statistical models and the computer code that implements those models; (7) offer guidance about how to improve inadequate models; and (8) not be a one-time exercise that ends early in the life of an ODSS, but rather an iterative process that repeatedly checks both old models and new models to assess the continuing reliability of the system.

In an ideal world, we would offer a ninth rule: T&E should be begun when the model developers have had their "best shot"; i.e., when they believe they can construct no better model with the available data and resources. However in the real world, T&E may begin whenever political pressures within the organization demand an assessment of the ODSS's ability to perform as well as advertised, or at least better than alternative systems.

Some brief expansion on our eight rules is warranted:

1. *Use real-world data.* Absent actual data, T&E is impossible; one can only rely on experts' judgments that the model represents beliefs accurately. But fitting a model with real-world data differs from T&E. Equation-fitting exercises, however closely grounded in real-world data, do not by themselves comprise a sufficient test of a model.

2. *Use data not used to fit the model.* Convenience tempts us to fit and test a model with the same data set. But prudence advises us to test a model with different data than those used to fit it because (a) predictions made within the sample underestimate the prediction error for out-of-sample forecasts; and (b) an equation may fit some particular data very well but fit subsequent data rather poorly—due, for example, to "overfitting" the data. Having "unused" data ready for T&E requires planning ahead; one must either set aside some data at the start of the model development cycle or else schedule the project so the T&E phase coincides with the release of additional data. Setting data aside at the outset assures that the data will, in fact, be available when the time for T&E arrives. However, if one has relatively little data at the outset, building the model may require all of that data; in such cases one may have to rely on future data for the T&E exercise.

3. *Check on how the model as a whole works.* Each module in a system should pass through T&E, but more importantly, T&E should test how the modules perform together. Decisionmakers seldom use modules in isolation. Knowing that each individual module works well in isolation is small comfort to the decisionmaker if in concert the modules perform poorly. And when models as a whole are tested, they should be tested in contexts similar to those in which they will be used.

4 *Simplify the problem.* A useful diagnostic tool for use in the test and evaluation of a model is to hold some portions of the model constant while varying others. For example, simultaneously performing T&E of the DMI across all of its dimensions (grade, years of service, AFSC, etc.) presented a daunting problem. Instead, some dimensions were held constant, and aggregate predictions were compared to actual data aggregated across the same dimensions.

5. *Compare the model's performance to that of available alternatives.* Organizations will be reluctant to give up a familiar model, even if that model has known flaws. (Better the devil you know than the devil you don't!) Therefore, decisionmakers will not adopt a new model simply because it works well enough to allow best decisions to be identified. To convince decisionmakers to abandon their familiar models, a T&E of a new model must demonstrate the superiority of the new model to the old.

6. *Check both the model's mathematical specifications and its computer implementation.* ODSS modules and models are frequently complex, and the computer code to implement the models is seldom simple. A good T&E exercise will differentiate between failures in the statistical work underlying a model and failures in the coding of the model, and will check for both kinds of failure.

7. *Provide feedback on how to improve the model.* T&E is an important component of developing an ODSS. When models are tested and found to perform poorly, they must be rebuilt to work well. A good T&E exercise will identify *why* a model is performing poorly, not just that it is performing poorly.

8. *Perform T&E periodically.*   T&E is not a one-shot affair that ends early in the life of an ODSS. A model that forecasts well today may forecast better or less well in the future. The world may change in surprising ways that were not anticipated when the model was built. The data used to implement the model may deteriorate or improve in quality, harming or enhancing the model's predictive power. And modifications to the model over time may either improve or hurt its performance. For users to sustain their trust in an ODSS's models, those models must be subjected to periodic T&E.

In the remainder of this chapter we illustrate several of these principles of T&E by reviewing two T&E exercises: (1) the test and evaluation of the Disaggregate Middle-term Inventory Projection Model (DMI) and (2) the test and evaluation of the middle-term disaggregate loss equation module, a module that underpins the DMI. The DMI predicts the numbers of airmen in each occupation for several fiscal years into the future. Central to every inventory projection model is a loss module that predicts the rates at which airmen leave the service. In the DMI, this module is called the middle-term disaggregate loss module (MTL). The MTL predicts annual loss rates by Air Force Specialty Code (AFSC).

We choose to summarize both of these T&E exercises to emphasize the importance of testing and evaluating both the parts of a model *and* the entire model.

Our discussion of the DMI T&E exercise emphasizes that T&E must attend to the uses to which a model will be put. The Air Force relies on the DMI to inform decisions about occupational training. To make good decisions, the service needs to know both the losses from the occupations *and* the movements among occupations. Consequently, the DMI's T&E had to assess the accuracy of the composite forecasts of the numbers of airmen in each occupation, forecasts built with both the occupational mobility module and the loss module, and indeed, built from all the modules of the DMI.

The DMI T&E exercise also illustrates the comparison of a new model to existing competitors. When we built the EFMS, the Air Force was already predicting the occupational structure of the force with a model called ASKIF. Essential to the DMI's T&E was determining whether the DMI would outperform ASKIF.

Our second illustrative exercise, the MTL T&E exercise, raises measurement issues inherent in T&E. In that exercise we used numerous measures to assess the performance of the loss equations. Those measures are applicable to many other forecasting models.

The MTL T&E exercise also illustrates how one can first check the computer code that implements a model and then test the model itself.

The remainder of this chapter is organized in the same order as the original T&E exercises: First we discuss the MTL T&E exercise and then we discuss the DMI T&E exercise.

11.2 TESTING A PART: TEST AND EVALUATION OF THE MIDDLE-TERM DISAGGREGATE LOSS EQUATIONS

The middle-term disaggregate loss equations estimate the probability of loss and the probability of extending given nonloss for any year in an airman's career. (The unit of analysis for the data with which the equations were estimated is called a "year at risk." See Section 7.3 for the definition of a "year at risk.") The loss equation T&E asked how accurately the equations predicted the loss behavior of airmen in each decision group.

The loss equation T&E is described in three steps. First, we define the decision groups for which loss equations were estimated and describe the data used for the T&E. Second, we specify four complementary measures of forecasting performance with which to assess the loss equations. Third, we apply those measures to the loss equations. For a more complete description, see Abrahamse [1988].

Loss equations were estimated for 10 distinct decision groups. These groups differ according to term of service to which they apply—first, second, career (any nonretirement term beyond the second) and retirement—and according to whether the airman is at the end of a contract, in the midst of a contract, or in an extension of a contract. The 10 decision groups, along with an acronym for each, are:

1ATT	First-term attrition
1ETS	First-term ETS
1EXT	First-term extension
2ATT	Second-term attrition
2ETS	Second-term ETS
2EXT	Second-term extension
CATT	Career attrition
CETS	Career ETS
CEXT	Career extension
RET	Retirement

The equations discussed here were estimated with a 40 percent simple random sample of airmen and seven years of data (fiscal years 1977 through 1983). The T&E data consisted of a 10 percent simple random sample from each of three fiscal years: FY83, FY84, and FY85. Data from FY83 were used to estimate the equations, but the other two years were new. The equations are described in Section 7.3. Details of their estimation are provided by Carter *et al.* [1987].

We now turn to the prediction performance measures, which are discussed at some length because the heart of any T&E is the set of performance measures used to assess the models. The T&E exercise for the 10 equations will be illustrated using data on losses for a 10 percent sample of airman records from FY83. The data set contained 50,987 airmen at risk. Overall, the actual number of airmen lost was 5934; the equations predicted 5686 losses.

We now discuss specific measures and apply them to this information.

Prediction error (PE) is simply the number of predicted losses minus the number of actual losses. In our example, the prediction error is −248 (= 5686 − 5934). The size of the prediction error depends partly on the accuracy of the module. It is positive if the module overpredicts losses, negative if the module underpredicts losses. But its size also depends on the number of airmen at risk of loss, and unless this number is known, prediction error is almost meaningless.

Note that a loss prediction also implies a survival (retention) prediction. The survival prediction error (number of predicted survivors minus the number of actual survivors) is just the negative of the prediction error, so there is a certain symmetry in this measure.

Percent relative error (PRE) is the prediction error divided by the number of actual losses, times 100. In our example, this rate is −4.2 percent. Since our equations are loss equations, PRE seems to be a natural measure of performance. However, it has two peculiar properties.

First, if loss rates are already low, the PRE can be quite large, even though the prediction error itself is small. If the cost of bad forecasts is driven by the *number* of losses mistakenly forecast, and the number of airmen at risk is small, a high PRE does not indicate a poor forecasting performance.

Second, the PRE measures of losses and survivals are not symmetric. If the number of survivors, rather than the number of losses, interests us, the survival percentage error rate would be the survival prediction error divided by the number of survivors. If losses are low and the number of airmen at risk is high, then the survival PRE will be small, while the loss PRE will be high. (In our example, the survival PRE is 0.55 percent—an order of magnitude lower than the loss PRE.) Thus, PRE is an ambiguous measure of performance, unless the model's user has some reason to value accuracy in one prediction (e.g., loss prediction) over accuracy in the other (e.g., survival prediction).

A more symmetric measure is the *prediction error as percent of number at risk (PEPNR)*—the prediction error divided by the number of airmen at risk, times 100. In our example, this rate is –0.49 percent. If we think of our equations as predicting, on a case-by-case basis, whether an airman will be lost during an applicable year at risk, PEPNR measures the net error rate [the net number of false negatives (if PEPNR is negative) or false positives (if PEPNR is positive)] as a percent of the number of predictions made. Note that PEPNR for survivals is just the negative of PEPNR for losses.

These first three measures (PE, PRE, and PEPNR) are purely descriptive. The fourth measure, called the *standardized prediction error (SPE)*, has more analytical content. Its definition requires some discussion.

Each middle-term disaggregate loss equation is a linear combination of the form:

LOSS = constant
     + parameter(1) * variable(1)
     + parameter(2) * variable(2)
     + ...
     + parameter(n) * variable(n)

Each equation applies to individual airmen. In any particular year at risk, each airman is described by the variables in the equation, and each equation is characterized by its variables and the estimates of its parameters.

Generally, the value of LOSS is a number that lies strictly between 0 and 1. Since an airman either leaves or does not, we interpret LOSS as a probability. For any group of airmen, we can add up the values assigned to LOSS for all airmen in the group to predict the number of losses within this group. But since we interpret LOSS as a probability, we expect that the actual number of losses in any group will not agree exactly with the predicted number; such disagreement does not necessarily invalidate the equation.

The actual number of losses will differ from the predicted number "by chance alone" even if the equation represents reality "perfectly." It may even differ by a large amount. But, as the difference gets larger, the probability of that difference gets smaller.

Calculating the "true" probability of observing a given difference between the actual and predicted number of losses is no simple matter. Generally, the equations do not in and of themselves give a complete description of what we think, or at least what we are willing to hypothesize. More specifically, we do not wholly believe either the homogeneity or the independence that our equations assume. We consider these two assumptions in turn.

Are the airmen homogeneous with respect to their probability of leaving the service? That is, do the equations assign each airman his or her *exact* loss probability, or do they assign each airman only the *average* loss probability for all the airmen who share the airman's values for the independent variables?

Homogeneity is especially questionable because most of the variables in the loss equations are categorical—they take on just a few values. In fact, most are "dummy" variables—taking on only the values 0 or 1. (The two important exceptions are the unemployment rate and the military/civilian pay ratio; but for any given fiscal year, the unemployment rate changes very little and the pay ratio changes not at all [because it is only updated yearly]. So, for the purposes of evaluation we can regard these two variables as part of the constant term.) Thus, in effect, each equation partitions the force into a relatively small number of categories and assigns the same loss probability to each airman in any one category. The question of homogeneity is whether, within each of these categories, the loss probability assigned to each airman is exactly his or her loss probability, or whether it is simply the average loss probability for all airmen in that group. If the latter is true, then the sample is homogeneous (with respect to our model).

If the sample is homogeneous with respect to some model, the probability distribution of the predicted number of losses in any particular sample can be calculated (but see the discussion of independence that follows), and then a probability can be assigned to observing any specified difference between actual and observed losses.

Of course, our samples are not homogeneous. In each stratum our equations define, other variables surely exist that are not now in the equation that would partition the stratum into further groups of airmen where the loss probabilities would be substantially different from group to group. But we do not know what these new variables are, nor how different the new loss probabilities would be.

Though samples are rarely homogeneous, it is not clear what to assume instead. Consequently, probability calculations are commonly made assuming homogeneity, but the results are then interpreted with the understanding that the assumption is likely to be wrong.

Homogeneity alone is not sufficient to allow us to calculate the distribution of losses in any given sample from the loss equations. Information is also needed about whether airmen's loss decisions are independent of one another.

Do airmen decide to leave the force independently of the decisions made by other airmen? That is, is one airman more or less likely to leave the force because some other airmen left or stayed? Whether the airmen choose independently of one another influences the distribution of the actual number of losses. The effect of this influence can be illustrated by looking at the variance in the actual number of losses.

If we act as though the sample is homogeneous with respect to our model, then for any decision group whose size is n and whose predicted loss rate is p, the predicted number of losses will be np. If within this group the airmen act independently, the actual number of losses will be a binomially distributed random variable with mean np and variance $np(1 - p)$.

At another extreme, the airmen could always act in concert (i.e., all leave together or stay together), but still all leave with probability p or stay with probability $1 - p$. This situation could still be appropriately represented by one of our equations, and the best prediction of the number of losses is np. The average number of losses will still be np, but the actual number will be a random variable equal to n with probability p and 0 with probability $1 - p$, and its variance will be n times bigger than the variance of the independent case.

As a third alternative, it could happen that all the airmen want to leave, but some kind of policy constrains airmen from leaving, so that once the fraction p has left, no further losses are allowed. In other words, exactly the fraction p leaves—no more, no less. Our equations still appropriately represent this situation, and the best prediction of the number of losses is np. In this case, the actual number of losses will be exactly np, the variance will be zero, and our predictions will always be perfect.

Thus, the variance of the actual number of losses depends on the kind of independence of choice among airmen in any homogeneous group. Different kinds of dependence can lead to greatly differing variances.

In fact, airmen probably do not act independently. Situations like those mentioned above probably occur to some extent. Current events within the Air Force or in the civilian world probably influence the loss decisions of many airmen. Also, after a certain number of losses, the service might impede further losses or offer special inducements for airmen to stay.

So, our fourth prediction performance measure (SPE) tests the hypothesis that our predicted loss rate is the "true" loss rate, under the assumptions that airmen are homogeneous with respect to the model and act independently. Under this hypothesis, the number of losses in any group will be a random variable whose mean m is

$$m = Np$$

and whose variance v is (slightly) larger than

$$v = Np\,(1 - p),$$

where

N = number of airmen at risk in the group, and

p = predicted loss rate for the entire group.

If N is large enough, under this hypothesis the standardized prediction error (SPE), given by

$$SPE = PE/sqrt(v),$$

is approximately normally distributed with variance slightly less than 1. This means that the probability of observing a given prediction error can be estimated from tables of the standard normal distribution

$$Prob(|SPE| > z) > Prob(|Z| > z),$$

where z is a normal random variable with mean = 0 and standard deviation = 1.

Generally, if the absolute value of SPE exceeds 2, we can reject the hypothesis that the predicted loss rate is the "true" loss rate, or we can reject the hypothesis that the airmen are homogeneous with respect to the model and act independently.

For the above FY83 example, SPE is 3.5, which means the hypothesis of a perfect statistical fit can be rejected. Such a lack of fit is not surprising. We do not believe the airmen are homogeneous with respect to loss rates, or we would not have developed so many decision groups. But more importantly, with large sample sizes statistical models rarely "fit" the data, especially when the models attempt to predict human behavior. Given the complexity of the process modeled here, and the size of the sample (more than 50,000 cases), a 3.5 standard deviation error is indicative of an acceptably well-specified model.

These four measures of performance (PE, PRE, PEPNR, and SPE) are now applied to the loss equations for the 10 decision groups.

First, the predictions of all 10 decision groups are combined to estimate the net number of losses for the entire sample. Next, these estimated losses are compared to the actual number of losses in FY83, FY84, and FY85. Finally, the predicted and actual losses for each of the 10 decision groups are compared to each other, first for FY83 and then for FY84 and FY85.

FY83 was in the estimation sample. Why include it in the T&E data too? Because making forecasts for 1983 and seeing that the predicted and actual loss rates are close modestly confirms that our computer programs are correct. Had large discrepancies between the actual and predicted loss rates in 1983 been found, we would have suspected the computer code was in error.

However, even though 1983 data were among the data used to estimate the equations, there is no guarantee that the equations will necessarily perform well for 1983. It might be the case that loss rates in 1983 differed markedly from previous years; the equations will predict average loss rates perfectly only if the averages are taken from the entire seven-year period. Thus, making forecasts for 1983 by itself is a weak, albeit worthwhile, test of the computer code.

Table 11.1 summarizes the overall performance of the 10 equations for the three years.

Table 11.1

Overall Performance of the Middle-Term Loss Equations by Fiscal Year

	FISCAL YEAR		
MEASURE	1983	1984	1985
Number of airmen at risk	50,987	51,769	51,933
Predicted losses	5,686	5,567	6,299
Actual losses	5,934	5,592	5,966
Prediction error (PE)	−248	−25	333
Percent relative error (PRE)	−4.2%	−0.4%	5.6%
Error as % of N at risk (PEPNR)	−0.5%	−0.1%	0.6%
Standardized prediction error (SPE)	−3.5	−0.4	4.5

The table suggests that the overall performance of the equations is quite good. The PRE is at most 5.6 percent (in FY85, which is two years beyond the data used to estimate the equation). But even in FY85, the equations taken together predict only 333 losses too many, out of nearly 52,000 airmen in the sample. The standardized prediction error has increased (in absolute value) by 1 standard deviation over the level in FY83.

Table 11.2 summarizes the performance of each of the 10 equations for FY83. Recall that data for 1983 were used to estimate the coefficients of these equations, so good performance for this year's data is likely if the evaluation code was correctly written.

Four of the equations, 2ATT, 2ETS, CATT, and CEXT, exhibit large relative errors. However, in the case of CEXT the number of losses is low, and the fact that the standardized prediction error is low suggests that the prediction error could be due to chance alone.

The second-term and career attrition equations exhibit errors that cannot be so easily dismissed. In each case the actual number of losses is more than 3.5 standard deviations from the predicted number. Apparently, 1983 is quite different from other years in the estimation sample.

The error seen in the second-term ETS equation was large enough to be noted, but not large enough to be alarming. Predicted losses exceed actuals by a little over two standard deviations. While the probability of such an event is under 5 percent, the probability of its occurrence in 10 trials exceeds 20 percent, so it might not be surprising to see a difference this large at least once in a list of this sort.

On balance, the performance of the equations in FY83 made us confident that there were no serious errors in the T&E computer code.

Table 11.3 presents actual and predicted loss rates for FY84 and FY85. Data for FY84 and FY85 were not used to estimate the parameters of these equations, so Table 11.3 represents a better test of the loss equations themselves than does Table 11.2.

Considering standardized prediction error only, six of the equations (1ATT, 1EXT, 2EXT, CETS, CEXT, and RET) perform exactly as one would expect an unbiased equation to behave. Of these six equations and three fiscal years, there is only one example where the SPE exceeds 2 (2EXT in FY85).

As in FY83, the four decision groups 2ATT, 2ETS, CATT, and CEXT exhibit large SPEs in both FY84 and FY85. As in FY83, CEXT loss rates

Table 11.2

Performance of All Models For FY83

MODEL	AIRMEN AT RISK	LOSS RATE		PERFORMANCE MEASURE			
		Pred	Actual	PE	PRE	PEPNR	SPE
1ATT	19461	9.57%	9.95%	−74	−3.8%	−0.38%	−1.80
1ETS	4283	34.47%	35.86%	−60	−3.9%	−1.39%	−1.91
1EXT	2850	30.81%	31.23%	−12	−1.3%	−0.42%	−0.49
2ATT	7117	1.98%	2.61%	−45	−24.1%	−0.63%	−3.82
2ETS	1203	14.26%	12.05%	27	18.3%	2.21%	2.19
2EXT	1037	14.71%	14.27%	5	3.1%	0.44%	0.40
CATT	9169	0.68%	1.06%	−35	−35.8%	−0.38%	−4.43
CETS	1617	1.76%	1.67%	1	5.4%	0.09%	0.28
CEXT	829	3.77%	4.34%	−5	−13.1%	−0.57%	−0.86
RET	3421	25.78%	27.27%	−51	−5.5%	−1.49%	−1.99
TOTAL	50987	11.15%	11.63%	−248	−4.2%	−0.49%	−3.50

are extremely low, and since the standardized prediction error is small, the error seen in that equation is no cause for concern.

The two attrition equations 2ATT and CATT continue to display the large SPEs seen in FY83, suggesting something may be wrong with either the specification or the implementation of these two equations. In both equations, the problem lies in the failure of the equations to predict big changes in the actual loss rates—in other words, the equations are unresponsive rather than over-reactive.

The second-term ETS equation exhibits the same marginal performance seen in FY83, with standardized prediction errors a little too large to be satisfactory, especially when seen in three successive fiscal years.

The T&E of the loss equations was encouraging, and it also pointed the way for making improvements in the loss equation specifications by indicating that the models for several decision groups needed further analysis.

Not every T&E exercise will prove encouraging. Indeed, an earlier EFMP T&E exercise exposed serious misspecifications in an earlier version of the 1EXT equation. Indeed, more detailed examination of the T&E reported here pointed the way to needed changes in the models that required months to complete.

11.3 TESTING THE WHOLE: TEST AND EVALUATION OF THE DISAGGREGATE MIDDLE-TERM INVENTORY PROJECTION MODEL

Whatever the success of the loss equations, *per se,* their success did not sufficiently test middle-term loss modeling in the EFMS. Policymakers have no direct interest in the loss rates forecast by these equations; they are little heartened by reports that loss rates they cannot put to immediate use are accurate. The decisionmakers' real confidence in the loss rates ultimately rests on how well the DMI, in which the loss rates are embedded, predicts the Air Force's occupational structure. The predictions about the Air Force's occupational structure are pertinent to decisions about the Air Force's trained personnel requirements (TPR). If the DMI is accurate enough to improve decisionmaking in the TPR exercise, then the loss equations are a success.

The test of the DMI focused on the number of airmen in each occupational group. This reflects the rule that a T&E should reflect the uses to which a model will be put. The T&E of the loss equations did not focus on occupations, but on the 10 loss decision groups. The focus on decision groups sufficed for assessing the loss equation modules' statistical reliability. No more detailed attention was required in the loss equation T&E for two reasons. First, occupational detail in the loss equation T&E would not have sufficed to establish credibility with the decisionmakers. Second, the DMI T&E exercise would indirectly check the acceptability of the loss equations' performance at the occupational level.

Occupational structure depends not only on losses, but also on the occupational mobility of airmen who remain in the service. The DMI combines the loss equation module with an occupation mobility module (and several other modules) to produce forecasts of numbers of airmen by occupation over the next several fiscal years. The purpose of the DMI T&E was to establish whether the DMI forecast these occupation counts accurately enough to improve decisionmaking in the TPR.

Unlike the loss decision groups, where the numbers of airmen usually number in the thousands, occupational groups (AFSCs) usually number in the hundreds. Clearly, the accuracy of forecasts in percentage terms is unlikely to be as good for such small groups as it was for large ones, so typical values of PEPNR were higher in the DMI analysis than they were in the loss equation T&E. Fortunately, Air Force policymakers are not particularly concerned about the smallest AFSCs (those with fewer than 50

Table 11.3

Performance of All Models for FY84 and FY85

MODEL	FY	AIRMEN AT RISK	LOSS RATE		PERFORMANCE MEASURE			
			Pred	Actual	PD	RPE	PEPNR	SPE
1ATT	84	19043	9.04%	9.00%	8	0.4%	0.0%	0.19
	85	18301	9.07%	8.69%	70	4.2%	0.4%	1.79
1ETS	84	4810	38.92%	36.45%	119	6.3%	2.5%	3.51
	85	4949	47.73%	37.91%	486	20.6%	9.8%	13.83
1EXT	84	2076	30.95%	30.49%	10	1.5%	0.5%	0.45
	85	1706	32.75%	31.65%	19	3.4%	1.1%	0.97
2ATT	84	8702	2.07%	3.92%	−161	−89.4%	−1.9%	−12.12
	85	9308	2.26%	4.86%	−242	−115.0%	−2.6%	−16.88
2ETS	84	1410	15.72%	13.26%	35	15.6%	2.5%	2.54
	85	1390	21.88%	17.27%	64	21.1%	4.6%	4.16
2EXT	84	759	14.92%	14.10%	6	5.5%	0.8%	0.63
	85	736	19.09%	14.67%	33	23.2%	4.4%	3.05
CATT	84	9631	0.67%	1.09%	−40	−62.7%	−0.4%	−5.05
	85	9910	0.70%	1.49%	−78	−112.9%	−0.8%	−9.43
CETS	84	1741	2.16%	2.35%	−3	−8.8%	−0.2%	−0.55
	85	1639	2.55%	2.93%	−6	−14.9%	−0.4%	−0.98
CEXT	84	690	4.10%	2.90%	8	29.3%	1.2%	1.59
	85	679	4.67%	5.15%	−3	−10.3%	−0.5%	−0.59
RET	84	3360	24.51%	24.40%	4	0.4%	0.1%	0.15
	85	3315	27.76%	28.02%	−9	−0.9%	−0.3%	−0.33

airmen) for which large percentage errors (though small *absolute* errors) are most likely.

Figure 11.1 shows the distribution of PEPNR (prediction error as percent of number at risk) across AFSCs for October 1988 forecasts of the number of airmen that would be in an AFSC on September 30, 1989. Attention is restricted to AFSCs with more than 50 airmen in October 1988. More than half the AFSCs have errors (plus or minus) of 3 percent or less. More than 95 percent of the AFSCs have errors of 10 percent or less. Only two AFSCs of the 230 have an error greater than 20 percent. Clearly the model forecast ahead one year quite well—well enough for the Air Force to rely on the DMI in the TPR exercise.

The model performs almost as well forecasting two years ahead. Figure 11.2 shows the distribution of PEPNR across AFSCs for October 1, 1987 forecasts of the number of airmen that would be in an AFSC on September 30, 1989. Attention is restricted to AFSCs with more than 50 airmen in 1987. More than half the AFSCs have errors of 4 percent or less. Ninety-five percent of the AFSCs have errors of 16 percent or less. Rela-

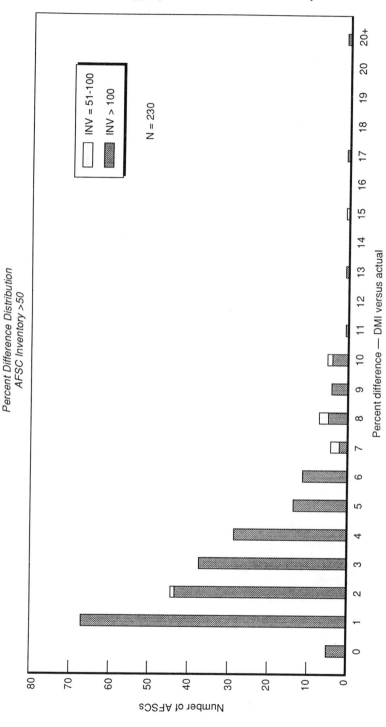

Fig. 11.1   Comparison of FY89 Actual Inventory with DMI one-year projection.

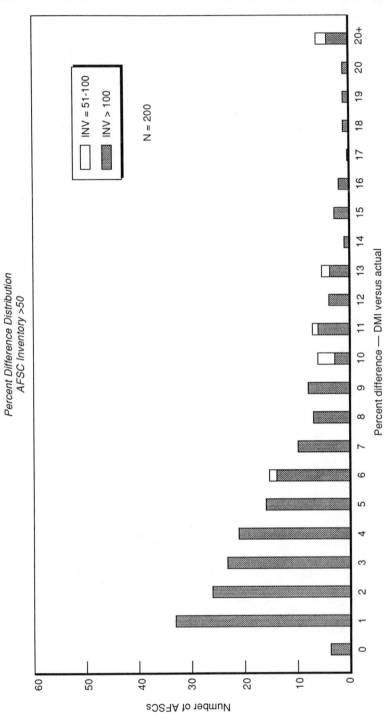

Fig. 11.2   Comparison of FY89 Actual Inventory with DMI two-year projection.

tively large errors are more frequent with the two-year forecasts: 7 AFSCs of the 200 had errors greater than 20 percent. On balance, these errors are modest and do not preclude the Air Force from relying on the two-year-ahead forecasts in the TPR exercise.

The attentive reader has noticed that the loss equation T&E data were from 1983–1985, while the DMI T&E data were from 1987–1989. In fact, the DMI has now been tested four times: in 1986, 1987, 1990, and 1991. Four major lessons have been drawn from these repetitions.

Lesson 1: Half-way steps toward testing whole models add little to the model's credibility. In the 1986 T&E exercise, the entire DMI was not tested. Instead, a partial test of the DMI was constructed by extending the loss equation test to examine loss forecasts for fiscal years (the unit of analysis of interest to the policymaker), instead of loss forecasts for years at risk. This involved combining the loss equation module with another DMI module, called the "blending module," that transformed year-at-risk loss rates into fiscal year loss rates. The blended fiscal year loss forecasts were not, however, a full implementation of the DMI. The forecasts did not model flows of airmen from training into occupations, and the full fiscal year forecasts were not what the users would ultimately need. The users would need partial year forecasts. These limitations of the forecasts prevented the relatively successful test of these forecasts from increasing the users' trust in the system as much as had been hoped.

Lesson 2: Politics may dictate when a model is first tested, and such tests may doom the system. In 1987 the DMI contained known programming errors, which some analysts feared might impair the performance of the system in a test. The principle that T&E should come after system builders have had their best shot at building the models advised against testing the system at that time. However, some clients and competitors in the Air Force believed the time had come for the EFMS to prove its worth; they demanded a test of the DMI and, in particular, demanded that we compare the DMI with ASKIF, the Air Force's old model for forecasting the occupational structure of the force.[29]

The comparison to ASKIF proved crucial to the success of the DMI's 1987 T&E. The programming errors in the 1987 DMI moderately eroded the model's performance; the levels of prediction error were markedly

---

[29] A new model that some in the Air Force favored over the DMI was also tested. It soon fell from contention.

higher than in the 1990 T&E described above.[30] However, the ASKIF model still forecast less well than the DMI. Consequently, most clients agreed that a continued investment in the DMI (and the EFMS) was warranted.

Needless to say, we would have rather conducted the DMI's first T&E exercise later—after we had corrected the DMI's bugs. Indeed, had we not been confident that the ASKIF model would perform poorly, we would have fought harder to postpone the test. But if ASKIF had surprised us, or if the program bugs had hurt the DMI's forecasts as much as some analysts had feared they might, this unwelcome early T&E could have brought an end to the EFMP. (Better forecasts were not the only factor that favored the DMI. For several clients, the determining factor was the bells and whistles in the DMI that allowed it to account better for both occupational mobility and promotions than ASKIF could.)

Lesson 3: This lesson does not pertain to T&E, but to data management. It is that the assembling, organizing, and cleaning of data (including the data needed for T&E) will absorb more resources than anyone expects. The 1986 T&E of the DMI was conducted by the analysts at RAND. The 1987 T&E was one of the first attempts by the Air Force to run an EFMS model in house, albeit in a test mode. The single greatest difficulty the Air Force encountered in conducting the 1987 DMI T&E exercise was compiling the actual data needed for the evaluation of forecasts. In 1990 and 1991, compiling the data was still a major part of the T&E effort.

Lesson 4: T&E should be an iterative process. Each year the Air Force refits the loss equations, and each year the AFSC codes change. Over time, such changes in the modules and variables of the DMI could erode (or improve!) the model's performance. Periodic reevaluation of the DMI, and of other ODSS models, will maintain users' confidence in the system.

---

[30] The programming bugs were not the only difference between the 1987 and 1990 DMIs. Three years of further research continued to improve the DMI.

PART V

IMPLEMENTATION

Chapter 12 | Principles for Implementing an ODSS

Implementation is the key to a successful decision support system. It is the point at which all of the individual pieces of the system have to come together and where the important transition from development to system operation takes place. However, it would be a mistake to look at implementation as a single point in the life cycle of a decision support system. It is a process that should begin in the earliest stages of system planning and continue through the entire development cycle. Few elements of the development process are not affected by the possibilities, constraints, and requirements of the environment in which the system will be implemented and operated. In fact, implementation can be thought of as the process of taking all of the disparate elements of system conceptualization, design, and development and turning them into a working decision support system.

While modeling often receives the most attention and visibility in discussions or written materials concerning decision support systems, it is only one of the elements that will determine the project's success. Data must be assembled and organized rapidly enough for the decisionmaking processes being targeted. Operational software must be robust enough to cope with the complexities and dynamics of the world the models are designed to address. Users must be brought into the project and become an integral part of its development. If any of these responsibilities is neglected, it can bring down the entire project, leaving the organization with thousands, or even millions, in investment dollars that at best may realize only a marginal return.

Organizational decision support systems should be viewed as on-line, interactive management information systems that include models and that provide some or all of the information required by the functions being supported. While technology and the nature of the processes or operations being supported may shape the development process for an ODSS, a structured and disciplined approach is still required. Many of the lessons learned in building more traditional information systems can be applied to ODSS development—the trick is to pick the ones that are appropriate. This and the following chapters in this part of the book should be of help in meeting that challenge. They deal with the process of transforming model specifications and prototypes into an operational information system. This chapter provides a context and guiding principles for this process. The remaining chapters show how the principles are applied to various aspects of the system. The process of transitioning the models from the modelers to the system developers is covered in Chapter 13. Chapter 14 deals with the need to choose the system software carefully and the fact that the hardware should be chosen after the software. Chapters 15 and 16 examine the issues of designing and building the database and application software. For the user, the system is what they observe or interact with. ODSS builders must, therefore, devote considerable attention to the design of the user interface. Chapter 17 discusses this aspect. The final chapter deals with updating and maintaining an ODSS. An ODSS must continue to evolve if it is to meet the changing external and internal environment of the organization. A static system will become increasingly irrelevant and will gradually cease being used. This chapter describes what must be done to keep the system alive and well.

12.1 DEFINING THE ARCHITECTURE OF AN ODSS

The components of an ODSS are all of the pieces of hardware and software that compose it. The architecture of the system is the specification of what those components are, the form they take, and how they fit together.

An architectural approach to ODSS development is the recognition that all its components are interrelated and that they need to be procured or developed with their relationships in mind. Rather than selecting or developing the pieces and then attempting to fit them together, the architectural approach looks first at the system as a whole and systematically uses that knowledge to select and shape the pieces. It recognizes and incorporates the goals of integration and interoperability from the very beginning. It imposes an overall discipline on building the ODSS that is essential for large-scale integrated systems that would not be required if the applications were truly to be "stand-alone" or "stovepiped." It also takes into account that ODSSs are not going to be developed all at once (as they would be if the System Development Life Cycle paradigm were being used), but will be implemented on a phased basis over an extended period of time. Applications will not be stagnant, but change as the environment they attempt to model changes or as new information is incorporated into their structure and operation.

Design of an ODSS's architecture begins during the conceptual design stage of development. As noted in Chapter 3, being a participant from the very beginning of the project is extremely important for those who will be charged with building the system. This accomplishes a number of objectives. It gives them an opportunity to obtain a real "feel" for the project itself, both in terms of the tasks to be performed and problems to be solved. It also offers them the chance to shape the initial planning for the ODSS in ways that can smooth implementation, simplify maintenance, ensure reliability, meet performance requirements, and facilitate operation.

The architecture of the system can be viewed from different perspectives. Two of the most obvious are the software and hardware views. In the EFMS, we addressed the software first (see Chapter 14). We believe that this is the correct choice for any system that does not have a definite hardware constraint (e.g., a corporate policy with regard to what hardware will be used or a key hardware-related component that is not readily available on the commercial market). Given the range of hardware options and the almost amazing growth in performance and functionality per dollar expended, software is much more likely to be both the driving factor in terms of capabilities delivered and the major constraint on what can be accomplished. Ironically, this approach ran contrary to Air Force practices at the time. However, in this case the software-first approach prevailed, with the hardware architecture largely evolving as a result of the software decisions that were made.

There are two components to the ODSS software architecture—the external architecture and the internal architecture. The external architecture is composed of those elements of the system that the user sees or experiences—the interfaces, controls, and specific inputs and outputs. Issues in the design and development of the external architecture are discussed in Chapter 17. The internal architecture is composed of the software tools employed, the interfaces or linkages among those tools, the data structures, and the application and support software.

Defining the internal architecture involves focusing on those aspects of the ODSS that tie the system together, are common to multiple applications, or serve the needs of large portions of the system itself. The internal architecture can be thought of as being composed of the following:

- The data residing in the system, from a content and structural standpoint.
- Functionality, processes, or operations that are either common across a number of identified applications or can be considered key elements in determining the overall success of the system.
- Linkages between the system and external users or sources of data.

Issues in the design and development of the internal architecture are discussed in Chapters 14, 15, and 16 and, to some extent, in Sections 12.4 and 12.5 of this chapter.

12.2 AN INTEGRATED APPROACH TO IMPLEMENTATION

A broad-based and integrated approach is necessary when implementing an ODSS. Some of the integrated approaches to manufacturing that have gained prominence over the last few years can be applied to develop successfully organizational decision support systems. Traditionally, in manufacturing concerns, marketing took the lead in determining the need for a new product. Product design was the sole province of design engineers. It was up to the manufacturing unit to figure out how to translate that design into the actual product. Maintainability and serviceability, if considered at all in the process, were of secondary importance. The analogous information system is one in which the users state the requirements, analysts do the analysis and design, programmers code the system, and the users live with the consequences—for better or for worse.

Today, a number of forward-thinking manufacturing firms, notably in the automobile and electronic industries, have taken an integrated approach to product design, development, manufacturing, and maintenance, thereby significantly reducing life cycle costs and time to production. Production, maintenance, and operational concerns are explicit considerations in product development and design. Design is not only the responsibility of design engineers, but the product of the cooperative efforts of all parties responsible for the various phases of the product life cycle.

This paradigm can be productively applied to building an ODSS. That is, all phases of the system life cycle need to be addressed from the very beginning. None of the principal elements can be worked in isolation from the others. One of the reasons that the EFMS achieved the success that it did was the fact that this principle of close cooperation and integration across the various phases of development was adhered to from the very earliest stages, even though specific tasks and responsibilities were divided among different organizations working on the project.

Some features of the ODSS development process differ from the industrial model. There is no sharp dividing line between design and production. The implementation for large-scale systems is often better managed on a phased, rather than "turnkey," basis. Model development most likely will not end at the point of implementation. Implementation will probably reveal factors that will require at least some modification to the models as they were originally developed.

In the case of EFMS, for example, changes in enlisted behavior required restructuring and refitting some of the models, even though those models fit the original data very well. In fact, several months were spent in tuning the models even after they were implemented in an operational mode. It is likely that future changes in behavior will again require restructuring the models. This kind of effort should be factored into project planning.

A number of specific areas of activity should be addressed in an integrated approach to implementation. Some of these have not been traditionally considered as part of implementation, but when implementation considerations are incorporated as part of these activities, almost every phase of the project benefits. Several of these areas require significant work well in advance of the actual implementation date. They are discussed below.

12.2.1 Requirements Development

Decisions concerning the conceptual design need to be guided by knowledge of the resources available for development. The scope of the system must fit within what can realistically be accomplished with the staff and other resources that are likely to be available. It is much better to address this issue as part of a requirements development process than for developers to deliver a system that does not meet what the users thought were the requirements or to surprise the users with the fact that their requirements cannot be met at all.

The detailed requirements also cannot be realistically separated from how they are to be fulfilled. To be feasible and practical, system requirements have to be developed in light of how the final results of these processes are to be implemented and the operational environment in which the system will reside, including such factors as expected machine capacity and software availability.

Traditionally, users often generate sets of "functional requirements" from which a project team then produces a system. Unfortunately, this approach does not generally work well in practice. Often, users are unaware of solutions and opportunities available that would expand the range of what should or could be done. In practice, functional specifications often turn out to be incomplete and disjointed, lack a systems perspective, permit a wide range of interpretations, and create confusion in the minds of those trying to interpret them. The final system definition often results from systems personnel trying to make sense out of what they were given as the "final" requirements by the users.

Bringing the project team, especially those concerned with actual implementation, into the requirements process can ameliorate many of these problems. This brings the expertise of the project team members to bear very early in the process, combining their unique set of skills with those of the users. As the project team absorbs information from the users, they can begin to integrate what might appear to be a disparate set of requirements into a "systems" solution. The project team can also bring time and attention to the development of the requirements that is not available within the using organization. In most organizations, requirements development is just an additional task that must be borne on top of the normal day-to-day workload. A "hot" new project or unexpected crisis can divert user attention from the ODSS effort. By having the project team develop the requirements with the users, continuity can be maintained.

The generation of the detailed requirements for the EFMS proceeded from the conceptual design for the system, which identified solutions for dissatisfactions and frustrations of the users and the shortcomings of the then operational system. Most of the detailed requirements were developed by the EFMS team and then coordinated with the users.

12.2.2   System Design

Considering implementation and maintenance issues as an integral part of the design effort can be a useful method for tempering the design by emphasizing standards of performance or accuracy that are acceptable, rather than reaching for degrees of accuracy or performance that may in the end not be justifiable in terms of the cost of development. This technique can be used throughout the system development cycle to adjust what may be competing interests or points of view in such a way as to create a system that represents a balanced approach to meeting the major needs for the system.

12.2.3   User Involvement

Systems that are perceived to have the greatest benefit to an organization, and those that are the most readily adopted and used, are those for which the using organization has developed a sense of ownership. This feeling of ownership does not spontaneously take place when the users are handed "the keys" to the system. It is slowly and patiently nurtured over time as a conscious element of the development process.

Although continuous user involvement is necessary, there are some phases in the development process where we recommend especially heavy user involvement, including conceptual design and definition of the system architecture. Here, the users can be extremely valuable in providing form to the system. In addition, heavy user involvement is essential in the design of user interfaces. This design is all too often left as an afterthought, but should be given a prominent role from the very early stages of a project. There are a number of different variations of the cartoon shown in Fig. 12.1 floating around. It is humorous because it is an all too accurate characterization of how information systems projects often turn out. It is really a comment on the shortcomings of current processes for defining, specifying, and communicating information systems requirements.

While there are no guarantees of success in defining interfaces, tools and methods exist for coping with the problem. As discussed in Chapter 17, we devoted significant attention to prototyping the user interface before the actual coding of an application. The prototype generally proved to be of substantial value in defining the content and the form of the infor-

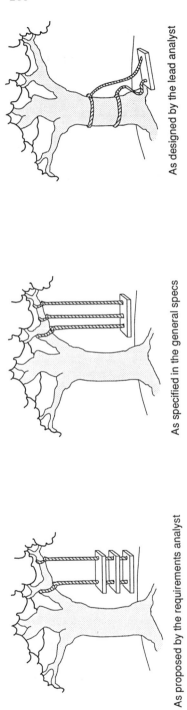

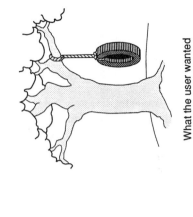

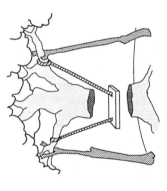

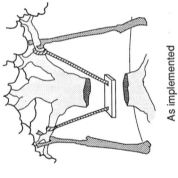

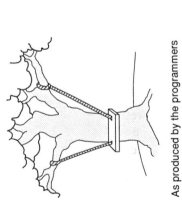

As designed by the lead analyst

What the user wanted

As specified in the general specs

As implemented

As proposed by the requirements analyst

As produced by the programmers

Fig. 12.1 How Information Systems Projects Often Turn Out

mation needed by the user, and we believe it was a key to the successful implementation of several models.

It is unlikely that a significant decision support system application is ever going to be initiated without the potential users of the system perceiving that they have a major problem to be solved or a significant deficiency to be overcome. This may seem obvious, but many proposals coming from the outside, including the MIS department, often appear as technological solutions in search of a problem. People and organizations are going to be very reluctant to buy into a project unless they can tie it directly to a need already felt. Unless this connection is made from the very beginning and maintained throughout the system development cycle, chances of success are greatly reduced. The EFMS was able to be developed and achieved the degree of acceptance it did in large part because the final configuration of the system fit a set of needs that had already been clearly expressed and closely matched a conceptual solution that was already in the process of being developed internally. Areas in which the system failed to make inroads, or received only lukewarm support and a lack of commitment were areas in which the perceived urgency or severity of the problems was not as great or potential users had "other" concerns that overrode any advantages they saw coming from the system itself.

12.2.4   Staffing the SMO

As discussed in Chapter 3, the SMO should be formed at the beginning of the project and has roles to play throughout the ODSS' life. It is, however, during implementation of the system that the SMO has the most to do and will reach its largest size.

For successful implementation, the SMO requires personnel to address both the modeling and information systems aspects of the development process. The modelers will be responsible for the models they build as well as for the successful transfer into the SMO of models developed by outside analysts. The information systems specialists will be responsible for transforming abstract models and concrete prototypes into routinely used computer programs. However, the modelers and systems analysts must interact continuously throughout both the development and implementation stages. This interaction may ebb and flow, but it never entirely goes away. Simply leaving the information systems people alone to implement what the modelers have created is equivalent (in a manufacturing setting) to having the design engineers throw the specification over the transom and letting manufacturing figure out how to get it out the door; disaster lies along this road. Similarly, leaving modelers alone to build the models without continuously assessing the feasibility of the implementation invites disaster.

Having an integrated set of skills on the information system development team is important. The SMO should include operations research personnel, mathematicians, and statisticians in the modeling group as well as analysts, software experts, programmers, data personnel, and operators in the information systems group. The team must also include some people with detailed knowledge of the operational procedures and needs of the parent organization. Such a mixture of skills in the SMO is essential to success. Neither analysts nor modelers can do the job alone. Information systems professionals are unlikely to have the requisite quantitative knowledge to effectively interpret, implement, and test the modeling portions of the system, let alone assume long-term responsibility for maintenance of those models. The modelers, on the other hand, are unlikely to have the computer skills necessary to translate the results of their work into a robust operational information system. We were very careful to ensure that the information systems team in the SMO supporting the EFMS was partially staffed with quantitative professionals in addition to information systems personnel.

One particular requirement for the SMO is an expert in the core computer language used in building the system. This may come as a surprise, since one of the most touted benefits to be derived from the use of recent software tools such as fourth-generation languages and application generators is the ease with which applications can be built and implemented sometimes with little or no assistance from a professional development staff. Nonetheless, the vast scale of ODSS databases and the complexity of tying together ODSS applications into something approximating an organized system do require an experienced professional, one steeped in the system's core language yet with a broad knowledge of alternative software tools that might supplement that language within the system.

12.2.5 Software and Hardware Selection and Acquisition

Unless significant decision support system activity is already under way within an organization, it is very likely that the current software suite is inadequate for the task at hand. The software selection process, which is discussed in Chapter 14, is the very foundation on which implementation takes place. The selection criteria should be an extrapolation of how the system will be operationally implemented. The larger and more complex the decision support system applications to be implemented, the greater the expenditure of time and resources required to make the right selections.

12.2.6   Data Management

In an operational situation, time may be a luxury that cannot be afforded, and the data may need to be very current. Creating the capability to have up-to-the-minute data with which to operate the system may require a major effort, one that differs significantly from the data gathering to support model development (see Chapter 9). The data used by the models in the operational system may be very different from those used to develop the models. For example, the research for the majority of EFMS models was done on a database that contained records from a 30 percent sample of all individuals who had been in the enlisted ranks of the Air Force since 1971. The inventory projection models use aggregated data from the entire force as it exists at the time the models are run. In doing research for model development, apparent anomalies in the data can often be eliminated or ignored. This may not be possible in an operational system, where anomalies may have to be resolved to produce credible results from the models.

This potential divergence of data needs should be anticipated and the development strategy should ensure that the models developed for the system have data requirements that can, in fact, be supported in an operational environment. This might mean that the modelers will have to tailor their models to function with operationally available data or that systems personnel must begin laying the groundwork for collecting new data.

12.2.7   Organizational Issues

Rather than automating the current way of doing business, the real opportunities for major advances from the ODSS will come from changing the manner in which business is done. In essence, implementation becomes more than putting the system into operation; it may mean the creation of and transition to a new organizational structure.

As a practical matter, organizational change should not be a major focus of an ODSS project without an unambiguous and strong mandate from the highest levels of management affected by the restructuring. Organizational change can be a very touchy subject. It was very clear to the builders of the EFMS that it would realize its maximum potential in an organizational setting that would look very different in several aspects from the one that existed when the project started. The EFMS team chose to soft peddle these organizational impacts. Emphasizing the creation of a new organizational structure in addition to the changes required by the EFMS tools might have sparked additional internal resistance, since it would have meant not only using new tools, but using them in new jobs. Given the political climate that existed, it was not deemed a prudent thing to do.

In the absence of an organizational commitment to restructuring, the best course of action is to let organizational changes evolve as part of the development process or as a response to using the system in an operational setting. However, by considering the potential organizational impacts of the new system, the developers place themselves in the position of being able to influence the course of organizational change and to take advantage of opportunities in this area as they occur.

12.3   ORGANIZING THE SMO FOR IMPLEMENTATION

One of the major decisions facing an ODSS or other relatively large-scale project is how to organize the personnel to carry out the implementation. In implementing the EFMS, we built two teams for each application—a development team and an independent testing team. The development team was a variant on Brooks's [1975] "surgical team approach" discussed in an earlier chapter. We'll discuss the advantages and disadvantages of an independent testing team and then conclude with a discussion of the duties involved in database administration.

12.3.1   Development Teams

We built teams around an individual developer who had primary responsibility for an application, from design through analysis and implementation. Exceptions were made for complicated models such as the middle-term disaggregate loss models, whose development was divided among several staff members. The primary developer was augmented by a number of personnel with specialized skills. Although the needs of other ODSS projects will clearly vary, we found the following types of personnel to be useful members of most application development teams:

- *An operations research specialist* who was knowledgeable about the underlying mathematical models in the application. This person helped the application developer translate the mathematical models into operational code. He helped in correcting, validating, and verifying the results of the modeling effort, and refitted the models to current data as necessary. Because the operations researcher had a good understanding of the results expected from the individual modules, he contributed to finding problems that might have gone undetected for some time if they had not been tested in an integrated mode with the application as it was being developed.
- *An application tester* to assist in all phases of testing beyond the initial checks made by the developer.
- *A data manager* who was responsible for meeting the data requirements of the other team members. The building, testing, and running of an application required significant amounts of data—many requests necessitating the processing of hundreds of thousands of individual records in various forms of aggregation to meet a specific requirement. This person tended to specialize in particular data and worked on several applications simultaneously.
- *Software specialists.* Software experts were periodically assigned on a full or part-time basis to assist the primary application builder in choosing the best approach to structure selected elements of the application efficiently, to construct some of the more difficult aspects of the application, and to evaluate the code being produced. In some instances, the primary application developer played the role of architect and the coding itself was the task of a technical specialist assigned to the team. In addition, these software experts were always available to the application developer on an advisory basis.

One of the advantages of a team approach compared to an approach that assigns a single individual to all phases of development is that it enables less skilled personnel to be used. This lets the most highly skilled developers concentrate their efforts on those pieces of the system that require the highest level of skill or specialized knowledge. Some of the tasks that might be turned over to less skilled personnel include:

- building data structures
- loading and validating external data
- inputting and validating user data
- writing reports and graphs
- building screen displays and menus.

12.3.2   Independent Testing Team

The testing of sophisticated decision support applications can be a complex undertaking, much more so than testing stand-alone applications. Variables can interact with each other to produce results that differ significantly from what one would expect based on single variable effects. In addition, applications may manipulate data in ways that go beyond the limits of the validity of the mathematical models embedded in them.

One aspect of ODSS testing that is extremely important and requires special emphasis is the independent testing of the models within the operational system. Even when acceptable results are obtained in tests of the models in their development environment, there is no guarantee that the same level of performance will be attained in an operational environment with production data. Implementation testing activities must not only test to ensure that the model specifications are implemented correctly as computer code, they must include a step to evaluate the performance of those models. Our EFMS experience was a confirmation of this view. When first tested using operational data, the middle-term loss models, for example, failed to provide the same degree of accuracy as obtained during the formal test and evaluation due to changes in behavior since model development and problems in using operational data that were not evident in an artificially created testing environment.

We set up an independent evaluation team to examine the performance of the software and models for each application. Having an independent testing team accomplishes a number of objectives. By assigning an independent tester, a second pair of eyes is brought to bear on the complex and difficult problems related to software accuracy. Progress is accelerated because the tester can simultaneously work on setting up test conditions, independently generating expected results, and creating software to analyze and validate outcomes. An independent evaluation reduces the effects of developer biases and provides a vehicle to conduct integrated testing across and between applications.

Some additional cost to the project will be incurred from having independent test teams. There will be a dilution of responsibility for the accurate working of applications. Both the development team and the testing team can point the finger at the other when a problem develops. In addition, some duplication of effort will be required, since the testing team will need to become as familiar with the application code as the building team. The developer and the operations researcher (if a different person) have special knowledge about problems within the application and thus are likely to be in a unique position to design critical tests that the application might fail. If the testing team designs the test plan, it is incumbent on management to ensure that there is major involvement by the development team. In any case, management must ensure good communication between the teams throughout the life of the project. One person who plays a special role in this communication is the database administrator, whose role is discussed next.

12.3.3 The Database Administrator

The person in the SMO who is likely to be most critical in determining the success of an ODSS is the database administrator (DBA). One of the principal tasks of ODSS project management should be to ensure that the DBA function is structured along the lines required by the system, that it is staffed by people with both the technical qualifications and proper orientation for the job, and that the DBA receives the support he or she needs to accomplish assigned duties.

Selecting the "right" person to fill the DBA position can present some of the same problems as are likely to be encountered with other members of the technical staff. DBAs require a degree of technical proficiency, proficiency that has often been been gained through a lot of hard work and experience on the job. Unfortunately, that experience may have established a pattern of thought processes and behavior that is in conflict with role the DBA is being asked to assume in an ODSS project. Breaking old habits and changing from methods that may have proved successful in the past is not always easy to do. For some, the tried and true ways of doing business may be so ingrained that change becomes impossible.

Personality may turn out to be one of the most important characteristics in choosing a DBA or other technically oriented members of the staff. A willingness to try new things or approaches is certainly an important attribute. A person who does not have the capacity to adopt to changing circumstances can become an obstacle to progress and a true impediment to project success. Substituting personality for technical competency in the selection process is not the answer. Not everything that was previously learned is obsolete. While new technologies often change the process of getting things done, many of the fundamentals remain the same. Building an ODSS still requires a disciplined and managed process.

The DBA must be able to get along with a variety of types of persons. In particular, he or she must be able to work efficiently and effectively with users, application builders, technical support people, and the ODSS project management. We discuss each of these types of interactions below.

WORKING WITH USERS

To develop an ODSS, the DBAs must be brought out of the "back room" to meet face-to-face with their user community. DBAs should be involved in the early stages of analysis so that the creation of the data model, resulting data structures and data views, and the acquisition and processing of data can proceed in tandem with other aspects of development. By doing this, the workload of application developers is reduced, and the progress between project milestones is reduced, pleasing the users.

On the other hand, if the DBA does not attend design sessions, application builders do not benefit from the DBA's global perspective. Various groups can repeat each other's work. Inconsistent data definitions may be used. If the DBA insists that data structures must be revamped, application builders may resent the interference and rework, and users will resent the schedule delays. At that point, it is too late to realize the benefits of generalized programs since application-specific code has already been written. The DBA's workload also increases, because additional time is spent in problems resulting from their lack of participation. Problems can be exacerbated as the DBAs are forced to spend more time correcting problems instead of focusing on moving forward with database design.

WORKING WITH MODELERS

Modeling, database administration, and application building are different disciplines, each with its own perspective, approach, and techniques. There is no substitute for building the database as a team. In this way modelers learn the capabilities and constraints of the software and hardware early in the development process. DBAs and application builders can learn the modelers' objectives, perspective, and language, and anticipate areas to be generalized. One of the most valuable aspects of this collaboration is that it gives the modelers, along with everyone involved in the development effort, a common understanding of the data needs of the system from an "output" perspective. However, this may only solve a portion of the modelers' data problems.

WORKING WITH APPLICATION BUILDERS

A natural tension can build between DBAs and application builders, because each group is looking at the system from a different point of view. To fulfill their responsibilities adequately, DBAs must take a global perspective of the ODSS. Their emphasis is on creating a database structure that will serve both the needs of the applications from a processing standpoint and the users' desire for information. They must balance these requirements against each other as well as balancing one application against another and the needs of one set of users against another.

On the other hand, application developers tend to be concerned only with the needs of those applications for which they are responsible. Their bias is to localize the data required for their applications, giving them greater control and flexibility. Individual applications may benefit from this approach, but usually at the expense of others, and many of the benefits may be more apparent than real. The strength of an ODSS, or any other management system that cuts across organizational lines, often lies in the ability of applications to share data, or for one application to build on the data produced by another. Failure of the DBA to maintain centralized control of the data where required can lead to suboptimization throughout the system.

One of the DBA's major tasks is to convince application builders and modelers of the benefits of centralized data control and to sell the message that the long-term benefits of data consistency and data sharing more often than not outweigh any short-term advantages gained by a single application having complete control over its data. In fact, by holding the line on data, the DBA can often demonstrate productivity gains for application developers because they are able to take advantage of data structures already in place and can customize generalized software designed to use those structures. Data that might be costly to produce on an application-by-application basis can often be economically produced when it can be made to serve several applications.

WORKING WITH TECHNICAL SUPPORT

On large ODSSs, the DBA can be overwhelmed with opportunities to write generalized programs to support application builders. Even more overwhelming is that most of the generalized programs are needed at the start of the ODSS. It is important that the DBAs not devote so much time to writing generalized programs that they have no time to work with users, modelers, and application builders. To compensate, project management should consider augmenting the DBA staff with programming support to handle some of these chores under the DBA's direction. The DBA has the technical background, the global perspective, and the detailed knowledge of how to prioritize requests to ensure that this support programming is properly directed.

WORKING WITH ODSS PROJECT MANAGEMENT

Because so many of the issues pertaining to building a DSS are data-related in some form, the DBA should be represented in a wide range of project management meetings. This is especially true during the analysis and design phases, when many of the most critical data-related decisions are being made. When in doubt, have the DBA present.

12.4 ESTABLISHING AND ENFORCING SYSTEM STANDARDS

12.4.1 Definitions

One of the early development goals of any system that crosses organizational boundaries or functions should be the creation of a common set of definitions and standards. In many organizations, the existing systems were originally developed to serve rather narrowly defined groups of users. In this circumstance, terminology usage can present a significant problem to the system developer. Groups may be using different terms to mean the same thing; terms may not have the same meaning to different groups; or the meanings may change depending on the context in which they are used. Even when there is apparent consistency, subtle differences may arise that are only discovered when attempting to achieve the level of precision required within the confines of a computer program, and then those differences may be missed. The project may also be creating entirely new data elements, or deriving new elements from combinations or extrapolations of existing data, some of which were created to serve other purposes. Again, seemingly subtle or innocuous shadings of meaning can have major impacts on the performance of the system.

To deal with these problems, the project team should develop a glossary of terms that becomes the definitive authority on how they will be defined in, and used by, the system. The goal is to ensure consistent definition across applications and to identify definitional problems early in the development process. This approach facilitates the accuracy of verbal communication, documentation, *ad hoc* reporting, the transfer of data among applications, code validation, and programming. The glossary should be considered a living document to be continually updated and revised as necessary throughout the development cycle and beyond. Depending on the technology used, much of the functionality of the glossary can be incorporated in "data dictionary" functions, which are becoming increasingly prevalent as standard features of DBMSs.

Many, but not all, of the terms in the glossary will eventually end up in the system's data dictionary (see Section 14.5.1). However, there is a long period at the beginning of ODSS design and implementation when a glossary is needed and no data dictionary has yet been built. In addition, another reason for developing a glossary that is separate from the data dictionary is that the two have overlapping but different sets of users. The data dictionary is referenced primarily by the database administrator and application builders. The glossary is referenced by users and managers as well.

12.4.2   Other Standards

Efficient programming of a large system such as an ODSS requires the establishment of standards, procedures, and naming conventions for data structures, data dictionaries, interfaces between modules and models, interfaces between users and programs, program libraries, and documentation. Each standard should include a statement of what to do, the reason for doing it, and an example of how to do it. Examples taken from the EFMS are:

- Show the program identifier of the program that generates each report in the upper left-hand corner of each page of the report. This information allows application builders to identify the program to be reviewed if users suspect that the report information is invalid.

- In the source code, label the components of the system, outputs, and databases consistently and uniquely with an acronym based on the first letter of the words making up the name. (For example, SAMFBYL for Short-term Aggregate Model, Force by Year Listing; the first three letters of the acronym reference the model or application, the remaining letters provide supplementary information.)

12.4.3   Enforcing Standards

Unfortunately, merely defining standards is rarely sufficient to guarantee that they are followed. The time constraints and pressures of the development schedule will lead almost all applications builders to circumvent the system at least some of the time, unless there is some external review process. The importance of uniformity for efficiency argues strongly for imposing reviews that check for the enforcement of all system standards.

Enforcement mechanisms that are appropriate for any large-scale information system development are also appropriate here. In the EFMS, each model was assigned to an internal review team comprised of project leaders, the database administrator, and application builders. Before coding began, the team reviewed the project team's approach to building data structures and programs. The goal of this review was to ensure that the approach was integrated with the overall EFMS and to catch mistakes before they were implemented. After coding on an application was completed, the same team reviewed how the approach was implemented. Here, the goal was to ensure that the implementation was efficient and maintainable and that standards, procedures, and naming conventions were followed.

While *ad hoc* project reviews may sometimes be required, the emphasis should be on scheduled reviews conducted at specified points in the development process. These reviews should be documented in the project schedule as milestones in the development process.

12.5   SYSTEM SECURITY

ODSSs are designed to be accessible by persons throughout an organization. This accessibility, which has been discussed as one of its important benefits, can also be one of its liabilities. It offers opportunities for abuse by unauthorized personnel, such as looking at confidential information, changing data, and harming programs. ODSS implementation must make system security a high priority. There are three major requirements for system security:

- *Confidentiality.* Controlling who gets to read information in order to keep information from being disclosed to unauthorized recipients.
- *Integrity.* Assuring that information and programs are changed only in a specified and authorized manner.
- *Availability.* Assuring that systems work promptly and that authorized users have continued access to information and resources.

The weight given to each of the requirements depends strongly on circumstances. For example, confidentiality may be the chief concern of a national defense system. Integrity was of highest concern in the EFMS.

The problems of information security are widely recognized, but not well dealt with. In 1991, the System Security Study Committee of the National Research Council, under the chairmanship of David Clark of MIT, issued a report entitled *Computers at Risk* [Clark, 1991]. The report concludes that the lack of a clear articulation of security policy for general computing is a major impediment to improved security in computer systems. It calls for the establishment of a set of generally accepted system security principles (GSSP) for computer systems. It also describes some potential elements of such a GSSP, including:

- user identification and authentication
- access control on code as well as data (control over which users can perform which operations on which pieces of data or code)
- protection of executable code against improper modifications or replacements
- security logging (for audit of security-relevant operations)
- security administration
- data encryption (for protecting communications in distributed systems)
- operational support tools (to assist the user and the security administrator in verifying the security state of the system)
- independent audit (analogous to an annual business audit by accounting firms).

The EFMS includes several levels of security. At the system level, password protection prohibits unauthorized users from logging onto the system. Users must enter a unique user identification code and password when logging onto the mainframe computer system on which the major

EFMS models and databases reside. Once logged onto the system, the ODSS software (EXPRESS) provides access control to the data in the database at the variable level. A specific user could be (1) denied the ability to see a given variable, (2) given the ability to read, but not change, the value of the variable, or (3) given the ability to read and modify the value of the variable. The presence of these security features was one criterion used in choosing the software for the system (see Chapter 14). Since many of the parameters for the EFMS models are specified through changing their values in the database, these security features also provide control over the operation of the various models.

An additional level of security is provided for dial-in users of the system. When dialing in, these users are required to provide a separate user identification code and password before being granted access to the system. They must then get through the system level of security. Facility security at locations containing the system's terminals or mainframes is provided either on a twenty-four hour per day or after-hours basis, depending on the overall security requirements of the using organization.

12.6   EFFICIENT USE OF APPLICATION BUILDERS

Efficient use of an application builder's time is absolutely necessary for the development of an information system on the scale of an ODSS. In turn, this requires designing, writing, and documenting generalized programs that are stored in program libraries and that can be called repeatedly throughout the system. These generalized programs also increase maintainability, because they reduce the number of places where code must be modified to reflect new circumstances. Generalized programs can cover any portion of the system including not only the type of computations that would traditionally be defined as a subroutine, but also data structures, input screens, and output screens.

Another way to increase programming efficiency is to build or purchase application generators. An *application generator* is a computer program that allows an application builder to build data structures and programs by answering prompts or completing forms. It usually works in one of two ways. It may be a standardized shell that is manually completed by the application builder; or the application builder may provide data and parameters to a computer program that will actually generate the application's code. In either case, the application generator functions as an expert system for building applications. It combines the standards, procedures, and naming conventions for the system with the expertise of the best application builders to automate building applications and increase the likelihood that the application will adhere to system standards.

The application generator used to build the EFMS was the RCG SYS-TEM,[31] a set of utilities within EXPRESS, pcEXPRESS, and MDB (the mainframe and microcomputer programming languages used as the ODSS Generator for the EFMS). The application generator represents about 50 percent of all of the code comprising the EFMS. Of the remaining 50 percent, roughly 80 percent is code that was generated from the application builder answering prompts; the other 20 percent was custom code inserted within redefined shells.

12.7   CONTRACTING

So far, this chapter has been written from the perspective of providing guidance to ODSS projects that are managed and largely staffed internally. For a variety of reasons, an organization may decide to have an ODSS built by contracting for most or all of the the work. One of the most common reasons for this is that decision support systems fall outside of the mainstream of information systems applications. They demand a variety of skills that may not be readily available within an organization. It can be all too easy to succumb to the notion of bringing in a group of "experts" in the form of an outside contractor to do the job. There are a number of potential problems with this approach that must be carefully considered.

One problem is the tendency to think that by contracting out you have passed responsibility for building the system to someone else, and all that remains is to wait for delivery. This attitude may go unstated, but it can crop up continuously as problems are encountered in the system development life cycle. This approach may also suppose, probably incorrectly, that lacking the skills to build an ODSS does not preclude the the ability to draft a statement of work or contract that provides adequate guidance and safeguards to ensure that a system is delivered that meets the objectives of the organization. In addition, contracting out may fail to recognize that while contract personnel may be experts in their specific disciplines, e.g., operations research, statistics, etc., they are neophytes when it comes to the client organization's data, policies, procedures, operational environ-

---

[31] RCG SYSTEM is a proprietary product of the Reding Consulting Group, 328 East Main Street, Barrington, Illinois.

ment, and history. In addition, even contract personnel who are computer professionals are not going to know your information systems and the environment in which they operate. Being able to integrate this kind of knowledge into the effort, however, is as critical to most sophisticated projects as the formal disciplines required to build a system. This knowledge must either be gained or brought to bear in some way for the project to succeed.

Assuming a system is delivered, it has to be thoroughly evaluated and tested. The skills required for these functions, to a certain extent, are the same skills required to build the system. Also, even if the system is delivered and works as required, it will probably start to become obsolete as soon as it becomes operational. It is unlikely that behavior, the environment, policies, or laws are going to remain stable over time. System performance will degenerate at a rate that correlates with the incidence and significance of changes to factors that influence the system. The maintenance effort will require the same skills as development, but the contractor will probably not have a thorough grasp of the decisionmaking environment or may not be retained under contract after implementation.

All of these factors need to be considered when making a decision to contract work.. One point that should be drawn from all of them, however, is that the potential client organization should not proceed with a contracting alternative unless it is willing to commit existing or specially acquired in-house resources to the project. If not already available, personnel should be brought on board well in advance of the contract effort to become thoroughly familiar with the issues.

Ideally, the client organization should be prepared to develop a comprehensive statement of work for the project that contains:

- detailed and complete requirements
- measurable and meaningful criteria for judging system performance
- specified deliverables
- a set of milestones that are meaningful in the context of the specific project
- provisions for reports and other forms of documentation at milestone points and on delivery of components of the system.

In addition to supporting the contractor's development efforts actively, the organization should be prepared to assume an active project management and coordination role, conduct thorough reviews of progress against predetermined milestones, and exhaustively test and evaluate components as they are delivered. Anything less than this level of involvement puts the success of the project at risk.

12.8   RISK MANAGEMENT AND SCHEDULING

The management of risk has got to be a major concern of any ODSS project. Projects that offer the most in the way of potential benefits to an organization often entail a significant degree of risk, not only in the project failing to meet its objectives—but of having schedule slippages, major redesign efforts, or initial results that do not meet expectations.

Risk management will become increasingly important in the corporate world as organizations seek competitive advantages through the strategic use of information technology. True competitive advantages through the use of information technology can probably be achieved only at considerable expense, risk, and time. If such a project were an easy or inexpensive thing to do, the organization's competitors might already be doing it, or could eliminate the advantage in a very short period of time by duplicating the technology.

The degree and nature of risk for any project is in many respects dependent on the unique characteristics of that particular effort. Some projects, such as the EFMS, have significant elements that can legitimately be considered as research. Much of the EFMS work addressed problems or issues that were new or where previous work had fallen short of acceptable standards of performance. In these situations, estimating levels of effort and cost can be an inexact exercise at best. If budgeted costs turn out to be too low, as they often do, the entire project can be placed in jeopardy.

The risk inherent in many ODSS projects can be ameliorated in the structuring of the system itself. It is important to divide the project into self-contained modules to the maximum extent possible so that if funding ends before the project does, or pieces of the project prove to be impractical or unfeasible to pursue because of cost, the entire project is not placed in jeopardy. Little thought is usually given to the possibility of "nothing" being produced, but the very high incidence of software-related project failures illustrates the downside possibilities.

Breaking a large project into logical modular components can reduce risk significantly over creating a project that requires everything to work for anything to work. It also provides management with better defined benchmarks against which to measure progress. Being able to look at discrete elements of the system that have been completed and measure them against established criteria and timetables is a better indication of project status than trying to measure everything against the final objectives.

Structuring the project into a number of discrete elements for implementation, each of which is tied to a specific set of benefits, is an effective way of producing early results, in addition to minimizing risk. Even if the project fails to achieve all of its initial objectives (and this may happen due to factors entirely outside of the project itself), it will still produce a set of tangible benefits to the organization that will have justified at least a large portion of the effort and expense.

Also, the larger and more complex a system, the longer it will take to implement. There are very few organizations that will have the patience or understanding to wait for extended periods of time to see results, even in situations fraught with risk or involving areas littered with the bones of previous failures. Many organizations require complete payback on their investments in less than two years.

Granted the value of a time-phased implementation, the question naturally arises about the sequencing of implementation of the various parts of the system. Obviously, the highest priority should go to those elements that provide the organization with the most important capabilities that are currently unavailable. In some cases it may be reasonable to allow higher than necessary developmental costs to meet an operational goal early in the system development project. As mentioned in Chapter 8, a decision was made early in the EFMS development cycle to put the bonus management subsystem on the air. This was done despite the fact that project personnel did not yet have a good grasp of the system's software at that point. Many of the interface and integration requirements had not been defined, and the project schedule was thrown completely out of kilter. This was definitely not a textbook solution, yet it paid untold dividends for the project. The users got a system that filled a critical void. It also eliminated constant criticism of the Air Force by the General Accounting Office. Both of these factors built user loyalty and instilled a sense of confidence that the project would actually produce tangible benefits. But, perhaps most important, that initial success could be used to deflect "politically" based criticism of the project by demonstrating the system's potential. A single application was put into operation that allowed decisions to be made and resulted in savings that would pay for the entire project in less than two years.

A second priority for early development is modules that will serve more than one purpose, such as the EFMS' loss modules that were discussed in Chapter 7. Completing development of such modules early allows more efficient specification and coding of the models that use these modules and may also increase the number of functions that can receive early support from the system.

Other characteristics that should increase the priority of module development include being easy to do, being informative to the organization, and being informative to the developers and/or implementers. Many management decisions can be improved if pertinent, timely information can be provided to the decisionmakers. Applications that provide information can frequently be developed more quickly than models and can provide useful interim decision support. Further discussion on the timing of model development is found in Chapter 13.

12.9 SUMMARY

This chapter has emphasized the fact that the implementation of an ODSS cannot be isolated and treated as a discrete set of tasks related to building software and converting to a new system. In reality, all facets of the development process can be thought of as being linked together in much the same way as the pieces in a jigsaw puzzle. The picture is not complete unless all of the pieces are there and in the right place. Implementation can be viewed as the process of gathering and fitting together all of the pieces of the System Development Life Cycle to form that complete picture.

While many texts focus only on the technical and mechanical aspects of building decision support or other types of systems, there are political and organizational dimensions to the process that are equally important. We have tried to cover those in some detail. Ignoring them adds an element of risk to any development project.

Chapter 13 | Passing the Baton: Implementing New Models

Relay runners who cannot pass the baton never win races. System developers who cannot pass on ODSS's new models to the SMO never achieve their system's goals. In this chapter we break down passing the baton into its constituent parts: timing, programming, modeling, documenting, and communicating. Timing refers to determining the point at which new models should be turned over for operational use. Programming, modeling, and documenting refer to three tasks that will compete for the SMO staff's attention when new models change hands. Communicating refers to a dialogue between developer and SMO staff that should be maintained until the models are securely in place within the ODSS—a dialogue that begins with the documentation that accompanies the new models.

13.1 TIMING

When should new models be turned over by the developers for operational use? If one listens to most analysts, the models should not be turned over until they are "finished products" with all blemishes removed. Analysts fear that unfinished models will draw criticism that will undermine users' confidence in the system's eventual reliability (and that will reflect badly on the analysts who built the system). However, if one listens to most system development managers, models should be used operationally as soon as they can make a positive contribution (however measured) to the organization's decisionmaking. These managers fear that funders of system development will become impatient with costs incurred for long periods without demonstrated successes in improving the organization's decisionmaking. Finally, listening to users of the system's output, one hears echoed the fears of both analysts and system development managers. Users are both quick to criticize blemishes in new systems (especially blemishes that suggest the new system is not in every way as good as the old) and impatient with development programs that swallow vast sums without offering immediate help in daily operations.

Offering unfinished models for operational use can indeed sour support among user groups, but delaying their implementation until analysts judge them unimpeachable can dry up support among funders of the system's development. Some models should be made inoperational until analysts bless them; some models should be brought on line before analysts are ready. But which models should be held back and which brought on line early must be carefully considered. In either case, users must be prepared beforehand to expect some blemishes and be taught how to interpret those blemishes.

Introducing models into use before they are fully developed offers five possible advantages:

1. The new model may already be better than what the old system provides, so decisionmaking may be improved.
2. The problems users encounter with the new model may suggest how the model should be changed in its final development.
3. Users may begin to anticipate the changes in their operations that will be required or allowed by the new model.
4. A successful new model may generate support for further development efforts.
5. Even an unsuccessful model may be better evidence that progress is being made rather than repeated claims that "we're not ready yet."

However, introducing models into use before they are fully developed poses six possible hazards:

1. If the new model never outperforms the old, introducing the new model with promises that it will eventually perform better may

lead an organization to make mistaken personnel changes ("we can let Steve go now that we won't be using the old model.") or mistaken operational changes ("we can stop collecting questionnaire x now that we won't be using the old model.").

2. If the model's final version differs substantially from the unfinished version, it may be costly to change from using the unfinished model to using the final model.

3. If the new model fails, user support for further development may be lost.

4. Running both old and new models can absorb excessive amounts of an organization's resources.

5. If running unfinished models operationally absorbs too much user time, the users may become reluctant to spend time in the development process as well.

6. Too much of the developer's time may be absorbed fighting fires, fixing bugs, and training or supporting users.

The unfinished models least likely to draw criticism from the users fill a current void—of them it can be truly said that "something is better than nothing." In the EFMS, the Bonus Effects Model (BEM) was such a model. The Air Force officers charged with recommending bonus levels had no analytical tools to support their decisionmaking. The BEM offered them capabilities they hadn't had previously. They could not possibly respond: "But this isn't what our current systems would tell us—and it's silly besides." The lesson? First offer unfinished models to the users most thirsty for analytical help.

Even "good" unfinished models can look "bad" if the data needed to run the models properly are not brought from the developers along with the models. In the EFMS, the "blending module" that supported the DMI required inputs such as the proportion of losses that occur at the end of any cohort year. At RAND, these numbers had been estimated for the time analyzed during model development. The Air Force did not initially have the data to update RAND's numbers, so for a substantial time outdated numbers were used that could have made the model look bad. Models that depend on data that the user does not have are poor candidates for early use.

The unfinished models most likely to draw criticism from the users are those that offer the most detailed output, because these models create the most opportunities for users' eyes to be caught by a preposterous number. Even when the number in question doesn't matter in the context of the users' application, a wildly wrong number can shatter confidence in a new model.

Any unfinished model can scare away users, most especially users not trained to asses the model's blemishes. In the EFMS, users frequently expressed dismay that the forecasts made for small AFSCs were not as accurate (in percentage terms) as the forecasts made for large AFSCs. Their dismay reflected a lack of statistical sophistication; no matter how good the forecasts for small AFSCs might become, the forecasts for large AFSCs were going to remain better—the Law of Large Numbers assured this. Sometimes, educating the users prior to introducing a new model can avoid adverse reactions to a new model.

Perhaps the most important lesson to impart to users is the dictum "models are to be used, but not to be believed" [Theil, 1971, p. vi]. Users understand half of this dictum; they are invariably eager to modify the output from models to reflect their own informed judgments. But knowing not to believe models isn't knowing how to use them; we often heard: "But if I'm going to fill in the numbers I want anyway, why do I need the model?" An early chore in developing an ODSS should be educating users about how they will be able to use their models. Users with this sophistication will be much less likely to complain about the unimportant blemishes in unfinished models and much more likely to appreciate what an unfinished model can do to help them.

Users should be informed early about what the models will and will not be able to do. Users should be encouraged to define tolerable limits for error—and should be reminded when the model in fact performs within those limits.

The users should be given the opportunity to educate the system builders early in the process. By presenting users with mock screens that show what a model's output may be, users may learn what error levels will draw fire and what levels will be tolerated. In the EFMS, the Air Force officers who brought the DMI on line never knew what error levels in forecasting individual AFSCs their operational counterparts would object to. Each time they brought "improved" versions of the model for the users to examine, these officers wondered if the users would find the forecasts "good enough." A better approach would have been to ascertain beforehand how accurate the models had to be in order to be useful.

"Beforehand" cannot be late in the development process. Once the users expect products, not prototypes, they will seldom hear the message that a model is not for their use, but for learning their demands for accuracy and detail. Hence, such belated offerings will probably receive critical reactions. In the EFMS we were still exploring the users' tolerances for errors in loss forecasts when the users were looking for finished forecasting models. The users harshly criticized the errors they saw in these unfinished models, and their resultant attitudes made implementing the finished models more tenuous than it need have been.

Unfortunately, users often don't know how good the models need to be. Technically unsophisticated users often say that the models must be "right" before they will be useful. This is most often heard from those users who currently rely on shrewd guesses rather than on models. Exercises with mock screens may not evoke much helpful information from such users, so trial and error may be the only recourse. It may turn out that developers will know how accurate the model has to be only when a version of the model is demonstrated that users are willing to accept.

In addition to education, care in presenting a model's output can alleviate the risks of introducing incomplete models. For example, if the model currently forecasts poorly for small AFSCs (but will forecast better when development is complete) presenting only aggregated figures for such AFSCs may forestall negative reactions. Users will react more favorably to "The next version will break those aggregates into the detail you need; meantime, we thought you'd like the better forecasts for the larger AFSCs that the model affords you," than to "Well, *those* numbers are silly, but they'll be better in the next version; meanwhile *these* are the numbers you should trust." However, when "packaging" the output from a model, be careful not to give the impression that you are hiding something.

Another device for avoiding the downside of introducing unfinished models is for the users to run the new and old systems side by side. By encouraging side-by-side runs, the SMO evidences its commitment to protecting users from the inadequacies of the unfinished model. Also, if the new results closely resemble the old results in which the user has the most confidence or confirms the user's skepticism about some results from the old system, the user's confidence in the new model will grow dramatically. Unfortunately, such parallel runs can be time consuming. Moreover, lack of data on actual outcomes often complicates comparing new and old systems. With no actuals in hand, the user may decide that discrepancies between the old and new systems reflect problems in the new system, even when the user is dissatisfied with the old system. Nonetheless, if unfinished models are handed over, the old and new systems should be run in tandem.

On balance, in the EFMP we believe we gained more than we lost by judiciously transferring models to the Air Force before the models were finished products. But transferring unfinished models is a risky business that requires careful deliberations among the analysts, the system development managers, and the SMO staff. Transferring unfinished models is the stage in passing the baton that is most fraught with potential disaster.

13.2   PROGRAMMING, MODELING, AND DOCUMENTING

When the developers pass the baton, the SMO staff must set off at a quick pace. The models must be used, maintained, and updated; the staff must find a cadence of programming, modeling, and documenting that best serves these tasks.

The staff members responsible for a particular model have a formidable chore: They must understand the model's computer code well enough to adapt it to the host operating system; they must understand the model and its data well enough to interpret the model's output and, eventually, to update the model itself; they must understand the user's operational responsibilities and the model's relation to other models in the system well enough to adapt the model, or at least its output, to institutional changes; and, finally, they must provide adequate documentation for the next people to fill the user's shoes. Few people will begin in these jobs already having all the requisite institutional and technical knowledge. Learning while doing is almost inevitable, and the most difficult period of learning while doing will come in the critical early months of implementation.

To appreciate the difficulties faced by staff members who implement the models, we will review the calendar of the Air Force analyst responsible for the middle-term loss models and their supporting data. This officer served another SMO analyst rather than a user outside the SMO. The calendar covers the officer's first seven months on the SMO staff, a period that coincided with the arrival from the developer of the models for which the officer would be responsible:

1 November 1986   Read RAND documentation; think; reread; derive some results for self. Talk with others in shop to learn personnel system jargon and notions relevant to the job at hand.

15 December 1986   Meet extensively with developers after becoming somewhat comfortable with documentation. Meet with operations folk to get a feel for environment. Learn enough about personnel operations to know how loss estimates will be used in practice.

1 January 1987   Study computer code intensively. Learn SAS computer language by reading code and a manual. Start with the simplest programs or with those for which most "actively" responsible. Leave complicated programs that might initially be treated as black boxes for last. Talk extensively with developers about code.

15 February 1987   Determine nit-picky changes in code required by shift to Air Force operating system. Worry about relationships within one's bailiwick. For example, what inputs does program x require? What program do they come from? Are they produced in the form program x requires?

1 March 1987   Try running programs. Make fixes. Try again (and again). Pore over output. Determine whether the output makes sense. Discuss output anomalies with developers. Talk with client. Establish a calendar for operational responsibilities and determine the programs required for each responsibility.

1 May 1987   Begin operational work. Start first update of loss models.

20 May 1987   Spend week with developer discussing first update. Continue operational job.

This calendar makes obvious the chief limitations the officer brought to his job: He was neither a personnel expert, nor did he know the computer language in which the code was written. His strengths were a facility with computers and strong background in applied mathematics. Such tradeoffs in skills inevitably arise in staffing an SMO. Unfortunately, the best personnel mix for starting up the system may not be the best mix for operating the system in the long run. Technical expertise is especially valuable when first introducing models. Institutional knowledge, however, grows in relative importance as running the system becomes more routine.

The calendar also exemplifies the tradeoffs analysts must make as the baton is passed. Models and programs need to be understood. Programs need to be made to run. Users' needs must be understood. Documentation must be created to enable others to perform the same job later. That documenting does not appear in the calendar is not a surprise, but it is a worry. Analysts and managers both give too little attention to good documentation. Less worrisome, in this particular case, is the user's low profile in the calendar. The officer's immediate client, another SMO analyst, sat back to back with this officer at an adjacent desk. Their informal discussions more than made up for a lack of formal discussions in the first four months. However, most analysts should schedule more interaction with users early on than appears in this calendar.

An analyst's inclination will be to understand every model and every program. Managers must make sure that this urge is resisted. Resources will be scarce in the first months of implementation, and tasks must be ordered in importance. Those programs and models that can be used for a time as "black boxes" (whose contents are unknown) should be so used, so that analysts can get on with making their programs run and with delivering their products to their clients.

Three criteria determine when a model or program should be left a black box: (1) The model or its computer code would take considerable time to understand; (2) the model's computer code is sufficiently well documented such that it can be run without understanding its inner workings; and (3) neither the model nor its program will need modification in the near future (which means, among other things, that the developers did some testing and evaluation of the model that justifies relying on it).

A model may satisfy criterion 2 yet not be especially well documented. In the EFMS, the computer code that created the data files used to estimate the middle-term loss models was extremely complex. The code itself (the "YAR code") was not well documented (perhaps unavoidably, given its complexity); analysts had to read the code itself and its embedded comments to understand what the code did. Nonetheless, the YAR code was used by the Air Force as a black box for several years because its documentation stated clearly how to run the program.

The YAR code illustrates how few programs can long remain black boxes. The YAR documentation said "update each year by conducting steps (a) – (f)." Unfortunately the documentation did not note that after four years yet another step would be needed to update the code. In the fourth annual update, no one understood why specific data were being lost by the program because no one understood the code. Only when one analyst undertook to learn how the code worked was the missing step identified.

Black box models seldom make their failures as obvious as the YAR code did. The Bonus Effects Model was for a long time treated as a black box. The computer program merrily produced estimated bonus effects whenever asked to. But, unbeknownst to the analyst who used the model, the coefficients in the model were based on a very early version of the middle-term loss models. Not until the analyst grappled with the computer code's inner workings did anyone realize that the bonus effects were being estimated with inappropriate coefficients.

Despite the perils of black boxes, managers must be ready to mandate that some models remain black boxes so that the analysts can get on with making the computer programs run.

As analysts come to understand their models, and as they try to make them run on the host operating system, opportunities arise for making the system work better, either by providing better results or by reducing run times. Managers must carefully assess the technical fixes analysts propose. "Sexy" technical improvements draw analysts like honey draws bears, but such fixes invariably take time, and frequently improve the system less than would more mundane changes. Managers must constrain zealous analysts, especially during the resource-scarce implementation period. The managerial monitoring of analysts necessary for identifying such overzealous analysis will not be welcomed by most analysts.

In the EFMS, two "sexy" improvements absorbed too much time. The first was an effort to create system code that would run the middle-term loss models with less keyboarding by the analyst. The system code was a sound idea that was implemented too soon; other, more pressing tasks, should have absorbed that programming time. The second was an effort to reduce the blending module's run time. The analytical challenge was clear, but the blending module's run time did not constrain the system, so reducing that run time should have been a long-term objective.

Problems should be given a high priority for fixing if they either threaten a model's credibility or keep a user from applying a model. On the first criterion, overcoming the poor forecasts of losses from extension had high priority in the EFMS. These poor initial forecasts threatened the credibility of the entire middle-term loss module. (The simple fix required to improve the forecasts would not excite most analysts, but that made the fix no less critical.) On the second criterion, fixing the short-term loss models had high priority. The Air Force was unwilling to use any of several short-term aggregate loss models that had been developed, so finding models that would be used became an important priority for the SMO staff.

Analysts and managers do and must maintain a creative tension among understanding, improving, and running an ODSS' computer programs. These four tasks will not be neglected altogether. In contrast, documentation has no advocates because tomorrow's workers have no voice in today's debates. Nevertheless, the long-term success of an ODSS rests heavily on the quality of its documentation.

Documentation did not appear in the above officer's calendar for a year and a half. Understanding the models, making them work, and making them better was a full-time job. But the lack of documentation created a grave risk. Had the officer been struck by a truck, or had he been transferred to another job, no one could have sat down at his terminal and taken up his job. The developers' documentation of the models would have offered a starting point, but the models were updated after seven months, and the changes that were made then were not documented for a year! All the code was in place, but there were so many programs—creating inputs, making cohort loss rates, blending loss rates, outputting the results for the clients—that another person could not have untangled the web.

One particularly nettlesome matter for documentation is specifying exactly what data a model requires: Where do the data come from, in what form do the data arrive, and how must the data be transformed before use? In the EFMS, analysts determined countless times precisely what was meant when a model asked for *"previous Palace Chase"* or *"early out losses."* The analysts arrived at the same conclusion each time, but wasted hours for not having written down the definitions in the first place. Eventually, they wrote down both the definitions and their rationales, making the determination routine.

In the EFMS, poorly written documentation posed special dangers because each job was understood by only one person, so the only institutional memory about the job was the scanty written record. For example, the officer who first oversaw the YAR code—an essential piece of the EFMS—left his job abruptly on a Monday. Only by chance had another officer asked him the previous Tuesday how to run the YAR code. Absent that accident, the first officer's departure would have been a calamity.

An organization can play fast and loose with documentation if it has several people trained to do each job. But when an organization is one deep at jobs, those jobs must be well documented. These observations indicate a dilemma for managers: *Documentation is most important when you have the fewest resources to create it.* When new models come on line, SMO staff will be reluctant to spare critical hours to document their work. But three rules should be strictly enforced: (1) the steps for running one's programs to fulfill a given task must be written down; (2) changes to the system must be documented in writing when they are being made, indicating (at least) what the old code was, what the new code is, and why the code was changed; and (3) a log must be kept recording all conversations with the developers that offered insights into the models or the code. The first rule ensures that someone could at least mindlessly run another person's models in an emergency; the second rule provides the minimum essential supplement to the developer's documentation; the third rule saves new people from having to rely so heavily on the developers—a group whose involvement with the SMO and whose system-specific expertise will surely fade over time.

An ODSS might be well served by having one person (a "project librarian") oversee the creation and maintenance of documentation. This person would train the staff to keep the records necessary for making good documentation and would assist staff members in documenting their jobs and the models they use in their jobs. In the absence of such a person, managers must identify what documentation is necessary, assign responsibility for creating it, allocate time for its creation, and make its existence known to others. In either case, the standards for documentation must be accepted widely by the SMO community or they will resist documenting their work.[32]

13.3 COMMUNICATING

Developers and SMO staff must stay in close contact during the implementation phase; otherwise, the baton will surely be dropped. Good documentation from the developers will smooth the transition process, but nothing can wholly replace conversations between the developers and SMO staff, not even a close electronic mail link and fax machines.

The best documentation does four things: (1) It tells what was attempted and why; (2) it provides an abstract, often mathematical, rendering of the techniques used; (3) it explains the mechanics of the computer code; and (4) it tells how to run the computer code on a given operating system. However, developers will seldom provide such good documentation, especially for unfinished models. Consequently, SMO staff must rely on reading the code and talking with the developers to fill in the gaps in the documentation.

The relationship between the developers and the SMO staff should go on long after the models are on line. (In the EFMS, two years after the

---

[32]The Department of Defense has formalized the role of a project librarian and describes the role in detail [Department of Defense, 1987].

DMI was operational, the officer in charge of updating the loss equations still spent more than a week per year with the RAND analyst who first estimated the equations.) Both the SMO managers and the development organization must budget transportation costs and allocate personnel time for these long-term interactions between developers and SMO staff. In particular, the development organization must sustain its system-specific expertise long after the models have been transferred. The RAND analyst who first estimated the loss equations stayed in consultant status for four years after he left RAND just so he could continue to work with the SMO staff.

Creating the rapport and respect between developers and SMO staff that will sustain such long-term engagements cannot be done hastily at the end of the development process. From the beginning, the developer must create an ethos that "development succeeds only if implementation succeeds." Everyone must share the conviction that the SMO and the development organization are partners from the outset and remain partners until the system runs routinely and successfully.

A close working relationship between developers and SMO staff is costly to achieve, and it is not without risks. The cost is the many hours of interaction between developers and their SMO counterparts throughout the development and implementation processes. The risks are twofold: (1) The SMO staff may rely too heavily on the developers—it may, therefore, never "take over" the system; and (2) the SMO staff may identify too strongly with the developers' perspectives and forget what their own jobs are. The first problem did not arise in the EFMS, but this book exemplifies the potential for the second problem. The analysts at RAND have a greater professional interest in writing a book about the EFMS than do the Air Force analysts, but SMO staff who have worked closely with the RAND analysts have been easily drawn into helping with the book.

Developers must also stay in close contact with their clients in the user organizations during the implementation period. Few organizations document their policies extensively in writing, so often the only way to get institutional knowledge is by word of mouth. One word of mouth mechanism that may prove helpful is to have SMO staff with extensive institutional knowledge brief their colleagues. In the EFMS this was done, but not early in the implementation period; rather, a series of informal seminars was organized two years after the first models were on line. If the resources can be spared, such briefings should begin sooner. An analyst who says (as one did in the EFMS), "Hell, all our models use 'Control

AFSC' and I still don't know what a 'Control AFSC' is" can't critically oversee the models. Such contact should not only start early, but it should continue. Users' needs may evolve over the long development life of an ODSS; continuing dialogue with users will enable the SMO staff to adapt the system to such changes.

Chapter 14 | Selecting the System's Software and Hardware

14.1 A TOOLBOX APPROACH

ODSSs include a large variety of types of users, types of models and databases, and types of applications. It is unlikely that a single piece of software or single type of hardware will meet the entire range of needs. The need for a multiplicity of tools requires a structured approach to the software and hardware selection issue. The selection process should be begun early in the development of the system. Rather than acquiring tools one at a time as a specific need is uncovered, the more strategic approach that we suggest—beginning with a specification of the system's software architecture (see Chapter 12)—allows the system to include a set of tools that truly fit together, and whose capabilities are complementary to each other.

In defining the software architecture, developers should be conscious of technologies such as application generators, fourth-generation languages, database management systems, screen builders, and microcomputer application packages that might be productively incorporated into the infrastructure. The software selected for an ODSS needs to be matched against the specific needs of the system. The challenge is to capture the possibilities that technology now offers within the development process in such a way as to meet short-term application goals without sacrificing long-term system objectives.

A general principle for building an ODSS is to choose the key pieces of software before choosing the hardware, if at all possible. (Remember, the structure of the hardware system—e.g., categories of equipment, networking, and communications—has already been defined in the conceptual design.) Tailoring the system to the problem situation and the needs of the user requires providing a set of specific capabilities. There may be few software products available that provide these capabilities. By adding hardware constraints, the number of possibilities is reduced even further, leading to the use of products that may seriously compromise the performance of the system.

Sprague and Carlson [1982] identify three types of software/hardware that are included in the label "DSS."

- *Specific DSS.* This is the combination of hardware and software that helps a specific decisionmaker or group of decisionmakers deal with specific problems. It is the ODSS that we are concerned with in this book—the end result of the system development effort that we have been discussing.
- *DSS Generator.* This is a software package that provides an integrated set of capabilities to build a specific DSS quickly and easily. It generally provides most of the software capabilities needed by the Specific DSS. The choice of the DSS Generator is a very important decision. We discuss an approach for making this decision below.
- *DSS Tools.* These are individual hardware or software elements that can be used to develop either a Specific DSS or a DSS Generator. They include hardware, such as workstations, and software, such as a C compiler, EXCEL, or more generalized CASE tools, application generators, and prototypers.

In general, development of a Specific DSS using a DSS Generator is faster and more economical than using only a set of DSS Tools (just as writing a computer program is usually faster using FORTRAN than machine language). But a DSS Generator will rarely have all of the desired capabilities, so other tools will generally be needed to fill in the gaps. For example, not every EFMS application is done in the DSS Generator language (EXPRESS). The software suite includes SAS, Lotus 1–2–3, Wordstar, FOCUS, and a set of CASE tools called the RCG SYSTEM.[33]

While multiple tools may go into the building and operation of an ODSS, at least three important reasons are mentioned here for selecting a single set of software or closely coupled and related sets of software for the heart of the system:

- It is important to provide a consistent look and feel to the system across all, or most, of the applications within it. This not only benefits the users, but simplifies the construction and maintenance of the system.

- Developers are building a system, not a series of individual applications; this implies the ability to readily transfer data from one application to another, and integrate data from multiple applications together at certain points. Attempting to accomplish this without a single integrated data management system that is linked directly to other important capabilities could create monstrous interfacing problems.

- Multiple application software packages mean multiple languages and construction techniques to learn, lengthening learning curves, fragmenting the staff, and decreasing productivity in development and maintenance. Using multiple tools will probably be necessary to some extent, as was the case in the EFMS, but it should be minimized and done in a way to ensure that the system itself can be integrated to a meaningful extent.

One aspect of hardware and software selection that may be overlooked, but can be critical to successful implementation, is deciding the type of hardware and software that will be placed in the hands of the users (e.g., should they receive 3270-type terminals or high-powered workstations?). While the introduction of almost any type of hardware alternative may be feasible in a computer-literate organization, it can be a real problem in those organizations whose employees are not using computer technology

---

[33] For example, the programs for determining the parameters of the middle term loss models, which are an extremely critical element of the system, have been programmed in SAS. There are important differences between the data manipulation requirements and data used in fitting the loss models and those of the inventory projection models (which are programmed in EXPRESS). The loss models require the processing of thousands of individual personnel records to determine the loss rate coefficients. The inventory projection models operate across aggregated data in the form of multidimensioned matrices, which are the kind of data structures that EXPRESS handles best. SAS is also used to aggregate the thousands of individual personnel records to form the baseline inventory for use by the inventory projection models.

as an integral part of their jobs. In the case of the EFMS, it was decided soon after the choice of software that the workstation of choice would be a DOS-based microcomputer.[34]

At the time the project was under development, the vast majority of potential users had little or no experience using computers. We addressed that problem by bringing in the microcomputers well before implementation, and introduced the potential EFMS users to many of the stand-alone applications that were available to them, such as word processing, spreadsheets, and database management systems. Through classroom and on-the-job training, the users became very familiar with these tools, and the transition to specific EFMS applications was made much less traumatic than it might have been.

14.2 PROVIDING HARDWARE INDEPENDENCE

An important principle in building an ODSS (which will strongly influence the choice of the system's software) is that applications should able to be transported from one hardware environment to another with few if any programming changes. This approach allows development and production to be distributed across a variety of personal computers, minicomputers, and mainframes, and ensures that the ODSS will survive and grow long after its initial hardware becomes obsolete.

Hardware independence or "semi" independence can be accomplished in a number of ways. In the case of the EFMS, a set of software platforms was chosen in which the differences in underlying hardware and operating systems are transparent to the developer, because the vendor has absorbed the cost of concealing these differences by providing similar capabilities across different underlying software solutions (in this case microcomputers running with DOS, and mainframe computers with the VM or MVS operating systems). In other cases, manufacturers such as DEC provide operating system commonality across a wide variety of platforms in their line.

The continued market penetration of UNIX offers the possibility of a single operating system that is hardware independent across a variety of

---

[34] DOS-based microcomputers were chosen for a number of reasons. The most important was the fact that the architects for the system wanted to be able to take advantage of and integrate the wide variety of application packages available as part of, or in addition to, the EFMS architecture. Given the marketplace at the time, they also felt that any microcomputer-based applications being built as part of an integrated DSS generator would be written for DOS. They also believed that DOS was fast becoming the *de facto* standard for Air Force microcomputer operating systems.

hardware, even those made by different manufacturers. (Although the failure of the industry to agree so far on a common UNIX standard may make migration more of a potential possibility than a reality without significant software modification.) Another way of achieving hardware independence is to utilize "open systems" standards, such as those being enforced within the U.S. government through mandatory procurement of certain standard systems, or those being more informally enforced through vendor-independent standards like X-Windows.

Independence can also be provided in the design of the software. One mistake that is often made when writing for multiple hardware environments is to restrict all programs to the lowest common denominator of capabilities available over all of the hardware environments. This mistake can be avoided by separating the services needed by a program from how the services are implemented. For example, picking choices from a list may be accomplished using a mouse, cursor keys, or numbers. In this case the service is to pick choices, and the implementation of picking choices is dependent on the availability of a mouse and full screen cursor support. By separating the functionality of the pick list from the means for linking to it and exercising it (the mouse, cursor, etc.), migrating the software to a new platform may require changes only in the linking modules, which are isolated, therefore requiring fewer changes to the code that provides the functionality.

14.3 SELECTING THE ODSS GENERATOR

A Specific ODSS is built by system programmers in the SMO using a DSS Generator and other DSS Tools. Most users will never learn about most of the capabilities of the Generator or the Tools because they will not be writing their own programs. This situation is distinctly different from the relationship between the DSS Generator and user that is often recommended for a traditional DSS (TDSS). In this case, the user is often expected to build his own Specific DSS using the modeling language provided by the DSS Generator. (For example, Reimann and Waren [1985] say that one of the purposes of a DSS Generator is to "enable nonprogrammers to develop customized DSSs for specific applications.")

In the case of an ODSS Generator, some capabilities will be helpful to end users, some only to the systems programmers, and some to both. For example, it should provide the benefits of a nonprocedural language to users to make it easy for them to operate the models, generate reports, and make inquiries against databases. It should also ensure that systems professionals have all of the facilities within the package to write complex applications programs without having to resort to other packages (e.g., for graphics, statistics, or modeling) to a large degree. This demands a language that combines simplicity for one category of user with a powerful and varied syntax for another.

The process of choosing an ODSS Generator is similar in some respects to that recommended for choosing a TDSS Generator. But there are some major differences. For a TDSS Generator, end users should be extensively involved in the process from beginning to end, the capabilities should be directed toward the needs of the end user, and the end user should control the selection process (see Meador and Mezger [1984] and Reimann and Waren [1985]). For an ODSS Generator, we recommend little end user involvement, capabilities directed toward the needs of the applications, the SMO, and the system programmers, and SMO control of the selection process.

Since it is such an important decision, and since there are potentially so many requirements and so many alternative packages to be evaluated, a structured approach should be used. The process that we used on the EFMP is described in detail by Walker, Barnhardt, and Walker [1986]. The basic idea is to match carefully the specific features and capabilities of the generators under consideration with the characteristics and requirements of the applications to be supported. The approach involves six steps:

1. Identify the overall objectives for the Generator (what it should accomplish and why).
2. Infer the general capabilities that the Generator should have to respond to the objectives (see Turban [1988, p. 203] for a fairly extensive list). The general capabilities are likely to be very similar for most ODSS situations (e.g., provide a common database manager and allow customized menus).
3. Infer a set of specific capabilities that will satisfy the general capabilities. The specific capabilities will generally differ for different applications (e.g., allow the use of data names that are consistent with the organization's naming conventions).
4. Identify specific software products that appear to have some or all of the specific capabilities.
5. Perform an initial screening of the products that are obviously over- or underqualified (if overqualified, you will be paying too much to satisfy your needs). Screening can usually be done by

using reference services, reading product documentation, and/or having vendors demonstrate their products and answer questions about their capabilities.

6. Perform a detailed analysis of each of the remaining products. This phase should be a systematic examination of product capabilities against requirements. It might also include benchmark runs, coding of test problems, an analysis of the reliability of the vendor, and the likely life of the product and its support system.

On the EFMP, we identified ten general capabilities that the ODSS Generator for the EFMS should have:

1. data management (a robust and comprehensive data dictionary, and the ability to build, maintain, and manipulate complex and sparse data structures, to provide access to information in a flexible and responsive manner, and to facilitate use and sharing of data)
2. external interfaces (ways to exchange data with statistical, graphics, worksheet, word processing, and desktop publishing applications, and the provision of hooks to other programming languages, such as SAS or FORTRAN)
3. data analysis (including a library of mathematical and statistical routines)
4. inquiry (an interactive database inquiry facility that would allow users to view the data they need for a given task selectively)
5. report generation (default formats and customization)
6. graphics
7. command language (including a modeling language)
8. multiuser support
9. system management facilities (including the ability to port an application between microcomputers and mainframe)
10. support for distributed computing.

Most of these capabilities are displayed graphically in Fig. 14.1. Note that all but the last three of the general capabilities are ones that are likely to be specified for many TDSSs. The last three apply primarily to ODSSs.

After specifying these general capabilities, we defined specific required capabilities within each category. For example, there were four specific required capabilities within the Multiuser Support category, including "Provide safeguards for the security and protection of data at the record level or below."

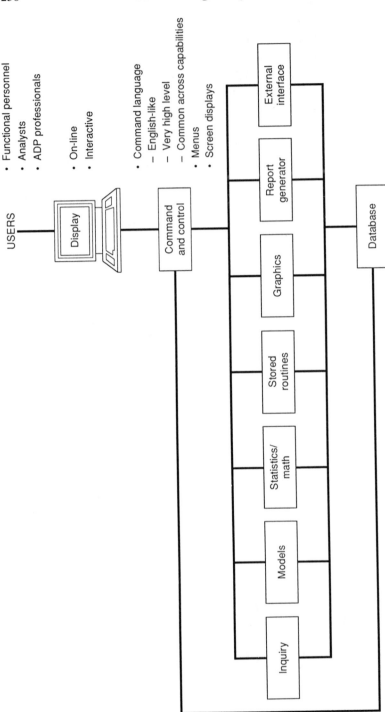

Fig. 14.1 Elements of the EFMS DSS Generator

Then we began the search for and selection of the ODSS Generator, which involved the following steps:

- Reading technical publications and systems documentation.
- Interviewing system users and talking to vendors.
- Screening (12 of the original 20 products were screened out).
- Detailed analysis of the remaining eight products:
  - rating each product (yes/no) on each specific capability
  - giving a summary rating for each product on each of the 10 general capabilities
  - comparing the summary ratings of all eight products across all ten categories (Table 14.1 shows this summary scorecard)
  - performing a benchmark test on a sample application.[35]

Once the search was begun, it took approximately two years until the necessary approvals were received to purchase the selected product. Three important factors, other than our desire to do a careful and thorough search and evaluation, contributed to the time and effort required to acquire the ODSS Generator: federal procurement directives, the large number of products, and internal resistance. The last is a factor that is likely to be encountered by most builders of ODSS, and is not generally addressed in the DSS literature.

There was considerable organizational reluctance to accepting a DSS Generator as a means of developing and operating the EFMS. Part of this reluctance stemmed from the fact that DSS Generators are fourth-generation languages and were a new concept to many, so a certain amount of education was required before gaining acceptance for the idea. The selection of the Generator was driving the supporting hardware options, and the Generator chosen required equipment that was incompatible with the systems then in use. There was also concern about assuming the additional burden of operating and maintaining these new computer systems. Also, historically, the emphasis had been on developing and maintaining computer systems that emphasized transaction processing. The unique needs of the Air Staff, which emphasized flexibility, user control, quantitative and analytical capabilities, responsiveness, and the use of summary data,

---

[35] Table 14.1 shows the EXPRESS met all of the required capabilities established for an ODSS Generator for the EFMS. Although that is true, as development proceeded it became clear that there were additional capabilities needed for the EFMS that EXPRESS did not possess. Therefore, other software tools were purchased (see Section 14.4). But in most cases, EXPRESS had hooks (e.g., for SAS and FORTRAN) to facilitate their integration.

Table 14.1

Summary Evaluation for DSS Generators for the EFMS

	EXPRESS	DSS/A	DSS/B	DSS/C	DSS/D	DSS/E	DSS/F	DSS/G
Data management	Yes	No	No	No	No	No	No	No
External interfaces	Yes	Yes	Yes	No	No	No	No	Yes
Data analysis	Yes	Yes	Yes	No	Yes	No	No	No
Inquiry	Yes	No	Yes	No	No	No	No	No
Report generation	Yes	No	No	No	No	No	No	No
Graphics	Yes	Yes	No	Yes	Yes	Yes	Yes	No
Command language	Yes	No	No	No	No	No	No	No
Multiuser support	Yes	No	No	No	No	No	No	No
System management	Yes	No	No	No	No	No	No	No
Distributed data processing	Yes	No	No	No	No	No	No	No

were not immediately apparent. In the end, the compelling nature of the arguments won most people over, and many Air Force personnel worked diligently to acquire and implement the Generator.

Once the software was selected, the system's hardware configuration was specified in detail (see Fig. 2.7 for an overview of the hardware configuration), and the process of procuring both software and hardware began. Since there are many books that deal with hardware issues in the development of distributed computing systems (e.g., Ananda and Srinivasan [1990] and Sloman and Kramer [1987]), we will not discuss hardware selection issues any further.

14.4 CUSTOMIZING THE ODSS GENERATOR USING APPLICATION GENERATION UTILITIES

The ODSS Generator is a general-purpose tool for building an enormous variety of possible applications (as is the case with any programming language). However, any Specific ODSS is likely to contain certain special operations and subroutines that are directly related to the context of the organization, but may be common to many applications. This provides the builder with an opportunity to improve productivity by creating a set of software utilities that can be used throughout the system. Utilities can also be written that automate the process of writing certain types of subprograms.

EFMS development benefited greatly from the use of utility software built on the application generation capabilities of EXPRESS and pcEXPRESS. Like a number of other DSS Generators, EXPRESS's fourth-generation language characteristics significantly reduced the amount of coding and number of steps required to build the software for the system. However, further reductions in workload and improvements in productivity were obtained by building on the capabilities of the EXPRESS and pcEXPRESS software to further automate the development process. For example, providing functionality to a report screen that has been generated requires the data that appear on it to be resident in a data set linked to the screen. EXPRESS and pcEXPRESS make it very easy to generate these databases and the code necessary to populate them, but the builder still has to go through a number of steps to complete the process. A utility built using the EXPRESS or pcEXPRESS software simplified the process even further by turning those steps into a standardized, forms-driven application. Developers merely had to fill in information on a screen form, and the underlying software (built in the EXPRESS language) automatically went through all of the steps to create the database, and even the associated code, when the form was completed. Not only did that speed up the process, but it provided a number of other benefits. For example, the discipline necessary to standardize database structures and nomenclature and foster system integrity was built into the database generation software.

Other functions that might be considered for customized automation in the form of utilities include:

- loading flat files from external applications into database data structures
- unloading database data structures into flat files
- routing output to any screen, printer, or plotter, and selecting fonts automatically
- saving reports and graphs in disk files for later printing
- allowing programs to run in batch (unattended) mode.

A customized utility for the application generator would normally take the form of a screen menu. The actions required on the part of the application builder would depend on the amount of commonality inherent in the activity being automated. For activities that are very close to being the same, regardless of where they appear in applications, the menu could consist largely of filling in the blanks on the screen to indicate the controlling parameters. For those that might have more differences from application to application, or use to use, the application builder would be required to provide additional information to tailor the activity to a specific occurrence.

Decisions should be made early in the ODSS implementation phases about which aspects of development should be further automated by extending and customizing the existing functionality of the ODSS Generator. The criteria used in determining which application generation utilities to build might include the following:

- *The pervasiveness of the development activity.* For example, EXPRESS is very much a data structure-driven DSS Generator, so the example used above was a natural one to undertake, not only in the EFMS, but for any application using this tool.

- *The characteristics of the application generation process.* EXPRESS and other powerful application generation tools require that developers overcome a conceptual hurdle to take full advantage of the capabilities that they offer. EXPRESS, for example, has a very rich and comprehensive language structure. It is relatively easy for persons familiar with more traditional third-generation languages such as COBOL to begin building applications as if they were using that type of tool. This is exactly what should *not* happen. Many of the benefits of using a fourth-generation package are lost in the process. A set of utilities can channel development along lines that best fit the tool being used.

- *The stability of the activity.* Some operations or processes are, or should be, performed in a similar fashion almost every time. Others may take various forms, depending on the circumstances in which they are undertaken. Automation can best be applied to those that are repetitive in nature.

- *Whether the way the activity is carried out really makes a difference.* Most application generators provide many ways of accomplishing the same result. But in most cases, some ways are more efficient than others (because of the way the generator works). Automation can be used to assure that the application builders use the most efficient ways.

- *The desire to enforce an important design principle.* In the EFMS, project management wanted to implement some of the principles of object-oriented programming in the building of applications (i.e., the packaging of objects—in this case the data sets—with the associated code for populating, transforming, and manipulating them). This allows the object to be reused across applications, or multiple times within an application. Even if objects, or the code associated with them, have to be altered to be used under different circumstances, this is made relatively easy to do. It also makes maintenance easier by placing objects and code together in self-contained modules. As noted above, utilities were developed not only to automate the construction of data sets, but also to generate the code associated with them.

- *Cost versus benefit.* Like many automation decisions, the choice of which activities to turn into utilities should be driven by the cost of doing it in contrast to the benefits derived. For example, the development team may choose to expend significant resources in automating an activity if there is a high probability of generating bad code that would require a large amount of work to correct. Selectively using automation may also allow less experienced developers to create applications that would otherwise be beyond their level of expertise, reducing project costs by requiring fewer highly skilled, more expensive personnel. Some application generation may be able to be automated to the extent that some of the responsibilities can be transferred from application builders to users (e.g., generating *ad hoc* reports and graphs).

In many cases, even given the resulting benefits, the cost of building this type of utility software cannot be justified to support a single system, or even a single organization. However, these types of CASE tools may be available on the commercial market. Their developers can recover their costs and make a profit by spreading development costs over a large number of units sold.

Much of the utility software employed in the EFMS was commercially available in a set of prepackaged utilities, which was called the RCG SYSTEM.[36] The RCG SYSTEM provided the EFMS with an application generator, a data dictionary, cross-referencing, standards and naming conventions, run time utilities such as menus and routing of reports and graphs, on-line help, and the ability to transfer code and data among applications. The RCG SYSTEM also allowed the applications to run on PCs and mainframes without any recoding. (See Section 17.4 for a description of some of the interface design capabilities built into the RCG SYSTEM.)

Serious consideration should be given to factoring the availability of software utilities into the process of selecting and acquiring the ODSS Generator, especially for large-scale systems.

---

[36]The RCG SYSTEM is available from the Reding Consulting Group, 328 East Main Street, Barrington, IL. 60010

Chapter 15 | Database Design and Management

15.1 INTRODUCTION

A new generation of applications generators and data management tools has provided the potential for building large decision support systems more quickly than in the past. They have also allowed developers to focus more of their attention on getting the data "right." But the use of these new technologies also presents new challenges—challenges that highlight to an even greater degree one of the oldest, but still most relevant, sayings in the data processing community "Garbage in, garbage out."

Along with these new tools and technologies has come a change in management's attitude toward information. According to James Martin [1984], "Information is becoming regarded as one of the basic resources of business along with capital, personnel and production [capability]." This change in attitude requires a change in the way an organization's information systems are designed and databases managed. Data must cease to be linked directly to applications and must begin to be treated as organizational resources. Standard descriptions of shared data to be used throughout the organization must be developed. Data directories must be produced. Databases must be defined that can support multiple applications.

This chapter treats some of these issues in the context of the development of an ODSS. For a more general description of such an information resource management methodology, see the Information Engineering Management Guide [Pacific Information Management, Inc. 1989].

15.2 LOGICAL DATA MODELS AND DATABASE MANAGEMENT SYSTEMS

One of the most important criteria to the success of any ODSS is the logical data model on which the database management system is based. The model represents the logical data structure that is used to portray the data at the level at which it is managed by the database administrator (DBA) and used by application builders to construct applications. Identifying important data entities and attributes, the relationship of the entities to each other, and the relationship of the entities to specific processes or models within an ODSS are important steps in constructing logical models of the data and databases residing within the system, as well as in formulating data management rules.

Data can be customized for display to users of a system in many different ways, depending on the requirements of the applications that define it, but these various user "views" of the data are often quite different from the logical structure observed by the application builder and DBA. The data that the user sees as output from the system are normally derived from this more "basic" underlying logical view structured in a way that supports a variety of applications and user views. In many instances, the user is completely unaware of the underlying data form.

Over the years, a number of underlying logical data models have been developed and implemented in database software to improve the data management capabilities of information systems. The thrust behind these efforts was to improve the capability to use a variety of data elements in different ways to support multiple applications, and to facilitate the extraction of data from the associated applications in many contexts to support the range of information needs of the users of these applications. Database management systems (DBMSs) provided an efficient means for tying a number of applications together that could not be achieved with traditional "flat file" technologies. They freed users from the restrictions of having to obtain information from individual applications and attempting to associate the various data elements outside of the supporting mechanized applications or through inefficient and complex interfaces. This was often a time-consuming and frustrating process, one that in many cases was not even possible on a practical or cost-effective basis. Database management systems also freed users from some of the restrictions of having to obtain data in predetermined and programmed formats.

Today, most, if not all, DSSs are built using a variety of DBMSs based on one of a relatively small number of underlying logical data models. It is not the purpose of this book to engage in a lengthy discussion of the various models, but the authors believe that their experience and resulting insights could be of significant benefit to those undertaking the development of an ODSS. The logical data model that is gaining ascendancy among data processing professionals today is the relational model. This model consists of a series of tables (relations), with each table composed of records (tuples) somewhat analogous to flat-file records. The power of relational systems is that data can be selectively extracted from these tables, or the tables combined through the use of a relational "algebra" or "calculus" to form new tables that can be used for processing purposes, or to extract data selectively. Part of their appeal also lies in the fact that relational tables, or relations (see below), display data in a straightforward two-dimensional array, whose structures taken one at a time are often easily understood. The data in them can be portrayed in a form that is analogous to a printed report. IBM's DB2 is probably the most well known of the systems based on the relational model. When combined with the related Structured Query Language (SQL), it provides a powerful tool for managing and making a wide range of information available to end users.

As with most DBMSs, relationally based systems are geared to maintaining data at an entity level, which implies that the information is maintained in the database at the lowest level that can be used to distinguish one entity from another (e.g., for transaction processing of updates to the database). To use a familiar example among data processing professionals, one table may contain information on "parts." There would not be a record in the table on each part because one of the same kind of part is not distinguishable from another, but there would be records maintained, for example, by part number, with attributes such as quantity, supplier, color, and location contained in the records. If a part were to be furnished by more than one supplier, come in more than one color, or be stored in more than one location, separate records for each unique occurrence could be maintained in the database because these attributes can be used to distinguish parts from each other, even though they have identical part numbers. In a relational database, those attributes that serve to uniquely identify a record in a table are called "keys."

For certain types of DSS applications, a DBMS based on the relational model may not be the best choice, even though it could be made to work. As noted, relational database management systems are geared to the maintenance of data at the lowest level required to distinguish unique entities. They are oriented to both update and query operations, with update transactions at the lowest level of detail being added as records to a relation. Through a process of "normalization," the data are often broken down and distributed among many relations or tables to eliminate redundancy and provide data integrity. As a result, a single relation is unlikely to carry all of the information required by a decisionmaker, even for the simplest of inquiries. Time dimensioning of data can also add further complexity. A series of relational operations referred to as relational algebra or calculus is used to aggregate data through the creation of new relations to bring the data iteratively into a form required by the user. These are not mathematical operations in the conventional meaning of the term. They are really operations designed to combine or limit parameters within tables for the selective extraction and structuring of data.

In DSSs, especially those that are model based, more conventional mathematical operations such as add, subtract, multiply, etc., are required. Relational records and tables do not lend themselves readily to this type of data manipulation. Aggregating data to serve the needs of a DSS can result in tables with varying and complex key structures that may be difficult to manipulate. The potential user or developer in these types of circumstances may be faced with creating, for example, a fairly lengthy set of SQL operations to put the data into a form where these operations can be applied, but in a less efficient manner.

Similar problems will occur in attempting to query operations on the database. Management queries will rarely take the form of a request for information at the lowest level of detail, or one that can be satisfied from a request against a single relation. The data first have to be transformed through a number of operations to put them into a form suitable for the query. Some of this complexity can be masked by software, but issues such as flexibility and performance must then be considered. In the end, relational models are applying a two-dimensional solution to a multidimensional problem.

A more familiar data model is the spreadsheet model, as exemplified by EXCEL. (Note: EXCEL would not be a candidate for the database management of an ODSS such as the EFMS; however, it is one of the most well-known products that use a spreadsheet model as its database. This model is also the basis for some of the database management systems that underlie software packages.) Spreadsheet models can display data at any level of aggregation required; however they have other drawbacks that limit their effectiveness. One of the most obvious is that spreadsheets present a two- or three-dimensional view of the world. While this is adequate for a number of applications, it can be a significant constraint in many common situations. Suppose a user wants to aggregate data from offices within a division, divisions within regions and regions within a company. While aggregation is possible, it is a lengthy and cumbersome process. It would mean creating numerous spreadsheets and then linking them. And, assuming they are finally linked and the data produced, attempting to extract data selectively from them could be a difficult and time-consuming task. (For example, "How many offices had sales of over $3 million for Product X?" Or, even more difficult, "How did sales compare this quarter as compared to last quarter and to this quarter last year?") The limitations in answering these types of inquiries are also inherent in the relational model, but are overcome through the use of software, such as SQL, to transform the data iteratively into a form that allows them to be satisfied.

In developing a data model for EFMS while defining the software architecture, the architects examined a number of data models. The limitations and problems cited above with the relational and spreadsheet models were of major concern. In examining the requirements for the EFMS, there were three characteristics that seemed to be paramount in defining a data model:

1. Other than external data that required transformation, the data in the system for processing purposes and those data needed by the users for informational purposes would be stored at some fairly high level of aggregation. Unlike the users of the Personnel Data System at the Military Personnel Center or other operational organizations, the users on the Air Staff would have almost no need to obtain or use information on individual airmen. For most purposes, data would be required for selected categories of personnel on an Air Force-wide basis.

2. When data needed to be aggregated, it would normally require two or more attributes, or dimensions, to define the result. The aggregated data could be derived from a data set with additional

attributes that was capable of serving multiple purposes. For example, a requirement for manning data by grade and career field could be satisfied from a data set that contained those data by grade, career field, years of service, term, years to expiration of term of service, and point in time. This was true from both a computer processing and user perspective.

3. Potential inquiries against the databases required data with more than two attributes. For example, "At the end of 1985, how many personnel were in the 732XO career field at the grade of E–8, with less than 20 years of service? How does this compare with the end of 1984? What percent of the total E–8 manning in the 732XO career field does this represent?"

From a logical point of view, the architects believed the data tended to be best defined by the use of multidimensional matrices. The inventory of personnel, for example, could be categorized and grouped based on each individual in a group having exactly the same values for a common set of parameters used to describe the entire inventory—parameters such as grade, career field, years of service, etc. Rather than dealing with individual records composed of a single data element and multiple keys, as would be the case in attempting to use a relational model, data elements (cells) would be able to be logically specified within the matrix, based on a cell's relative position with respect to each of the dimensions. To use the "parts" example above, the parts matrix might consist of the following dimensions: (1) part numbers, (2) color, (3) location, and (4) supplier. Residing in the cell would be the number of parts corresponding to the unique combination of these attributes. If comparisons across time were needed, for example, to show the inventory at various points, a fifth dimension, signifying the beginning or ending of day, week, month, quarter, or year could be added.

Instead of using relational algebra operations such as join, union, and intersect, which are oriented toward data retrieval, matrix mathematical operations such as multiply, add, and subtract could be directly applied to transform data within matrices, combine matrices, or populate matrices based on mathematical manipulation of the data within other matrices. This would be an obvious advantage in building models that required mathematical calculations to derive results.

By selectively aggregating across dimensions, or by limiting the dimensions of a matrix selected in an inquiry to two, conventional two-dimensional displays comparable to spreadsheets, reports or other two-dimensional displays could be produced.

The multidimensional model's utility is not unique to the EFMS application. It could apply equally well to a wide range of ODSS and other management applications.

As implied in the previous paragraph, just as with a relational or spreadsheet data model, the data model alone, even though it forms the heart of the DBMS, is dependent on a number of other characteristics of the DBMS to realize its potential. The DB2 relational-based data model is useful to the extent that the data in the database can be selectively combined and extracted by using the capabilities of SQL, and for the ability of other languages such as COBOL to use embedded SQL statements for a wide range of processing applications. EXCEL has achieved the prominence it enjoys, not only because it uses the familiar spreadsheet model, but also, in part, because of the power of its user-friendly interface, the ability to define relationships between cells, and to define cells in a variety of ways, the easy manipulation of data on the spreadsheet, and the ability to program via the use of macros.

Similarly, a DBMS based on a multidimensional matrix data model is only useful to the extent that other tools are present in the associated software to utilize effectively the full potential of the data model. Some of the most important are listed below:

- a programming language, preferably integrated with the DBMS, that is capable of supporting the processing requirements of the potential applications that will be built using these facilities
- data retrieval capabilities that conform to the generic meaning of "user-friendly," and allow selective extraction and display across a broad range and combination of parameters on an immediate basis
- functionality that does not restrict the system to operating within the confines of a single data set, but allows the data in multiple sets to be used or selectively combined for processing and data retrieval.

The multidimensional data model coupled with the above functionality can significantly simplify and accelerate the development process. The application builder is using the logical data model directly, eliminating the necessity of working with data structures that are less efficient or awkward to use. In contrast to a relational-based construction, the developer would not be required to create additional data structures or processes to reformat the data for specific modeling or other application functions.

One of the major factors that led to the choice of EXPRESS as the basis for EFMS development (see Chapter 14) was that it is based on the use of a logical multidimensional matrix data model and provides the functionality identified above as well as meeting other critical software requirements for the system. EXPRESS was selected, however, after a determination of the logical data model that constituted the best fit to the applications to be supported—not before. No one data model is best for all situations. While the project team did not find the relational model suitable for its applications, the relational model might be suitable under other circumstances. Systems that rely heavily on variable selection and formatting of data in many different ways as an input to the decisionmaking process may benefit from a relational system. This is especially true if those data have to be assembled from several sources within the database. (Relational tools are especially powerful in selecting, aggregating, and summarizing data for presentation on an *ad hoc* basis.)

Technology has progressed to the point that data users, and even system developers, can be shielded from the logical method of storage in the underlying database. Software tools can present different logical views of the data to different users and allow them to proceed as if the data were actually stored in those different forms. In this case, the software overcomes what would otherwise be a constraint on the data model. However, this choice may come at the expense of the "horsepower" needed to make something happen, awkwardness and inefficiency in achieving results, and acceptance of limits on the range of operations that can be performed. Fitting the data model to tools specifically designed to take advantage of the potential strengths of that model is the best choice in most situations. Thoroughly understanding the data needs of the system should be an important precursor to evaluating potential software alternatives.

15.3 DATABASE DESIGN CRITERIA

Determining the proper data structures for an ODSS requires balancing competing objectives, such as ease of use, maintainability, disk requirements, memory requirements, access/update times, etc. In many types of information systems, efficiency considerations (e.g., memory utilization) are heavily weighted. In an ODSS, the overriding consideration should be ease of use for end users.

If data structures are simple and easily understood, they are more likely to be used across the full range of capabilities defined into the system by the developers. Complex and less well understood data structures are likely to inhibit users—they may not feel comfortable with the data, job pressures may make them reluctant to invest the time to master the data, they may not believe the system is responsive enough to meet time-sensitive requirements, etc.

Too much emphasis on optimizing disk storage, memory utilization, and access/update times can work against the more important objective of ensuring end user ease of use. The focus on the end user may be a hard one for the less flexible, more traditionally minded DBAs to accept. They have been trained to build databases for applications, not for end users. That training reflects a time when computers were less powerful and more expensive. Their objectives reflect the fact that efficiency is more easily measured than effectiveness. It is much easier to measure the immediate disk, memory, and time savings than to measure how much end users will benefit from easy reporting or how much application builders will benefit from easier maintenance. Disk, memory, and time savings can be measured right now and their achievement are signs of the traditional DBA's technical skills. For an ODSS, project management must stress the importance of simplicity, ease of reporting, and maintainability. This does not mean that hardware and software constraints can be ignored altogether. In the real world they often present constraints that cannot be easily overcome within the scope of the ODSS project management structure.

15.4 FUNCTIONS OF THE DATABASE ADMINISTRATOR

The DBA plays a pivotal role in any ODSS project. This role begins very early with the selection of the DSS software, and continues through the entire system development life cycle.[37] Aside from software selection, the DBA's job encompasses two major functions:

- Data management within the parameters of the ODSS, i.e., the construction and management of data sets, their associated data, and software in a form and in ways that best serve the needs of the users of the system. (Note: The DBA's users also include application builders and other information system personnel associated with the project.)

---

[37] The selection of the DBA is one of the most critical personnel decisions to be made when building an ODSS. It is discussed in detail in Section 12.3.3.

- The gathering and manipulation of data from external sources required for the operation of the DSS.

Not only is the DBA's DSS role important (data completeness and integrity, both critical DBA responsibilities, are important parameters in measuring the success of any decision support system), but it is a role that differs significantly from that played by the DBA in more traditional types of systems. The differences arise from the nature of the applications, the degree of integration required, and the necessity of dealing directly with users in addition to application builders and maintainers.

Traditional DBAs work with application builders to implement transaction-oriented, application-specific design problems. The DBA's strength is in knowing how to store and retrieve data efficiently in a multiuser environment, e.g., reducing storage, improving retrieval times, and using memory more efficiently.

In an ODSS, the DBAs are building databases for use by end users as well as application builders. While technical proficiency is still an important component of their jobs, DBAs in this environment must have a greater appreciation of the applications making up the system, not just from an information systems perspective, but from that of the users as well. They must understand how the applications relate to each other, and how the end users will actually use the data. Since ODSS data needs are often *ad hoc* and irregular, the DBA rather than the application developer is often in the best position to make critical design decisions involving data. DBAs must reconcile the competing, sometimes conflicting, data needs of users, modelers, and application builders. The ability to inspire confidence in the user community and communicate effectively, especially in translating technical concepts into language that is easily understood by nontechnical personnel, are important characteristics of the DBA's role.

15.5 DATA MANAGEMENT

15.5.1 Data Standards and Data Definitions

A well-defined logical data model includes a data dictionary, which establishes a framework of rules that govern data acquisition and guide data application. (Data acquisition is the process of capturing, storing, and maintaining facts. Data application is the process of assembling information from facts that have previously been acquired.)

The data dictionary can serve as the primary mechanism for data management in an ODSS. The construction of the database for a DSS is an incremental and evolutionary process. As the system is developed, more and more information must be stored. This information includes the identity and content of data structures, the format of the fields on a form or report, and the contents of the menus. For small systems, such as a TDSS, keeping in touch with such information is fairly easy to accomplish. But data management can make or break an ODSS. It is the key to the realization of an integrated, organization-wide information system.

Since a data dictionary is normally maintained by the ODSS Generator or by the application generation software, it is instantly available to all developers and to project management. It can be used as a more traditional dictionary, i.e., to obtain information about the system, or it can be used by project management to ensure that the standards and naming conventions established for the project are being adhered to. Within the capabilities of the dictionary, written documentation is replaced with real-time direct access to definitional information that can be cross-referenced and correlated with other definitional information in seconds. The dictionary can also serve many of the documentation needs of the project, eliminating the requirement to create much of the system documentation in paper form.

The amount and kind of information that is provided, as well as the tools for accessing it, are a function of the system development software being used on the project. The capabilities can vary from the very rudimentary to highly sophisticated. The existence of an automated data dictionary and the capabilities that it provides should be included in the criteria used to select the system development software.

Some words of caution, since many large-scale systems such as EFMS rely on more than one set of application tools: A single data dictionary that encompasses the entire spectrum of the software for the system will probably not be an achievable goal. This does not eliminate the need for some form of centralized control; it only makes the problem somewhat more difficult, and increases the need for written documentation to fill in the gaps in the software packages and their capabilities. Also, the data dictionary is only going to be as good as the planning that goes into the establishment of the standards and definitions, and the rigor with which they are implemented and enforced in the dictionary.

15.5.2   Centralized and Distributed Databases

We have already discussed the fact that data definitions can be centrally managed through the data dictionary and software libraries. However, the question still remains as to how the data themselves will be maintained and managed, i.e., should they be stored in a central database, distributed databases, or a combination of both? The choices made should be a reflection of the applications themselves and how the data are to be accessed and utilized by the users of the system.

In the EFMS, data were maintained on both a centralized and distributed basis. The alternative chosen in a particular circumstance was determined by a general set of criteria that might serve as a guide in making choices in similar situations. Data were stored in the central database when they were:

- received from or sent to an external application
- used by multiple applications
- used to produce *ad hoc* reports and graphs.

All other data were maintained with the application that used them. Centralizing data received from external applications ensured that they were validated before being accessed by applications and that the validation occurred only once. Centralizing data sent to external applications ensured they were validated before being sent and that they were, in fact, sent and transmitted on a timely basis. Centralizing data shared by applications eliminated the need to write an interface between each combination of applications, and ensured that all applications used the same definitions and data sharing programs. An application sent data to another application by sending it through and updating the central database. These centralized controls and the establishment of "official" versions or views of the databases can be extremely important when a number of different versions exist, such as work files, or when different views may contain the same data, but for slightly different time periods.

When data are to be shared among a number of applications, it is critical that controls be implemented to manage the sharing. In the EFMS, data were managed by retaining them in working data sets until the person or persons responsible for that application took positive action to release it to the central database for general use. Various versions of the data were clearly labeled in the database so that users obtained the version they required. For example, the Department of Defense planning, programming, and Budgeting process was composed of several iterations where identical or similar data were produced, but at different points in time and for varying time periods. There were occasions where previous versions of the data were used, e.g., when comparing actual to forecast data. At other times the most up-to-date data were needed, e.g., preparing the current version of the budget. To complete the linkage between data producer and data user, the user was required to take positive action to obtain the data needed—an additional step to ensure that the right version of the data was being transferred.

15.5.3   Data Stewardship Versus Data Ownership

Ownership implies control; stewardship implies responsibility. Traditional information system methodologies view data as an application resource rather than as an organizational resource, thereby fostering the belief that the sponsor of the application is the owner of the data. Often, these owners do not want to share the data with others. Nothing aside from conflicting data definitions could do more to undermine ODSS integration.

In an ODSS, neither the organizational units, nor individual users, nor any computer applications should own the data; they are owned by the organization as a whole. Stewardship of data is delegated; ownership is not.

Users often take the position that systems personnel are responsible for all aspects of the system, including data accuracy. But there are areas of data stewardship that properly belong to the users. Provided the system is operating correctly, users should be the stewards of the data that they generate within the system. Clearly, if one group produces a forecast that is used by other parts of the organization, that group must take responsibility for the data it produces. Responsibility for external data used by the system is less clear, but a strong case can be made that, other than providing edits and other measures to ensure that the data are entered correctly into the system, the responsibility for those data belongs to their users. For the most part, these are data that relate directly to the functions they perform, and therefore they have the best knowledge of its validity and accuracy.

As a general rule, systems personnel should be responsible for the accuracy of the applications they create and maintain, and for the composition and structure of the data sets that are part of the system. Users have responsibility for the data themselves.

15.5.4   Linkages With External Data Sources

While some ODSSs may be self-contained from a data standpoint— i.e., all data creation is done by the system or entered by the users directly, with all outputs going only to the primary users—these are probably exceptions. Most systems will require data from external sources. Gathering and transforming these data into a form that can be used by the system can be a daunting task, one that should be addressed as part of the system's architectural design. At least six potential data issues pertain to this aspect of the system design—either on the input or outside side:

- source
- accuracy
- validity
- form
- content
- availability.

For this aspect of the design, the architects are also dependent on the modelers and the results of their work to define a complete interface architecture. Many of the potential problems that need to be overcome will, in all likelihood, be identified first by the modelers as a result of their research efforts. This is especially true of data accuracy, validity, and content. The large amount of time expended by the EFMS modelers on data-related issues described in Chapter 9 is an indication of the magnitude of the problem. However, as with the internal data issues, the architects need to approach this as a "fill in the blanks when the information is available" problem. Most of the broader issues, especially those concerning source, form, timing, and availability, can be identified and addressed early in the design process.

Chapter 16 | Building Applications

16.1 APPLICATION BUILDING VERSUS PROGRAMMING

As explained in Part I of the book, most decision support systems today go well beyond single program systems that serve a single narrow purpose. Decision support systems are characterized by their reliance on multiple programs linked together in overlapping subsets to serve multiple and complex purposes. Programs linked together in this way are referred to as *applications.* Underpinning applications, and essential to their success, are sets of files or databases that allow the manipulation and use of common data by multiple programs.

Building successful applications is at the heart of building a successful ODSS. But despite the fact that an application is made up of programs, the skills required to build an ODSS are not simply those required to write good programs. The array of tools available to an applications builder is too extensive for any one person to master completely. Consequently, application building will often require the participation of numerous people, people who collectively have a wide range of information processing skills. The person assuming a lead position in an application development effort, while not required to have extensive knowledge of all of these skills, will have to know enough about them to know which ones may be required and how they may be used in the application building process.

Just as applications are seldom built *by* a single person, they will seldom be built *for* a single person. Generally, the demands of several users will constrain the building of an application. The application builder must understand the organizational objectives that the application will serve and be able to communicate to the users how their competing and sometimes conflicting demands will shape the application.

Developers can be seduced into getting to the coding immediately because it appears so easy to do. However, a number of essential tasks need to be accomplished before actual construction begins. Apparent delay actually sets the stage for completing application development more rapidly, and in a way that produces a consistently structured and coherent system—not a loosely coupled set of applications. Important elements in the implementation phase include:

- identifying and standardizing software construction techniques
- forming application building teams
- customizing the ODSS Generator
- establishing common definitions
- determining development standards, procedures, naming conventions, and documentation procedures
- developing a data dictionary
- determining how to organize and share data
- setting up software libraries
- establishing data ownership.

These staffing, technical, and contextual requirements lead to a requirement for a new conceptual framework for building applications. The following section provides more information on this new conceptual framework by contrasting the role of the application builder with that of the more traditional role of the programmer. Succeeding sections present principles and procedures for the application builder to follow.

16.2 THE ROLE OF THE APPLICATION BUILDER

Programming is only a splinter in the tree of applications building. Programmers write code for users; application builders solve problems for organizations. Programmers can thrive by assuming that the user is always right. Such programmers write clean, efficient code that performs the chores dictated by a user. Application builders, in contrast, must understand that each user has a perspective that reflects the user's biases, the user's job, and the user's level within the organization. Application builders must serve a user from a wider perspective so as to design an application that will synthesize the user's requirements with the organization's requirements. For example, a user who is facile with computers may press for faster implementation at the expense of user friendliness in the design of output screens. Were the application to serve no one but this user, and if development costs were low enough to warrant redevelopment if this user were to leave the organization, then the user's choice might be correct. But if the application's output must be viewed by others, or if redevelopment for a new, less computer facile user would be prohibitively expensive, the user's choice is a bad one. A programmer might well not correct the user's error; an application builder must persuade the user that patience is worthwhile, that delay is necessary because the organization's needs call for more user friendliness.

Most problems an application builder solves do entail computation, but the solutions may be manual or automated, and the skills key to identifying and implementing a solution are not necessarily programming skills. Beyond technical programming expertise, an application builder must have a sophisticated understanding of the roles computer programs can play in an organization, must be skilled in the art of negotiating compromises, and must have the flexibility of mind to adapt to the needs of each new organization the builder serves.

A central tenet for application builders is that their works are meant for the long haul. Well-built applications anticipate that personnel will turn over; therefore, features are incorporated that will enable replacement personnel to learn more easily how to use the application. Well-built applications anticipate that an organization's objectives and constraints may change over time, and therefore incorporate flexibility to accommodate the most likely changes. Finally, well-built applications anticipate that new needs will arise, and are therefore built in such a way that their components can be reused to form new applications.

Application builders are more interested in improving decisionmaking than in automating it. Consequently, the application builder's first task is to grasp why an organization wants particular information from an application and how else the organization uses the information required by the application. By understanding how the information from the current application will be used, the builder can design the application to best integrate its output into decisionmaking within the organization. By understanding how the current application will rely on information from other applications or will share information used by other applications, the builder can design the application so that the running of many applications jointly becomes more efficient.

The application builder's perspective makes for durable, well-integrated applications. By determining how and why information is used, the application builder ensures that the application is built on the bedrock of organizational need.

Once the application builder has determined the requirements of the user and of the organization, he or she must obtain agreement on a design plan. Users will quibble over the useful features to be included or bypassed; managers will contest the cost or feasibility of higher quality solutions. In dealing with users, an able builder will try to raise the users' sights, getting them to settle on features with the organizations needs in mind. In dealing with managers, an able builder will help the managers to find novel ways to reduce the barriers to better solutions.

For these deliberations, the builder must combine an understanding of the organization with a familiarity with the models under discussion, the data sources to be used, the data structures required by these data, and the relationship of this application effort to other models and applications used within the organization.

Users will need most persuasion about two kinds of features in an application: (1) those that will serve others besides themselves and (2) those that are in service of simplifying data management. The builder must serve as an ombudsman for the rest of the organization in settling on a final menu of features.

The barrier managers most often raise before better solutions is time, either the time to develop the application or the time to run the application on the computer. An application builder who has carefully studied the organization's decisionmaking will often be able to identify for managers several people within the organization who have similar needs for information of the kind produced by or used by the application. In these cases, the cost of application development may be markedly lowered by relying on generalized code or by adapting existing code, spreading the cost across several applications and thereby making a higher quality solution more feasible. (Some organizations establish application support groups to write such generalized code. In other cases, deals are struck by departments to share the cost of developing such code. The net effect is the same: reducing the programming cost of better solutions.)

In settling on a design, application builders look to other applications for ideas—and for cost-reducing code already in place. Indeed, one contrast between modelers and application builders is that modelers see differences where application builders see similarities. Modelers see differences in computations, in variables, or in time periods being forecast, where application builders see similarities in data structures, programs, menus, and procedures. For example, from a modeler's perspective, the Short-Term Aggregate Model (SAM) and the Middle-Term Aggregate Model (MTA) of the EFMS are quite different. Their forecast horizons differ, their decompositions of the force differ, and their mathematical models differ. But from an application builder's viewpoint, the two applications are quite similar, requiring similar data structures, menus, and computational procedures.

Well-built applications isolate their peculiarities within the structure, making them as small a part of the whole as possible. Most components of a well-built application are generic elements that could be incorporated easily into numerous other applications. Thus, application builders expect that they can build much of their newest work with pieces already created by themselves or by other application builders. For example, building the MTA was simplified by using the already existing database structure and libraries of the EFMS's central database. This simplification allowed us to complete the project more quickly and with less risk than if we had undertaken to write brand new code for the application's data requirements.

Developing applications in modular fashion does more than just allow code sharing. By scheduling modules for completion sequentially, morale can be kept high because success is tangible and seldom far off; progress can be measured by modules completed, rather than just awaiting the far off day when the application is complete. Furthermore, each new application begins with more interchangeable parts already at hand, and the more experienced team members begin to reap the gains of almost an assembly line approach to building custom applications.

16.3 THE SIX PARTS OF AN APPLICATION

The modular approach requires seeing applications as decomposable into distinct parts. Most applications will be made from a subset of the following six parts:

- *Input data structures.* The design of input data structures should conform to the guidelines and standards established for the system as a whole and, where appropriate, to the mathematical specifications of the models embedded in the application. When data used in this application are also used elsewhere in the system, their data structures should be common across applications if at all possible. The programs and menus used when populating the data structures should be prepared in tandem so that they can be tested together and can be used to populate the data structures with sample data to test the appropriateness of the structures themselves.

- *Local data structures.* Not all data needed by an application are input that can be drawn directly from the global data structures of the system. Sometimes variables must be transformed or created for the specific application. These local data structures supplement the global data structures available to all applications.

- *Computational modules.* The purpose of this type of module is to execute the computations required by a mathematical model's specifications.

- *Linkage modules.* The purpose of this type of module is to create derived variables from the input data. These modules connect the other modules of the application, shuttling data and other information among them.

- *Interfaces with other applications.* The interfaces must conform to standards established for the system as a whole. Interfaces imposed by one application on another invite chaos, but even interfaces agreed to by the application builders risk disrupting the ease with which people can learn or modify the system if they violate agreed-on standards that are in common use elsewhere in the system.

- *Application output.* Whether the outputs are data, screen displays, printed reports, graphs, charts, or tables, they should conform to standards established for the system as a whole. Violations of this principle will be especially costly when the outputs are data used as inputs to another application, but violations will add to development costs whatever the output. Three primary clients must be consulted and kept in mind when designing structures and formats for an application's output:

  1. users who will rely directly on the application's output in making decisions (see Chapter 17)
  2. other applications that will use the application's output as input data

3. the central database, which may be the repository for the
application's output if it needs to be generally accessible.

16.4 DOCUMENTATION AND COMMUNICATION

Bad documentation makes for bad applications. If the application
builder leaves the users clueless about the workings of an application,
adaptation to changing goals or changing constraints becomes almost
impossible. If the application builder leaves the user uninformed about
how the application runs, new users will be unable to learn how to run the
system if key experienced personnel leave the organization.

No application is complete until it is documented. Application builders
can further good documentation by integrating documentation into the
application building process: Don't build now and document later; rather,
document as you go. (Managers can make good documentation more
likely by taking documentation seriously in both scheduling work and in
evaluating workers' productivity. Managers can also further good documentation by ensuring that documentation standards are established early
and are embraced by everyone engaged in the development process.)

As each component of an application is built, the builder must communicate with other persons in the ODSS development team. Creating input
data components requires discussions with the data management team and
the model builders. Creating computational components requires discussions with the model builders and users. Creating linkage components
requires still more discussion with the model builders so that the the integrity of the mathematical specifications is maintained in translating the
specifications into code. Creating interfaces with other applications
requires discussions with other application builders and their users. Creating output components requires discussion with all parties who have an
interest in the output. Finally, creating documentation requires discussion
with those who will operate, maintain, or update the application.

Modular construction of an application allows several parts of the
application to be built simultaneously. But for this construction in tandem
to work, the team members building the application must coordinate with
one another carefully at the outset. The MTA application development
illustrates the coordination required.

The MTA application design team determined early in the process that
much of the input data to the MTA would be from a SAS database, but that

most of the application would be written in pcEXPRESS. The major separable tasks the team identified were to build:

- global data structures, their maintenance programs, and menus
- a SAS database
- SAS programs to create an input database for pcEXPRESS
- pcEXPRESS programs to load the SAS data
- local data structures, their maintenance programs and menus
- input forms and tables and their validation code
- process control, computation, and linking programs
- report and graph generating programs.

For these tasks to be completed in tandem, the team had to agree on three features of the application:

- the SAS data to be supplied to the model
- the formats for the data files to be transferred from SAS to pcEXPRESS
- the global and local data structures to be loaded by forms and tables, computed in the computational and linkage modules, and printed or graphed by output programs.

The team decided to document the MTA by requiring subteams to contribute to the documentation as they built their components. This required further agreement about the outline of the user manual and about the documentation file names to be used by each team member.

16.5   PROGRAMMING PRINCIPLES

Well-designed applications will not survive the test of time if they are poorly programmed. Maintenance and updating are made practically impossible by bad programming, and new applications become more costly to develop if the original applications were not written with reusable general-purpose pieces. Modeling tools, application generators, and other utilities, which are often grouped under the heading of computer-aided system engineering (CASE) technologies (see Winsberg [1988]), can be used to build applications efficiently.

The most important principles for programming applications are well known (see, for example, Yourdon [1975]). Five worth highlighting are:

1. *Programs should perform a single function.* Programs that perform a single function can be easily reassembled to perform dif-

ferent major functions without recoding. Each program should print a report, or calculate a variable using a specific algorithm, or perform some other task.

2. *Programs should be structured.* Structured programs contain no "go to" statements; each routine can be decomposed into:

   • multiple statements executed in sequence
   • an "if-then-else" statement
   • a "do while" statement.

Structured programs can be easily broken down into smaller, comprehensible pieces, speeding development, maintenance, and updating.

3. *Programs should be callable as drivers or as subroutines.* A driver is a program callable from an application's command level or from an application's menu; a subroutine is interior to an application and is called by a driver. Ideally, a subroutine performs its single function on the data specified by the arguments passed to it. Subroutines can then operate on any data structure, making them more easily transported to other applications and less likely to need modification over time. When code must be "bound to data" (i.e., made dependent on the data structures of a particular application), it is better to impose the dependence at the level of a driver or, better yet, to impose the dependence on a menu rather than on a driver.

4. *Do not hard wire parameters into subroutines; instead, pass arguments.* Application-specific parameters, such as the number of months spanned by a data set, should not be written into the code of a subroutine or driver, but should be passed as an argument to the routine or driver. This will facilitate both updating and transferring a routine to another application.

5. *Pass arguments by keywords, rather than by position or value.* Passing arguments by position requires tedious and error-prone attention to identifying the null arguments and the position of each argument in a sequence; this is unnecessary when arguments are passed as keywords or values. Passing arguments as values can entail passing variable numbers of arguments from one call to the next; this complication for debugging is avoided when arguments are passed as keywords.

While these five principles are widely known, they are also widely violated. An ODSS' development team must commit and frequently recommit itself to adhering to these principles in order to keep down the future costs of maintaining and updating the system. The application builders in the development team must keep vigil to ensure that all programming adheres to these principles.

In addition to these general principles for applications programming, programming with fourth-generation languages—especially those that are rich and robust—provides a number of alternatives for constructing programs and their subelements, subroutines, processes, operations, etc. But, while there may be many options for accomplishing a task, all are not equally efficient; and the obvious choice is not always the most efficient from a performance or computer resource standpoint. Using the information gathered in defining the system's software architecture—identifying key or common functionality, processes, and operations—it makes a great deal of sense to find the most efficient means to program them and to standardize development around them. Aside from the gains to be realized in performance and efficient use of computer resources, other substantial benefits are to be gained:

- Training can be simplified, allowing it to be focused on the general principles, rather than on specific applications.
- Developers can work more quickly, because they already know how to go about performing certain functions. There is less reinventing the wheel and consulting with other developers about the best ways to accomplish a task.
- The system is standardized and optimized across applications. Personnel can move from one application to another during development or in a maintenance mode without having to spend excessive time learning how the original programmer approached construction.
- The ODSS Generator can be customized using this information, further automating and accelerating the development process (see Chapter 14).

16.6   WRITING VALIDATION CODE FOR FORMS AND TABLES

One programming chore common in application building, writing validation code for forms and tables, differs from traditional program writing in ways worth noting here.

Forms are used to input one-dimensional data, while tables are used to input multidimensional data. Each field of each form or table requires determination of (1) the variable to be loaded into the field; (2) how to display the data; and (3) validation logic indicating what to do when the data are entered (fill the field with the data, fill the field with a missing value indicator, etc.). It is the last of these requirements that entails writing code with the following peculiar traits:

- The code must anticipate entry of data into any field. The code must judge whether a particular proposed entry is erroneous because other fields contain information that must be altered before the present datum can be entered. In such cases, the entry must be refused and a corresponding message displayed.
- The code should suggest the next action to be taken and move the cursor to that position.
- When the user aborts out of the form or table, the code must decide what to do with the data already entered—keep them or delete them.
- As data are accepted into fields, process control must be notified so that all derived variables dependent on the datum are recomputed.
- Users can often activate overlapping forms and tables to any depth. The code must eliminate all side effects of forms and tables upon one another, even in the case in which the user aborts out of a nested form or table.

16.7 CATALOGING PROGRAMS

Programs that perform a single function proliferate. As the number of programs in a system grows, so does the need to organize them. An application builder working alone may virtually memorize applications programs and their arguments while developing the system. But this memory will fade quickly. First arguments will be forgotten, then programs. Application builders working together may jointly know all the programs and arguments in an application, but not for long. Without a formal record of programs, their functions, and their arguments, updating and maintaining the system will become unwieldy and building new applications from old pieces will become impossible.

The EFMS has roughly 2000 application programs. A useful index of programs would list for each application the programs that appear in the application. A more informative system-wide library for the programs would organize the programs by major function. Major functions might be sorted:

- by whether the programs:
  - maintain one (table) data structure (e.g., maintain AFSCs)
    or
  - process multiple data structures (e.g., input, process and report loss information from the Air Force)
- by whether the programs:
  - are applicable to multiple applications (e.g., utilities)
    or
  - have a special purpose (e.g., convert AFSCs between time periods)
- by
  - inputting
  - calculating
  - outputting
- to screen
- to a file
- to a report.

Criteria for categorizing programs must be agreed on early if a system is to build a program library successfully. It is likely that a system's proto-type programs and the programs written by model builders designing an ODSS will not be very well indexed. The prototyping and model building exercises are much less structured than application building and lend themselves less well to the creation of program libraries. Thus, at some stage in the development of an ODSS, there must come a shift from the fluid, here today, gone tomorrow flexibility that inevitably marks creative exercises, to a structured, all accounted for architecture that will allow the system to succeed in the long haul. The champions of this conversion should be the application builders, acutely aware as they are that many, many pieces ready at hand are the key to the cost-efficient construction of an ODSS.

16.8   TOOLS FOR DEVELOPMENT AND MAINTENANCE

The success of an ODSS will be measured partly in terms of user satis-faction and the degree to which users (and top management) are able to achieve their objectives. It will also be determined by the cost effective-ness of its construction and maintenance, and the ability of the support staff to react to changing needs of users and the environment in which it operates.

A number of factors that contributed to the success of the implementation of the EFMS have already been discussed. Several of those relate directly to choices that were made in terms of the tools used to build the system. (Chapter 14 discussed the use of an ODSS Generator and application generation utilities). Others are associated with the manner in which the techniques were used in constructing the EFMS—standardization and the ability to customize individual application programs by modifying and tying together generic components (see also Section 17.6). Two other techniques were also used that are worthy of mention: automated generation of code and cross-referencing.

All information required to generate the interface components (program code) in the EFMS is stored as data in the data dictionary, so interfaces can be modified by altering the dictionary data. The program code is generated from these data. If a new capability is added to a component or a more efficient generation technique is found, all programs using that component are regenerated. This approach reduces recoding time and effort, and contributes to consistent and error-free programs.

Cross-referencing is a powerful tool for ensuring and maintaining system integrity. It allows the development of facilities within the system to manage associations or relationships by using cross-referencing to provide linkages. With this facility, the process of making modifications or changes that may ripple through can be automated or the software maintainer can easily locate all the components of a module. For example, if a menu is deleted, all submenu references to the deleted menu can be automatically removed and the menus rebuilt. Also an application builder can move among the components of a module by identifying the pertinent collection they belong to, such as:

- submenus of the menu
- programs called by a menu or submenu
- forms called by the program
- programs called by the form
- other programs that reference the collection.

Chapter 17 | User Interfaces

17.1 INTRODUCTION

One of the most neglected yet important aspects of decision support system development is the definition and design of the user interfaces. Not only are they critical to how the system will be accepted and used, but their design can also be an important element in understanding customer needs and determining their expectations for the system. By addressing the interfaces at the early stages of the development process, the developers can gain important insights about the proposed system by requiring the users to think about their needs in a detailed and structured way that is difficult to achieve using standard analysis techniques. New screen generators and interface simulation packages provide tools to assist in accomplishing this task in a rapid and realistic manner.

While the characteristics and structure of the interfaces themselves will vary from system to system, they tend to fulfill a common set of purposes. There are certain guidelines and standards that can be applied to enhance the functionality of most systems. This chapter concentrates on some important objectives to strive for in the design of user interfaces, the components that go into making up an effectively designed set of interfaces, and guidelines for developing and maintaining those interfaces. The discussion is addressed primarily to project managers, DBAs, and application builders. Actual EFMS pcEXPRESS screens are used to illustrate how design objectives can be translated into tangible results. For a more general overview of user interfaces for decision support systems, see Stohr and White [1982].

17.2 DEVELOPING THE SYSTEM WITH THE AID OF INTERFACE DESIGNS

The use of data modeling as a tool for system design has received a lot of attention over the last few years (see, for example, Tsichritzis and Lochovsky [1982]). It has become an effective tool in dealing with the growing complexity of data as technology has provided the means to build larger and larger systems with increasing amounts of data, often from multiple sources and used in many different forms. However, data models are often arcane, and certainly do not present data in a way that the users want to see it, or perhaps even understand it. What is important to the users are *their* views of the data, both from an input and output standpoint. A system development effort that addresses data from this perspective in its early stages, and then uses data modeling to define and build the logical underlying data structures of the system, maximizes the chances to capture the "real" user requirements, although the research and subsequent design of the models in the system may cause some alteration of these views and underlying data structures. However, a robust interface design should be able to accommodate reasonable changes without radical alterations.

Screen and report generators have become effective tools for rapidly prototyping user interfaces. Software is now available (e.g., C-Scape, Cooke et al. [1987]) that provides even greater capability by simulating the operation of the user interfaces in addition to providing screen mockups. Application generators (various combinations of screen building devices, code generators, and fourth-generation language facilities) also provide the means for prototyping interfaces, or quickly generating screens and report formats in addition to more rapid development of systems. These are powerful tools for ensuring that the systems being built are targeted to actual requirements. Users can see from the very early stages of the system development life cycle what they will be getting and can quickly confirm the designer's grasp of their needs.

17.3 OBJECTIVES

The primary objective of any set of interfaces, as with the decision support system itself, is to improve the quality of decisionmaking within the organization, whether that means "better" decisions, more rapid decisions, more cost-effective decisions, or fulfilling a combination of criteria. The extent to which the interfaces provide a means of obtaining information that is needed, when it is needed, and in a form that supports the decisions to be made is a measure of success for the entire system. From a user perspective, the interfaces *are* the system.

Because of the characteristics of the decisionmaking process and decision support systems themselves, an effective interface design will place a large measure of control directly in the hands of the users, making them self-sufficient in some aspects of system operation. Self-sufficiency can be determined by the extent to which users are able to run their applications and engage in actions in support of decisionmaking without having to rely on the application builders, DBAs, other users, and user manuals.

To allow users to attain self-sufficiency, a number of characteristics should be present in the interface. It should:

- be full featured, providing all the functions users could accomplish if the application was done manually, including generating reports and graphs
- be intuitively obvious to use; e.g., providing lists of valid responses, recommended responses, and suggestions for the next action to be performed
- allow users to control processing (e.g., the order of functions performed) without programming
- provide context-sensitive on-line help, directing users to the precise help information they need based on their error or question
- provide context-sensitive error messages, explaining the specific error and how to correct the error in language the users will understand.

Providing full features and ease of use are somewhat competing objectives. As more features are added, novice users are overwhelmed by all the options. If the features are spread over additional layers of forms to avoid overwhelming novices, experienced users become annoyed at having to traverse multiple screens to accomplish their tasks.

Novice users' acceptance of the user interface is primarily influenced by simplicity and visual appeal. Experienced users' acceptance is primarily based on having full features. To gain novice users' acceptance of the user interface, they should be thoroughly trained by experienced users.

An error that is often made in designing user interfaces is to design them with only the novice user in mind. This is often manifested in designs that present only a limited amount of information or choices on the screen at any given time, hierarchies that may be several levels deep as users are guided through options one step at a time, and the use of on-screen representations that require the movement of the cursor to select an option. This may be appropriate for systems where the personnel using them are relatively unskilled or the turnover is high. But most ODSSs, by their nature, require relatively sophisticated users, and the novice will soon become the experienced user. Thus the design of the user interface should be heavily biased toward "easy to use" rather than "easy to learn."[38]

A number of things can be done to make accommodations for both the novice and the more experienced user. Multiple menus can be displayed on the screen at one time, rather than presenting the user with a hierarchy that must be traversed one screen at a time. This is not to say that the screen should be packed with so much information that it becomes confusing and difficult to comprehend, but keeping each menu simple, and setting it off with a different background color, for example, can eliminate potential problems. Allowing the use of key strokes in addition to on-screen responses to invoke commands or choices can serve both the more experienced and novice user. For example, the novice Lotus 1–2–3 user will often move the cursor across the top of the screen to make menu and option choices, while more experienced users will rapidly type a series of letter commands to achieve their objectives. Help screens that truly provide "help" can often mean that users do not have to be presented with information long after they have ceased to need it as they traverse the system. Help screens can also be used to guide less experienced users to alternative choices for the next set of actions. Function keys can be preprogrammed to provide alternatives to more experienced users that might only confuse the novice if presented on the screen. Menus should not be linked in hierarchical form unless the nature of the tasks demands it.

---

[38] For a discussion of the distinctions among systems that are easy to learn and easy to use, see [Anderson and Shapiro, 1989].

Experienced users should have the freedom to move directly between menus without having to back out of a sequence or traverse through several screens to get to the menu desired.

While the careful development of the interfaces for an ODSS may require more time and effort to implement in the beginning, this attention to detail can provide significant dividends in the longer term. As capabilities are transferred from application builders to users, more work gets done, both by users and application builders. Ongoing communication between users and application builders is minimized, as are demands for system changes due to the inability of users to get what they want from the system when circumstances change slightly. As a result, application builders spend less time in maintenance activities and have more time to build new applications.

17.3.1   Standardization and Consistency

The standardization and consistency of interfaces should be addressed from two perspectives. A common "look and feel" should be preserved across the given set of interfaces. While the content of the various screens will differ, the general construction (e.g., where certain things appear on the screen and the methods used to implement commands) should be the same unless specific circumstances dictate differences.

Second, users, regardless of type—end user, application builder, DBA—should be using interfaces that are structured along the same lines. This approach reduces cross-training effort, improves communication, improves functionality, and reduces development and maintenance effort. Coordination is also improved. Virtually any user interface question can be answered by any other user, application builder, or DBA.

Standardizing across these two dimensions improves user capabilities in two ways. First, since each user interface component is used globally across all applications, each improvement to a component has maximum impact. Second, users are willing to use a greater percentage of the overall capabilities because they know that everyone else in the organization can help them if they have a problem concerning how something works. Also, their time investment in learning each new capability will be offset by the benefits of using the capability across all their applications for years to come. In addition, standardization minimizes development and maintenance effort. Application builders can design menus, forms, reports, etc., to an organizationally defined standard, rather than to each individual's taste.

Note that the common "look and feel" of user interfaces comes at a price in programming time and effort. This time and effort is worth it when the end user is not a member of the SMO. If, however, the end user of a model is a sophisticated user doing specific isolated tasks, the benefits might not outweigh the costs.

17.3.2 Customization

Standardization in interface design does not necessarily preclude customization to meet the needs of individual users. Standardization may, in fact, promote the customized use of system features. For example, a standardized method of producing *ad hoc* reports permits users across the system to have access to this facility, thereby allowing them to produce reports that are tailored to their specific situations. Other customized features may include the selection of screen colors, printer, plotter, and program function key assignments. In addition to creating *ad hoc* reports, experienced users might perform more sophisticated tasks, such as linking together programs into automated procedures that can be invoked at given points in time or under specified circumstances. The user interface can also be tailored to each user by automatically transferring or defaulting the application to a selected point or process based on a user's past responses to a set of prompts. (For example, the user interface can be programmed to remember answers to prompts, so that the user's last answer becomes the default for the next prompt.) Or, the user might set up a sequence to be followed that could be selected by the use of a function key. A similar (although less versatile) capability is the macro facility available on PCs.

17.4 INTERFACE DESIGN CAPABILITIES EMBEDDED IN APPLICATION GENERATORS

The cost, in terms of time and resources, to build from scratch an interface system as elaborate and multifunctional as the one that is part of the EFMS would be prohibitive in most circumstances. However, the EFMS interfaces were not built from scratch. While it was not a trivial task to build them or conceptualize their overall design and structure, they are really the result of taking full advantage of an underlying set of capabilities and possibilities that were present in the application generation software (the RCG SYSTEM) that was used to build the system itself. Some of the most important software capabilities built into the the RCG SYSTEM are listed below:

- a very high-level programming language that included a data dictionary and database/file building functionality, and provided full functionality to the interface system by integrating interface design and system building activities
- a screen generator that allowed the rapid building of screens, and the use of a wide range of associated features:
  - icons, mouse, and cursor functionality
  - window overlays and split screens
  - color
  - choice lists
- programmable function keys
- interactive analysis and presentation style graphics
- a full-function microcomputer-mainframe link that allowed interactive processing
- file generation and transfer capabilities, including the creation of file formats compatible with, or used by, popular applications (e.g., spreadsheets, word processors, statistical packages)
- a report generator that permitted end users to create simple to elaborately formatted reports
- a procedure generation capability in which users can choose up to 15 menu entries, answer all of the prompts, and save the resulting sequence as a procedure.

Because each of the user interface components was built and maintained by the application generator and supporting utility software, very little actual coding was required. Application builders constructed and now maintain these components using the user interface itself. The only portion of the user interface that required coding was the validation logic for each input field. However, in most cases code was able to be copied from existing validation programs and modified.

17.5   SYSTEM ARCHITECTURE AND INTERFACES

Anyone who has more than a nodding acquaintance with computer technology has probably noticed the differences in functionality and capabilities between the interfaces for applications on microcomputers and mainframes. Mainframe interfaces are not nearly as good. A number of reasons can be given for this. Today's mainframe technology has been built on a base that goes back to a time when applications were not envisioned to have the end user interaction that has become commonplace in the relatively newer world of microcomputing. For the most part, the tools are not there to build them. Also, attempting to provide the same kind of interface features on a mainframe that are present in most microcomputer applications requires large computer resources in a more expensive shared environment, with other large-scale processes competing for those same resources.

This situation can create a dilemma for the developer who requires the power and storage capacity of a mainframe computer to support the computational requirements of an ODSS. That dilemma was resolved in the EFMS by selecting an ODSS generator that provided integrated microcomputer and mainframe processing capabilities. While the mainframe version of EXPRESS provides the capacity for heavy-duty number crunching and storage of large-scale files, its user interface potential is significantly more primitive than pcEXPRESS, the microcomputer version of the product. However, because the two products can be linked together to provide an integrated processing environment, we were able to take advantage of the strengths of both forms of computing.

A microcomputer component of the system can serve as the platform on which to build the interfaces to the system, and the mainframe can be used to do the heavy-duty computational work and accommodate large-scale files. The user interacts with the microcomputer to invoke mainframe application processing, the results of which are then transmitted through the communication links back to the microcomputer for display. Other pieces of the application may run entirely on the microcomputer, depending on their processing and storage requirements. In either case, the underlying system configuration can be made transparent to the end user. This is commonly referred to as "client/server computing" [Francis, 1990].

17.6 COMPONENTS OF USER INTERFACES (USING EFMS AS AN EXAMPLE)

Because the interface developed for EFMS is fairly sophisticated, complex, and extensive it can serve as an example of the range of possibilities that exist for the user interfaces of an ODSS. Therefore, the remainder of this chapter will explain some important interface components, and we will illustrate them with EFMS examples.

The EFMS interface consists of roughly 20 types of components, such as menus, input forms, choice lists, and error messages. Learning how to use the components requires more up-front training than is required for a typical single user interface. However, once the components are understood, that knowledge can be transferred to all applications in the system. The same facilities that are provided to end users also form the basis of a set of development and maintenance tools that are applications used by software developers and DBAs.

Specification of the characteristics and components for a specific ODSS interface should be based on the activities that would be most commonly performed by the users of the system in accomplishing the major tasks that the system was built to support. In the case of EFMS, those user activities tended to fall into the following major categories:

- selectively retrieve and display data, either from one's own or another user's database(s)
- establish conditions, criteria, or parameters (e.g., time periods, economic assumptions, population segments, level of detail) to control the forecasting and production of data by the system
- initiate and control the timing of processes within the system (e.g., model runs, inquiries, job streams)
- store results or output from the system on a selective basis, either permanently or in temporary data sets
- analyze the results of a process or processes, including the comparison of runs made at different points in time or with different parameters
- produce *ad hoc* or preformatted reports and graphs.

All of these functions can be performed through the on-line EFMS interfaces, and all were created using a generic set of components, provided through the application generator. The most important of the components are listed and described below.

- menus and procedures
- report and graph routing
- scratch pad
- external software packages
- collections
- forms and tables

- progress messages
- error messages
- on-line help.

These components were either present in the application generation software itself (e.g., menus) or were created using facilities that were part of the application generator (e.g., procedures and scratch pads). Application interface building then consisted of tailoring each component to a specific application and assembling the components into a specific element of the interface. Frequently, already-developed interfaces were able to be slightly modified and selectively assembled to form a new interface in a short time.[39] The following sections describe these components and their use in the EFMS.

17.6.1 Menus and Procedures

As with a great many on-line systems, the EFMS is menu driven; i.e., the users operate the system through a series of preformatted screens. Screens may either be generic to the entire system, or tailored to a specific application or set of applications. However, the principles of standardization and consistency have been applied across the entire system, so that the "look and feel" of the screens is similar, regardless of where a user or data processor finds himself in the system. A sample menu is shown in Fig. 17.1.

When a user logs into the EFMS and selects a model to use, he or she is presented with the "top menu" for that model, in this case the Middle-Term Aggregate (MTA) model. Each top menu contains up to 15 menu entries, each denoting a submenu or operation. Submenus are labeled with trailing >'s (not shown) to distinguish them from operations. Eleven menu entries applying to all applications appear at the bottom of every menu screen.

As users select submenus, the list of preceding menus is displayed in the upper-left corner to provide a sense of location within the menu structure. While there may be a logical hierarchy within a structure of menus and submenus, users are not required to traverse through every screen in the hierarchy to accomplish a given set of tasks. With a single command,

---

[39] Some of the functionality described here is available on PCs through the Microsoft Windows system and with the new Macintosh operating system.

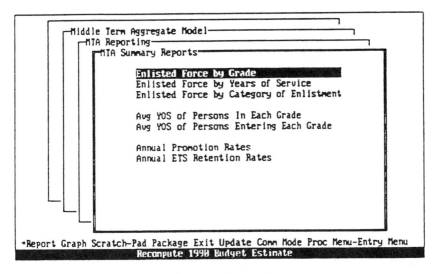

Fig. 17.1   A Sample Menu

they can go directly to any other menu screen from any point in the application. They are presented with an alphabetical list of menus. They pick one, and are placed immediately in that menu, just as if it were a submenu of their current menu. The next time that user attempts to move laterally (as opposed to hierarchically) across the menu structure, his or her last lateral menu becomes the current default.

EFMS also offers the option of changing the execution mode via on-screen mode selection. Users may indicate whether the programs should prompt at each step in a process, prompt only when the user must make a selection or enter data, or execute on the basis of commands without prompting for each. This allows the system to be adjusted by individual users to reflect their familiarity with a particular application.

Finally, if users change the parameters on the screen for a specific application, the system presents a message at the bottom of the screen to warn them that an operation must be performed to synchronize the derived data in the database with the current set of parameters.

Many of the EFMS menu entries actually represent commands to run a program or series of programs. To complete a task a user may be required to string several of these together to form a procedure. Rather than requiring them to choose each of these operations sequentially, they can establish automated procedures that will string the individual operations together. This is accomplished through a procedures menu. Up to 15 possible menu selections may be identified in the sequence to be run. Users can also specify that procedures be executed immediately or submit them to batch for overnight execution. Alternately, the operations can be performed by the DBAs supporting the system. DBAs can also limit users to a selected set of programs that can be sequenced in this manner. The use of procedures minimizes the documentation required to ensure all the programs of a collection are run together or in the right order, and reduces users' dependence on application builders and DBAs.

17.6.2   Report and Graph Routing

EFMS offers users the option of displaying reports and graphs on their screens or having them printed in hardcopy form. When users wish to display or print a report or graph, they may select from several options via an on-line menu. For example, they may decide:

- whether the reports and graphs should be printed to the screen, printer, or plotter
- which printer or plotter to use
- whether the reports and graphs should be printed, printed and saved on disk, or saved for subsequent printing
- whether page numbers should be assigned consecutively across reports, beginning page number, number of copies, etc.
- which forms and fonts to use.

The EFMS software knows for each hardware environment the available screens, printers, and plotters and their characteristics. It automatically selects and downloads fonts appropriate for each report. Users may specify whether reports printed to the screen are printed page by page or in their entirety for subsequent full screen editing and viewing.

Figure 17.2 illustrate how functions are layered for novice and experienced users. Novice users primarily toggle between printing to the screen and printer. More experienced users may choose to change printers, orientation (portrait versus landscape), and select specific fonts.

17.6.3   Scratch Pad

Reports and graphs can be saved in temporary storage areas on disk called scratch pads. Using the scratch pad selection, users can edit, print,

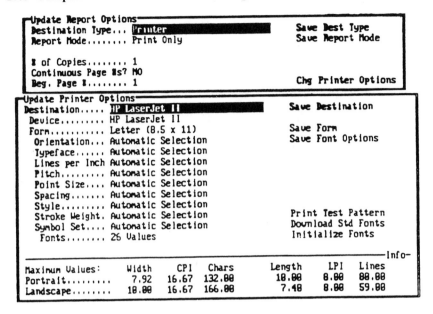

Fig. 17.2   Layered Functions

delete, archive, and restore the reports and graphs, send them to other users, and receive them from other users. Using the on-line editing facility, users can customize reports (e.g., enter columns of data not contained in the database), append footnotes, or make last-minute changes. Printing with a number of options can be invoked from the scratch pad facility. These include printing even/odd pages (for double-sided copies), selected pages, and reports as a group with a table of contents.

17.6.4   External Software Packages

Attempting to build all of the capabilities required for an ODSS from scratch can be a time-consuming, costly, and unnecessary task. Not only are there a number of application generation software packages available with many of the capabilities that might make up an ODSS, but by selecting one that provides file generation and transfer capabilities, data can be transferred from one package to another. For example, the builders of EFMS quickly realized the potential of integrating Lotus 1–2–3 into EFMS. While other packages have more elaborate graphics, those in 1–2–3 are very easy to use, and coupling them with its spreadsheet features, including some statistical analysis functions, make it a very powerful tool. During the development cycle, 1–2–3 was used to make comparative analyses of model results. Operationally, it gave users very clear graphical pictures of the projected results of their management decisions. Users were required to make some adjustments from the menu system of EFMS to the menuing of 1–2–3 in operating the system. However, since 1–2–3 had already been adopted as a standard within the organization, the adjustments were minor. Also, using the capabilities of the application generator, the transfer of files between Lotus 1–2–3 and EXPRESS could be done by menu selection, making it a very simple process for the users. For example, a program in the EFMS could generate a Lotus 1–2–3 spreadsheet. The spreadsheet could then be edited using the scratch pad editor or by invoking Lotus 1–2–3 from the Proc selection of the menus (see Fig. 17.3).

17.6.5   Collections

In most organizations, there is a group of core tasks that are repeated over and over—e.g., creating quarterly forecasts, preparing year-end reports, etc. Traditionally, when these are produced by some type of automation, they are based on entirely "hard-coded" computer programs, or the data are transferred to a microcomputer application form, where the users makes adjustments for time periods, etc. on a set of reports they have created. When time periods, or other parameters change, either the applications maintainers or the users have to expend time making these changes. Often, similar changes have to made to a number of programs or applications, duplicating effort and introducing the possibility of errors and inconsistencies. In the case of hard-coded programs, users are depen-

Fig. 17.3   Software Package Menu Selection

dent on the applications maintainers to make programming changes. This can be especially frustrating at critical times during the year (e.g., at the end of quarters or the year), when many users may require support.

To overcome these problems, important parameters, such as time periods, are maintained in "collections" within the EFMS. These collections are created and maintained separately from the program code. Many different programs within the the system can call the same collection, minimizing maintenance. Some types of collections that can be specified in the EFMS are:

- simple lists (e.g., months of the current year)
- formatted lists (e.g., accounts of a balance sheet properly indented with overlines and underlines, and leading and trailing blank lines)
- hierarchical lists, (e.g., Jan, Feb, Mar, Qtr.1, Apr, May, June, Qtr.2, Half.1,...)
- computed lists, where selection criteria are incorporated into the collection making up the list (e.g., months in which the goal is exceeded by 10 percent)
- prompted lists, where the user provides the additional information necessary to build the list (e.g., months in which the goal is exceeded by XX percent)
- sort sequences (e.g., ascending order of Air Force Specialty Codes within career field groups)
- list of programs to be run periodically.

The EFMS provides a variety of tools to allow users to define collections and to choose only a portion of a collection. In this way, maintenance is reduced, users are given much more power to obtain only the output they desire, and they are able to get it in a much more rapid fashion. It should also be understood that this process invokes more than a set of labels for the output from the system; in selecting and setting the status of collections the user is actually establishing and limiting the parameters across which a particular operation will take place. For example, if a user wishes to see a forecast of the enlisted inventory for the next two years, the limit on the forecasting horizon will be set in the system when the status of the collection to be used for that parameter is set (see below). Collections defined in the ODSS can also be used in creating new reports or graphs. This approach saves time and gives developers and users a great deal of flexibility.

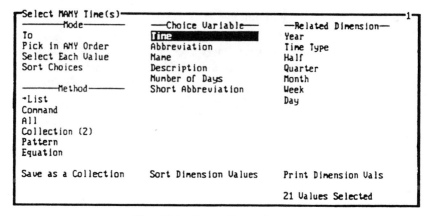

Fig. 17.4   Status Setter Screen

<small>DEFINING COLLECTIONS USING STATUS SETTERS</small>

In the EFMS, collections can be defined through the use of status setters. The primary purpose of the status setter is to establish the range of dimension values, sort sequences, or parameter values for a particular operation or procedure as described earlier. This software interface tool provides a range of options to the user in defining and using those dimension values. The user may:

- choose via one-dimensional variables of the dimension (e.g., number of days in the time period)
- choose via related dimensions (e.g., months, quarters, halves, or years)
- specify a pattern by completing a form on the screen (e.g., select from various options presented)
- choose a collection of dimension values (e.g., time periods covered by the current forecast)
- specify an equation by completing forms (e.g., time periods with less than 100 people in any grade)

The software tools associated with the status setters allow the users to perform additional operations such as selecting the union, intersection, and complement of two sets of dimension values, specifying whether choices should be sorted before presentation, and saving the selected dimension options for future use.

Figure 17.4 shows the EFMS's status setter screen.

DEFINING COLLECTIONS USING CHOICE LISTS

Sometimes it is easier to define collections by using choice or "pick" lists, because they present users with a list of electable options to choose from, rather than requiring the user to determine what can be chosen before taking action, or having the user refer to a separate listing first. They also save key strokes and time, especially if the lists offer the option of making more than one selection at a time. For example, there are almost 400 individual Air Force Specialty Codes that come under the control of the enlisted force managers. Selecting one, several, or from predefined groupings for a report, display, or inclusion within the parameters of a model is a much more simple task than keying in the choices one at a time. Choice lists also offer other advantages. For example, they can be used in an overlay mode with a menu, so the user can move from the menu to the choice list easily, without having to transition to another screen. Choice lists can also make more information instantly available than can be displayed on the screen at one time, the users merely scroll through the list, making selections as they do. Coding is also reduced since additional code need not be written to validate or edit user choices. When the basic choice list functionality is present in the application generation software, the developer is only required to customize it for a specific application. Documentation is reduced, because the choice list itself is a form of documentation.

An ODSS should allow users to specify the order of their choices, where applicable. Figure 17.5 illustrates picking in any order versus picking in order. In the first picture, choices are selected by pressing enter. In the second, pressing enter assigns the next sequential number, which can be overridden by typing.

17.6.6 Forms and Tables

Forms and tables are probably the most common and oldest of the on-screen display modes. They are also among the most useful, since they display information in ways that have proven their merits over time, even in the absence of computers. Forms represent one-dimensional data. Even if the data are arranged in a form to facilitate data entry, they are still capable of being displayed logically as a single normalized record in a computer file.

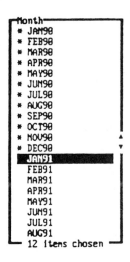
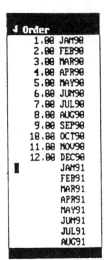

Fig. 17.5 Two Examples of Choice Lists

Tables are multidimensional and often mimic their noncomputerized counterparts. Their uses tend to be somewhat different. Forms are often oriented toward data entry, while tables are more often used for display. Examples of a form and table are shown in Fig. 17.6. The first picture shows the form for defining information for each user i.d. (one-dimensional), and the second shows the definition of each program function key for each environment (two-dimensional). Figure 17.6 (b) also illustrates how program function keys, and ODSS applications in general, can be table driven (i.e., controlled by data instead of program code).

The functionality and power of these displays can be increased by combining them with other interface tools (e.g., using choice lists linked to databases to select standard displays of information concerning each of the individual occupational specialties). Other options include the following:

- allowing one form to overlap another
- presenting slices of the data by paging up or down through the form or table
- organizing form fields into inputs, actions, and information so that the specific purpose of a field or group of fields on the screen is obvious to the user.

```
┌─Update Users─────────────────────────────────────────────┐
│                          Reding_Robert                    │
│                                                           │
│  Name................  Robert Reding                      │
│  Abbreviation........  Bob Reding                         │
│                                                           │
│  User Type...........  _Data_Base_Administrator           │
│  Password............  seCRet                             │
│  Host Userid.........  EFMSRR                             │
│  Identifier..........  RR                                 │
│  Default Menu........  Middle_Term_Aggregate_Model         │
│  Is Locked in Menus?.  NO                                 │
│                                                           │
│                    Select Screen Colors                   │
│ ───────────────────────────────────────────────────────  │
│  Last Login..........  Wednesday January 31, 1990 at 18:54:54 │
│  Last Password Change  90/01/31                           │
└───────────────────────────────────────────────────────────┘
```

```
┌──────────────────────────────────────────────────────────┐
│ ENVIRONMENT: _MDB-UM                                      │
│ PF Key              Name                    Commands       │
│ PF01   Help                          _EDPUPKM              │
│ PF02   Display PF Keys               _EDEPFK               │
│ PF03   Return to Top Menu            _MMM                  │
│ PF04   Return to Last Menu           _MMRTM               │
│ PF05                                 _EDPUPKM              │
│ PF06                                 _EDPUPKM              │
│ PF07   Page Up (Backward)            PU                    │
│ PF08   Page Down (Forward)           PD                    │
│ PF09   Quit                          QUIT                  │
│ PF10   Done                          DONE                  │
│ PF11                                 _EDPUPKM              │
│ PF12   Top                           TOP                   │
│ PF13                                 _EDPUPKM              │
│ PF14                                 _EDPUPKM              │
│ PF15                                 _EDPUPKM              │
│ PF16                                 _EDPUPKM              │
│ PF17   Group Page Up (Backward)      GPU                   │
│ PF18   Group Page Down (Forward)     GPD                   │
│ PF19   Up (Backward)                 U                     │
│ PF20   Down (Forward)                D                     │
└──────────────────────────────────────────────────────────┘
```

Fig. 17.6   (a) Form for Defining Information
(b) Definition of Each Program Function

17.6.7   Progress Messages

Time never seems to pass as slowly as when one is sitting at a terminal or microcomputer waiting for an operation or series of operations (procedure) to be completed. Very large-scale models or a long string of consecutive processes can take several seconds, if not minutes, to complete. This is true, even on a very large mainframe computer, especially when it is shared by a number of users. One of the most effective ways of minimizing frustration, as well as providing useful information, is to display prog-

```
                    Year End Processing

                                          19:03
     √ Change Data Measures                19:04 00:01 0:01
       Enlisted Force by Grade                          0:03
       Enlisted Force by Years of Service               0:02
       Enlisted Force by Category of Enlistment         0:04
       Annual Promotion Rates                           9:01
                                                00:01
```

Fig. 17.7   Sample Procedure Progress Message

ress messages at various points in the operation. The users then know exactly where the system is in completing a series of operations. As visible progress is displayed on the screen, it gives the users a sense that something is happening and reduces the potential monotony of waiting for the series to complete. After a while, users can estimate how long an operation will take to complete and can use this knowledge as a gauge in utilizing their time. For example, if it appears the operation will take an abnormally long time to complete, they might temporarily turn to other tasks. Progress messages can also aid in identifying portions of an operation that may be candidates for tuning by timing how long they remain on the screen before being replaced by a message for the next step in the process. The following is an example of an EFMS progress message:

    * _SMSP Loading Actuals from SAS

Procedures also have progress messages associated with them that display the beginning time, elapsed time, and estimated elapsed time for each step. A sample procedure progress message is shown in Fig. 17.7.

17.6.8   Error Messages

High on the list of user complaints about any system are indecipherable error messages and help screens that don't help. There is frequently good justification for those complaints. This aspect of system design is usually regarded as something to address after the real work is completed. All too often, the functions are designed without adequately considering the real needs of the users—who are not data processing professionals, and may not understand the details of the underlying operation of the system. Some actions can be taken to improve this aspect of design significantly. We first discuss the error messages. Help screens are covered in the next subsection.

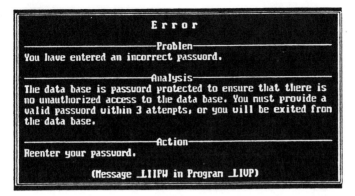

Fig. 17.8   Examples of an Error Message

Error messages should be context sensitive, i.e., having the message "SYSTEM FAILURE" appear under several sets of circumstances is neither useful to the end user or the application builder trying to track down the source of the problem. All EFMS error messages are designed to provide "real" information about the problem and are tailored to a specific situation. They contain three parts: problem, analysis, and solution, as illustrated in Fig. 17.8.

The error messages are stored in data variables, with programs supplying specific context-sensitive information that describes the error. This approach allows programs to share "skeleton" messages when appropriate, with a program providing the specifics. It also allows DBAs to review and clarify messages by completing forms, rather than having to modify the programs that issue the messages. Each message shows the message i.d. and program that issued the message. This information provides DBAs with direct access to messages and programs in error situations.

17.6.9 On-line Help

Help screens should be targeted to two major functions—providing information (e.g., defining the operations performed by programmed function keys) and guiding the user through a set of alternatives or actions in the context of a specific situation. While some users may look to the help screens as a means to learn a new system, attempting to design to this kind of standard is a mistake. On-line tutorials and system documentation are tools designed to serve that purpose.

A user perspective, context sensitivity, and clarity of communication are the keys to designing an effective on-line help subsystem. Users sitting in front of terminals or computers can be likened to student drivers operating an automobile. There is no instructor sitting next to them to provide guidance, but the on-line help subsystem's functions can be compared to the instructor's help. There is a certain amount of information the instructor will provide all students to acquaint them with the system: the location and function of the accelerator, brakes, etc. Rather than attempting to explain everything, the instructor is going to provide information on those things that will be of immediate relevance in getting started and performing basic vehicle operations. He is also going to have insight into the mind of his student, anticipating where problems are going to occur, and being ready with appropriate answers. Based on his experience with the system (in this case the automobile) and with his users (in this case the students), a good instructor will anticipate what and where problems will occur, and will be ready with appropriate answers or guidance. When the student driver encounters a situation requiring "help," he or she wants information directed toward the specific problem being faced. If the car is skidding out of control, a generalized lecture on the physics of friction and bodies in motion, or instructions on changing a tire are not going to be considered very useful in the context of that particular situation. The same can be said of help screens that are so general that the user has trouble equating them to his or her problem or of screens that do not offer the specific information needed for this situation. Designers need to understand their users, anticipate what and where problems will occur, and have appropriate messages readily available. They also must provide basic information on operating the system.

EFMS was designed with those principles in mind. Attention was also paid to features that made the system easy to use. A comprehensive table of contents was provided for users who wished to browse through the system looking for selected items of interest. Users are able to access on-line help from any screen. Once an on-line help screen is displayed, users are able to digress to related information without limit and then return to where they started. The text of each help screen contains highlighted keywords. When a user selects one of the keywords, a help screen for that keyword is shown, and so on. Users can return to the prior screen by pressing the escape key.

On-line help facilities can also be overdesigned. Many of the very good help systems now provided with some microcomputer applications packages are not necessarily models to be emulated in building an ODSS. It should be remembered that these packages were designed for a mass market, which includes potential customers who are relatively unsophisticated in the use of computers and who have few options for getting assistance. The ODSS designer should consider his projected user base and support capabilities in determining the level of effort to devote to help facilities. An ODSS operated by a relatively small number of people who have relatively stable job situations and a strong support staff has much different needs from a system that is widely dispersed geographically within an organization and may have relatively junior users with a high turnover rate.

Chapter 18 | Updating and Maintaining the Models of an ODSS

18.1 INTRODUCTION

Developers of an ODSS experience their greatest thrills when the models they have worked so hard to develop are implemented and work. The system is running! When this euphoria passes, a daunting realization emerges: The system will not perform well indefinitely unless care is taken to maintain and update its models. (By *maintenance*, we mean activities that allow continued use of the existing models or that monitor their performance; by *updating*, we mean activities that revise the existing models to improve their performance.) In this chapter, we offer guidelines for the effective updating and maintaining of a system's models.

Two forces work to undermine good maintenance and updating practice. First, the day-to-day demands for the system's output pressure SMO workers to neglect updating and maintenance. The degradation in the performance of models is frequently slow, so the glamor of adding new bells and whistles to the system will often tempt developers to emphasize new models or radical updates of existing models over the more mundane maintenance or modest updating of existing models. Managers must resist these tendencies and ensure that the SMO's work plan always contains a balanced program of updating and maintenance activities.

314

Marshalling the resources for updating and maintenance is never easy. Unless there are obvious problems, upper management will inevitably lean toward skimping on maintenance and updating costs because the rewards are too intangible for easy recognition. Whether the issue is maintaining urban infrastructure, corporate assets, or an ODSS, expenditures on new capital come more easily than expenditures on old. But the reality is that updating and maintenance of an ODSS can be as costly as operations (e.g., the DMI takes as many resources for maintenance and updating as for running the model). Developers of an ODSS must recognize, plan for, and budget substantial updating and maintenance expenditures from the inception of the ODSS project. This foresight won't make the cost any less, but it will make it easier in the long run to get the funds from top management (or it will enable top management to abort the project early if they are unwilling to pay the costs of maintenance and updating).

Who should be assigned updating and maintenance work: the SMO staff who operate the model or a specialized staff whose primary activity is maintenance and updating? Choosing between SMO staff and a specialized crew is not straightforward.

Having updating and maintenance done by those who operate the model brings the following advantages: (1) People become truly expert about their model, understanding all aspects of the model, from analytic concepts to operational details, (2) problems arising in an updated model during operation are likely to be fixed faster if the people operating the model are the people who updated the model, and (3) a consolidated staff is probably easier to sell to higher management because it looks leaner.

On the other hand, separating operators from maintainers and updaters brings the following advantages: (1) If the model is complex (for example, combines several extensive modules, such as the loss models and the DMI), separating duties avoids overloading one person with too many duties; (2) operators and updaters are likely to develop some expertise in each others' jobs, so by having both, the organization avoids ever being just "one deep" in any model and hence achieves more continuity in the face of employee turnover; (3) two heads are better than one—a pair of analysts is likely to catch some of one another's errors; and (4) having two people working on a model may bring a more diverse set of skills to the model, e.g., programming and analysis skills.

The more mundane and frequently a model is run, the more reason there is for separating operating from maintaining and updating. Humdrum operating requires few of the skills that are almost always important to good updating and maintaining. In the same vein, the more sophisticated the work of updating and maintaining a model, the more reason for separating running the model from updating and maintenance. Finally, if the models are operated not by SMO personnel, but by end users, the responsibility for updating and maintenance must be given to someone on the SMO staff.

In this chapter we discuss three genres of maintenance activities and four genre of updating activities. The maintenance activities are: (1) periodic test and evaluation exercises, (2) the training of new personnel to operate the system's models, and (3) fixing bugs. The four updating exercises are: (1) adding data to the system, (2) updating parameters of models, (3) creating new models or adapting old models to meet new functions, and (4) updating computer programs. A specification of maintenance and updating activities for the EFMS's middle-term loss prediction models is given by Murray [1989].

Spanning all the maintenance and updating activities is documentation. In all stages of updating and maintenance, rewrite documentation to keep it current with the system. Especially helpful is documenting *why* a change was made, instead of simply reporting the change itself; documenting why will help others to understand the new arrangement and to justify the changes to users. Such an audit trail of changes made in the system will help in fixing the system when bugs arise due to interactions among changes made. In the EFMS, the biggest barriers to creating good documentation of changes were (most importantly) time and (less importantly) writing ability. Too little time was explicitly planned for documentation and some analysts were not able writers and therefore found creating documentation daunting. Managers must ensure that time for documentation is part of their work plans and that analysts weak in writing are given assistance in creating documentation.

18.2   MAINTENANCE

18.2.1   Periodic Test and Evaluation

The continuous modification of programs will inevitably lead to errors in the documentation. As time passes, more and more small changes will be made that are not documented. Consequently, the broad outlines of the documentation will be more reliable than the details, so analysts should rely on documentation for "the big picture," but be more skeptical when it comes to the nitty gritty details. Caveat emptor.

Periodic test and evaluation of the system's models serves two major purposes: it sustains the credibility of the models when they perform well and it identifies which models are in need of overhaul when they perform poorly. An organization's environment is in constant flux. Periodic test and evaluation is needed to ensure that these environmental changes have not undermined the efficacy of the system's models. For example, the thaw in relationships with the Soviet Union and the onset of the Persian Gulf crisis had the potential for markedly altering people's tastes for the military. Were these changes sufficient to undermine the models of the EFMS? Only periodic testing and evaluation of the system's models can say.

Sometimes institutional changes may overwhelm a model. In such circumstances it may be necessary to throw away an existing model and switch to either a new relatively *ad hoc* model or to an existing alternative model better suited to the new circumstances. (In the EFMS, we built the retirement loss model to serve as a ready replacement for other loss models if specific substantial changes in the compensation system were introduced.) But don't be too quick to assume that an apparently momentous change will undermine your models. Grandfathering may slow a change's effects, and your models may prove more robust to changes than you anticipate. Rely on test and evaluation rather than quick judgments to decide if new models are needed. We were quite surprised when test and evaluation revealed that the middle-term loss models did extremely well even as the defense budget began to be slashed and the Persian Gulf crisis began to loom large.

The principles for periodic test and evaluation are the same as those for the initial test and evaluation of models detailed in Chapter 11, so we will not discuss them here. The major point we wish to make here is that such exercises may be expensive, and a system manager must anticipate these costs. For example, a periodic test and evaluation of the short-term and middle-term inventory projection models in the EFMS conducted several years after the system became operational absorbed about one person-year of resources! These costs were high, but they were also essential to sustaining the support of users of the system: The users needed evidence that the models they were relying on did indeed continue to perform well.

18.2.2 Training New Personnel

Even the best models are useless if no one knows how to operate them. Since turnover in personnel is inevitable, maintaining an ODSS includes training new people to run the models. A good manager will make such training less disruptive by anticipating turnover and by budgeting time for training in the SMO's work plan. In anticipation of turnover, a manager should ensure that as many jobs as possible are "two deep," with at least two people in the organization knowing what must be done to run any model.

Staying "two deep" in each job protects the SMO from sudden departures or illnesses. Such "cross training" also facilitates budgeting training time on a regular basis. Instead of only doing training when a departure is imminent, training can be scheduled as a regular part of system maintenance. When a departure is imminent (or has already happened) the training effort can be focused on the new person in the shop, with the old operator doing the training if he or she is still around, or with the "number two" operator doing the training if the old operator is gone. When there is no departure imminent, the training time can be used by the current operator to advance the training of his or her backup.

Good documentation will lower training costs. Designing programs to run the models with as little *ad hoc* intervention by the operators as possible will also make it easier to train people to run the models. (More generally, making as much of the updating and maintenance process as routine as possible is an important element in developing an "institutional memory" that ensures jobs can be done even when personnel turn over. The keys to routinization are good documentation and computer programs that perform as many tasks as possible with minimal user interaction.)

18.2.3 Fixing Bugs

No complex system is free from bugs. Throughout a system's lifetime new bugs will be found and fixes required. Fixing bugs will be a time-consuming activity in any ODSS.

The two guiding principles for fixing bugs are (1) document changes in models and code, explaining why the change was made as well as what change was made, and (2) remember that changes in one part of a computer program can have ripple effects elsewhere in the program—or even elsewhere in the system. Test all elements of the application software that might be affected to make sure that the changes did only what you intended them to do.

18.3 UPDATING

18.3.1 Updating the Database

Some updating tasks will become so routine that ODSS personnel will probably think of them as maintenance rather than updating. Chief among these is feeding the ODSS database.

Adding data to the database will be most routine when the additions consist of new observations on variables already in the system. Adding new variables will be less routine and will generally require greater adaptations to the data processing code and to the system's data dictionaries.

Anyone adding data to the ODSS database must be familiar with the structures of existing data sets and with the programs used to process data coming into the system. Anyone adding variables to the system's database must be able to document where each new variable came from and how it is defined. Anyone adding data to specialized data sets associated with particular models (for example adding new variables derived from variables in the system's database) must be clear about the definitions of the variables to be created. In all cases, the people adding data to the system must engage in the kind of data cleaning exercises described in Chapter 9.

Those persons assigned responsibility for updating the system's database should be sensitive to both the providers and the users of the data. Providers of data to the SMO will balk if the data requested from them change too frequently. Similarly, users will balk if the formats in which data are made available change too frequently. A sensitivity to the cost that change can impose on others will condition decisions to alter the database.

The addition of data can create requirements and opportunities for updating the parameters of the ODSS models. Many models will keep track, for example, of the number of months of historical data on which the model can rely. As new data are added, the number of months grows, and must be changed in the models. New data also afford the opportunity for making better estimates of the parameters needed in the models. New data may spur updating exercises in which statistical analyses of the new data may lead to changes in the parameters used in the system's models.

Changes required when data are added should be well documented and routinely made. When the changes needed to be made are poorly documented, disruptions of the system can arise. For example, in the original documentation of one model in the EFMS, there was no documentation of the fact that one array would become too small to accommodate the system's data after five years of use. Had this not been caught by an alert Air Force analyst learning about the model, the model would have suddenly started giving erroneous answers five years into the system's operation. Finding the glitch would not have been easy. Model builders must document the limits of their specifications carefully.

18.3.2   Updating Parameters of Models

When the reestimation of parameters from new data is a routine matter, the process for using those data to estimate new parameters for the models should be made as mechanical as possible, so that reestimating the models requires little more than understanding the programs that recalculate the parameter estimates. A "how to" manual should be prepared that guides such reestimation efforts.

However, purely mechanical updating of the parameters is only a first step in "best practice" updating. An analyst should examine the parameter estimate changes and determine whether they indicate that substantive changes in the model beyond simple reparameterization are called for. For example, in an early updating of the first-term loss model we considered whether the instability across samples of parameters on a time trend variable indicated that the time trend specification was inappropriate; we concluded that it was.

More generally, new data may afford the opportunity to estimate richer specifications of a model than was previously possible, or to consider new bells and whistles in the model that expand its capabilities or improve its performance. For example in a later update of the middle-term loss equations, we considered specifying distinct equations for some of the larger job categories, an enhancement we had not had time to explore in the initial model building exercise. (In this instance, we found the extension of the model would not improve performance, but even that finding added to the system's credibility with users—they were comforted to learn that the reason we did not distinguish more thoroughly among the job categories was because doing so would not improve performance of the models.)

Models whose parameters are routinely updated must also be routinely subjected to test and evaluation. Generating the data for the test and evaluation should be computerized to the greatest extent possible to make the process simple and less subject to error. In addition to this standardization of the process, the criteria for testing and evaluating models described in Chapter 11 should be followed.

18.3.3 Updating Models

Updating the models to accommodate new specifications demands more analytical expertise than just altering the parameters in the old specification. The analyst must first understand the statistical strategy that underlies the model and have enough institutional information to know which variables have been important explanatory variables in the past and which are likely to be important in the future. The analyst must also have a shrewd understanding of how the models are used and what benefits might flow to the user from an altered specification. A thorough understanding of the data is also necessary. The analyst must know what prospects additional data have for improving the model and be aware of the perils the data hold for estimation. For example, a naive analyst might think that adding explanatory variables to the retirement policy analysis model would be a good idea as additional data become available. However, additional data are in fact quite unlikely to overcome the computational problems the model faces when more variables are added; consequently, such an updating exercise would probably be a waste of time. Finally, the analyst must understand the model's computer programs well enough to adapt the programs to incorporate a new specification.

While test and evaluation is part and parcel of ongoing system maintenance, testing and updating is especially important when substantial changes are made to a model, either through large parameter changes or through respecification of the model's form. Testing and evaluation are particularly onerous when a new specification is introduced or when parameters are changed in a model that is not routinely updated. Routine parameter updates can be tested with tried and true software that is routinely used for that purpose; new specifications or nonroutine parameter updates will require new test and evaluation software that must be carefully constructed and tested itself before it can be used to test the new models.

Which models are given the most attention in an updating exercise will in part reflect the discontent of the user community. Which models' performances are causing users the most grief? But greasing squeaky wheels should not be the only concern. Analysts should be asked to assess which of their models they think might benefit substantially from an updating exercise.

18.3.4 Updating Computer Programs

The last updating activity we consider is the updating of computer programs. Computer code may be rewritten for several reasons. Common reasons include: (1) faster code may be wanted, (2) more modular code may be wanted, (3) institutional rule changes may require altering algorithms used by models, or (4) new code for new system tasks may be needed.

Common across all these reasons are the principles discussed in Chapter 16. We will not reiterate them here, other than to declare once more the importance of writing modular code whenever possible. Poorly written code is more difficult to modify than well-written code, so writing the code well the first time will make it easier to make changes later.

The greatest pitfall in rewriting code is making changes whose consequence is to create errors elsewhere in the program. The best safeguard against this problem is writing modular code in the first place. The second best safeguard is having the code rewritten by someone who understands what the program is for and how it works. This latter safeguard is especially important when the code in question is complex. Unfortunately, people who mix programming skills with the substantive skills needed to understand the purposes of a complex program are expensive people, so altering a system's most complex programs is likely to be an expensive activity.

The main point of the previous paragraph is worth repeating: rewriting code risks introducing new problems in other parts of the code. Never rewrite the system's code without testing and evaluating the results extensively.

Chapter 19 | Epilogue

In this final chapter, we review the 1992 status and future prospects of the EFMS. We then briefly highlight the major lessons we have drawn from building the system.

19.1   THE EFMS IN 1992

The Air Force began using the EFMS as soon as the first models were ready. The Bonus Effects Model, completed in 1986, was the first EFMS model used by the Air Force. By 1987 the Disaggregate Middle Term Inventory Projection Model was in place. The stable, and even increasing, levels of accuracy of this model's forecasts over the model's first four years were the foundation for a great sense of confidence in the system. By 1990, the remaining critical components of the EFMS were in place and had been validated against 1990 data. The success of this validation led the Air Force to discontinue operation and maintenance of the Airmen Skills Force Model, the primary model that had been used for disaggregate inventory projection and force management in the past. Since 1990, the EFMS has been the chief analytical tool used to support major policy and programming decisions affecting the enlisted force.

The conceptual design for the EFMS included support for making Air Force personnel policies and for implementing those policies (i.e., for both planning and programming activities). But as the EFMS was built, programming support took center stage. The programmers were the most eager for the help the EFMS promised, and their operations presented the most pressing deficiencies. As the models have come on line and proven their worth, their use throughout the programming community has continued to expand. Moreover, the uses of the EFMS have begun to expand into the planning arena, as originally envisioned. In several complex, high-visibility areas, the EFMS system has been adapted to provide critical forecasts. In particular, models have been used to portray both the dynamic and steady-state projections of individual career fields, as well as to assess the impact of various management decisions on career field reenlistment and promotion opportunities. These recent policy applications mark the entry of the EFMS into the planning arena.

Particularly noteworthy in the development of the EFMS is the fact that the accuracy of the models that predict airman losses has continued to improve over time, and that the predictions from the various loss models (aggregate and disaggregate, middle and short term) track closely to each other. The improvement in accuracy can be attributed to the fine-tuning of model performance, eliminating explainable anomalies in the data, and adding additional years to the cohort databases to capture complete data on those serving 30-year careers.

Equally gratifying from the Air Force's perspective is that the EFMS is serving as a catalyst for change in areas besides enlisted force management. For example, some of its tools and concepts are being adapted to the management of other elements of the total force. There is now an officer cohort file similar in concept to the YAR file, which is being used to address officer management issues. Advances have also been made for improving civilian force management capabilities. Also, new tools have been added to the SMO toolbox (e.g., FOCUS, a data management and inquiry product that provides easy access to the detailed personnel data in the system's database.) It now appears that the Air Force is well on its way to achieving its goal of EFMS becoming the initial element of what will eventually become a total Force Management System.

The office primarily responsible for personnel planning was merged with the SMO in 1991. The success in adapting the existing EFMS models to planning purposes, in integrating new tools, and in addressing issues beyond enlisted force management gives hope that the system will evolve into the full-service ODSS originally hoped for.

As dramatic changes in Eastern Europe and the Soviet Union continue to unfold, the challenges to restructuring our Armed Forces become great. A question yet to be answered is whether the EFMS will prove flexible enough to provide accurate information in a dramatically altered environment. The first efforts to use the EFMS models to make inventory projections in this changing world have been encouraging.

19.2   LESSONS LEARNED

The scale of an ODSS staggers the imagination. Building the EFMS absorbed more than 125 person-years; the software written specifically for the system amounts to hundreds of thousands of lines of code; and the system's database contains more than a billion bytes of information.. Building so large a system entails risks. (For example, in the 1980s the Bank of America invested heavily in the development of an ODSS, only to abandon the project before completion.) Once built, operating an ODSS remains a large chore. (The direct operations and maintenance costs for the EFMS run about $100,000 per year, excluding personnel costs. As of the end of 1991, there were 21 military and civilian person-years allocated to the development, operation, and maintenance of the system. Of course, this cost should be compared to personnel expenditures on the enlisted force of over $13 billion per year.)

We have written this book to reduce the risks to others who desire to build an ODSS. By sharing with them our experiences, we hope to enable them to build on our successes and avoid our errors. Here we summarize the major lessons we have drawn from building and implementing the EFMS. We offer lessons bearing on the purpose and structure of an ODSS; the people needs of an ODSS creation project; preparing the users to approach the ODSS with sophistication; testing, evaluating and prototyping models; data; standards; and implementation. In doing so, we wish to make it clear that the building of an ODSS is much more than an exercise in mathematical modeling. Even though mathematical modeling problems are fundamental and must be attended to, they constitute only one of a large panoply of issues, most of which we have tried to address in this volume.

One of the most important principles to be followed in building an ODSS is that sufficient resources and time must be made available to do the job right. The EFMS took nine years to develop, although it should not have taken nearly so long. It continually lacked adequate in-house resources to move the project along at a reasonable pace. Other factors that contributed to the long development time included significant time for data gathering and cleaning, long procurement time to obtain the system's hardware and software, and the time required to build consensus and support for the project within the Air Force's personnel hierarchy.

The development of an ODSS requires the employment of a project team with a wide range of skills. For example, neither information systems or operations research personnel alone have the skills necessary to design and develop the system. Each type of expert brings a different perspective to the project, based on his or her background and skills. This can be beneficial, since it brings into play a wide range of ideas and alternatives, but it can have a negative impact if the project members do not work closely together, supplying their individual strengths to a team effort.

To be worth the cost, an ODSS must do more than automate the current way of doing business; it must improve the quality of decisions. Introducing an ODSS may, in fact, also change the manner in which business is done, but, management changes need not be—and for political reasons often should not be—a major focus of an ODSS project. Rather, the major focus of an ODSS should be to improve overall organizational performance. Because the ODSS serves functions, not management structures, changes in management structure that occur after the system is built will have little effect on the ODSS.

Three major differences between ODSSs and traditional DSSs make an ODSS appear rather monolithic:

1. An ODSS relies on a single, centralized database shared by all users.
2. An ODSS serves functions rather than individuals, and indeed, coordinates and integrates decisionmaking across functions.
3. An ODSS strives to show a single face to users, with each user seeing, to the extent possible, a single interface no matter what model is being run.

However, the ODSS's database may be distributed, its users may be geographically dispersed, and its internal organization should be modular, not monolithic. Be prepared to build separate models for separate functions, decisions and circumstances. Be prepared to build multiple models to mimic a single phenomenon, with each model fine-tuned to meet the demands of a different decision, function or circumstance. Speed, detail and accuracy must be constantly traded off, with the uses of a model dictating the importance of each.

Combining modular construction with a seamless interface for the users requires care in construction. Because the models of an ODSS are highly interrelated in use, the builders of the various models must communicate closely with one another when designing and building the models. Models that will "speak" to one another, with the output from one becoming the input to another, must be especially well coordinated. An ODSS must be built by a cohesive team, not by semi-independent individuals.

Making the system modular allows timely introduction of models, while balancing the conflicting demands of model users and model developers. Analysts will drag their heels, wanting to provide a perfect product. Users will chafe at the bit, wanting models they can use right away. Modularity allows the introduction of some models while others are still being built. Modular development also hedges against the risk that ODSS development may be stopped or abbreviated. If funding is reduced, individual parts can be eliminated from the design without losing the entire investment.

Modularity should also influence the choices of software and hardware. Because both hardware and software technology are likely to run ahead of system development, software should be as independent of the system hardware as possible. During the lifetime of an ODSS, much may change in the world of computer technology. Independence of software and hardware will make changing one or the other less costly. To the extent that software and hardware are not independent, we recommend allowing software needs to guide the choice of hardware, not vice versa.

An effective ODSS will become part of the central nervous system of an organization. This makes installing an ODSS in an organization akin to transplanting an organ in a human body. The ODSS must be carefully matched to the rhythm and needs of the recipient organization. The prospective users must be readied for the new system, and must help ready the system for themselves. This readying must begin with the inception of system building. A turnkey ODSS, built by outsiders and handed over to the users as a *fait accompli* will usually be rejected by the users, no matter how good the system—the system will be too alien. The users of an ODSS must be among the builders, so that they "own" the system from the outset and so they can contribute to conforming the system to the organization's internal structures. When an ODSS incorporates new technologies, the engagement of the users from the outset becomes especially critical; users are unlikely to accept innovations that they see as imposed on them from outside. Had we not engaged the user community in building the EFMS from the very beginning, we believe the system would have never come to fruition.

Missteps early in an ODSS project can drastically increase costs incurred at a later date. To reduce the risk of such mistakes, the team that creates the conceptual design must see to the end of the project from the very beginning. The design team must include representatives of all the specialized skills that will be needed to build and maintain the system. Implementation and maintenance requirements must temper the conceptual design to ensure the envisioned system's efficiency and operability. Perhaps the most costly misstep we took in building the EFMS was not including more conceptually expert programming and data management people on the project team during the design stage of the project. We would then have made database issues a more important part of the conceptual design and would have given the conceptual design a more sophisticated view of user interfaces.

Having strong in-house management of an ODSS development project greatly increases the chances of success. Even if outside contractors are retained to help in developing the system, the using organization is unlikely to get a "turnkey" system just by writing a contract. If nothing else, there is a huge body of knowledge about the organization that must be brought into the development process. In addition, to fulfill its responsibilities, the using organization must be able to structure the project, measure progress, and evaluate results. Responsibility for system development and its management should be assigned to a separate office (a System Management Office) so that the system's unique character and needs will not get lost in the hustle and bustle of everyday business. The SMO must also be staffed by persons with both traditional skills and attitudes and by those who have the willingness, flexibility, and skills to open up the organization to new ideas and approaches.

An ODSS will touch many people within an organization, and some of these people will resist the intrusion of the ODSS into their domains. Consequently, the project leader for building an ODSS must have both political savvy and the respect of powerful members of the organization. An ODSS needs "sponsors," i.e., influential people within the organization with sufficient power to sustain budgetary and political support over the long development life of the system. An ODSS also needs "champions," i.e., enthusiasts within the organization who will bullheadedly push forward the ODSS agenda. Champions may be either system users or system builders. Since an ODSS takes a long time to complete, we advise that system builders continuously cultivate potential new champions or sponsors in case old ones leave their positions.

Despite the need for championing and sponsoring an ODSS, if the people who build and operate an ODSS are to endure as respected advisors in providing decision support tools, they must demonstrate a commitment to being colleagues with the user community. Candidly discussing both the strengths and the limitations of the ODSS will help build such collegiality. Sustaining an intimate relationship between the functional user and the technical expert will maintain a vital link in the continued evolution of an ODSS.

Decisionmaking with an ODSS requires users sophisticated in abstraction; achieving such sophistication may require that system builders educate the prospective users by discussing with them the aims and limits of models. Users must come to understand that models, whether descriptive or prescriptive, are only approximations of reality and need only identify the significant consequences of alternative decisions accurately enough to allow a best decision to be distinguished from others. Users, absorbed in the specific details of their work, will frequently find it difficult to accept that models may sacrifice realism for simplicity. An ODSS will be more easily embraced and better used as users come to understand that while the numbers produced by a model should be taken with a grain of salt, they can, nevertheless, serve many useful purposes. Put differently, model builders should share the insight that models are tools, not solutions.

Once users understand this characteristic of models, they will readily accept that they should not abandon judgment when using them. But it will be difficult to teach users to keep their professional judgments separate from the models. Users will need urging to heed the maxim: "When a model's results are judged to be wrong or inadequate, don't monkey with the model." The model's results are what they are; the user's judgment is what it is. Keeping the user's judgments and the model's results sharply distinct is essential to the credibility and integrity of the models. Judgment may well involve "fiddling" with the results from the models. That is fine. What is not fine is fiddling with the models themselves and then claiming that one has results from the models that conform to the user's judgments—because all one really has are the user's judgments.

Users will reject models that do not demonstrably improve their job performance. Consequently, before offering models for use, they must be tested and evaluated. Such testing and evaluation should ascertain whether the models perform well enough for the uses planned for them, not whether the models agree with reality. Analysts trained in more academic settings must keep in mind the practical purposes of the models and not subject them to the type of stringent validation that might be more appropriate in an academic setting. This less stringent form of assessment requires users to heed a simple caveat: Do not use models for purposes for which they have not been tested and evaluated. A model that performs well in one use may not perform well in another. Furthermore, because a model that worked well in the past may not work well in the future, we recommend periodic reevaluation and updating of models as a standard activity in an ODSS.

Prototype models are essential to building an ODSS. Analysts learn immense amounts from building them and from the users' reactions to them. Also prototypes can demonstrate to users the potential benefits of the ODSS, and thereby strengthen political support for completing the system. However, prototyping incurs two risks. First, users may confuse the limits of the prototype with the capabilities of the completed system, thereby undermining, not strengthening, political support for completing the system. Second, prototypes that users find helpful in their jobs can become entrenched, and users may be reluctant to replace them with different (albeit more advanced) descendants.

No matter how extensive one's prototyping and no matter how careful one's testing and evaluation, models benefit from good data—and good data are costly. Designing and cleaning the database for building the EFMS absorbed as much time and effort as actually building the models. (In retrospect, even *more* time should have been devoted to those activities.) Bad data invite bad modeling and risk inaccurate forecasting. Choosing data sources carefully and cleaning data well can reduce subsequent model building costs and can enhance model performance. However, good data cannot always be obtained. As a general rule, the more questionable one's data, the more one should rely on simple models; to perform well, complex models often require good data.

An ODSS must draw its data from multiple sources, from various branches of the organization, and, often, from government. Do not underestimate the problems caused by using data from multiple sources. Such data will be rich in inconsistencies. Reconciling these differences, and deciding when not to reconcile them, requires meticulous attention to detail. Choose your data managers accordingly.

When assembling the data for an ODSS, emphasize data quality. Clean your data; examine it; clean it again. But in contrast, when designing a database structure for operating an ODSS, emphasize ease of use for the end user. Whether the data are structured with spreadsheets, relations, or matrices, the keys to success are ease of access, ease in reporting, and maintainability.

Good data standards are one key to ease of use. Standards for data structures, variable names, and module interfaces must be explicitly defined. Unfortunately, just establishing standards does not ensure that they will be met. Managers must review compliance regularly.

Attention to standards extends to standards for documentation. Quality documentation is essential for a successful ODSS. The functions served by an ODSS may remain stable, but the personnel may turn over often. New actors must have good documentation in order to learn their jobs quickly and well. Unfortunately, documentation is often slighted when building an ODSS because, when time is tight, doing often seems more important than documenting. ODSS managers must impress on their staff the long-range importance of good documentation. Managers must force their staffs to create good documentation as they proceed and must force themselves to allow their staffs time for preparing documentation.

New technologies have the potential to shorten overall development time by speeding up analysis and design, reducing the amount of manual documentation, and decreasing the number of lines of code that need to be written. Realization of this potential, however, requires careful selection and employment of the appropriate tools.

The developers' jobs are not done when they deliver the models to the users. Developers must support the users in applying the new models, and must stay in touch until the first full cycle of use, maintenance, and updating has been completed. An ODSS is not successfully developed until it proves capable of evolution within the operational environment.

A final lesson from the EFMP is "don't give up." One of the members of the project team recently said about the project "If I had known beforehand what I was getting into, I never would have done it." This same thought, while unstated, probably crossed the mind of almost every person on the project. But the EFMS is up and running, its builders feel a sense of pride and accomplishment, and the Air Force has the best enlisted personnel management system of any military service in the world.

References

1. Organizational Decision Support Systems

Ackoff, R.L., **Redesigning the Future: A Systems Approach to Societal Problems**, John Wiley & Sons, New York, 1974.

Allison, Graham T., **Essence of Decision**, Little, Brown and Co., Boston, 1971.

Ananda, A. and B. Srinivasan (eds.), **Distributed Computing Systems: Concepts and Structures**, IEEE Computer Society Press, Los Alamitos, CA, 1990.

Anthony, R.N., **Planning and Control Systems: A Framework for Analysis**, Harvard University Graduate School of Business Administration, Studies in Management Control, Cambridge, MA, 1965.

Applegate, Lynda M., James I. Cash, Jr., and D. Quinn Mills, "Information Technology and Tomorrow's Business Manager," **Harvard Business Review**, November/December 1988, pp. 128–136.

Arguden, R. Yilmaz, **Principles for Dealing with Large Programs and Large Data Files in Policy Studies**, P–7409, The RAND Corporation, February 1988.

Ariav, Gad and Michael J. Ginzberg, "DSS Design: A Systemic View of Decision Support," **Communications of the ACM**, Vol. 28, No. 10 (October 1985), pp. 1045–1052.

Baccus, M. D., **Aids to Decisionmaking: A Review of the State of the Art**, N–3000-OJCS, The RAND Corporation, 1991.

Bidgoli, Hossein, **Decision Support Systems: Principles & Practice**, West Publishing Company, St. Paul, MN, 1989.

Bots, P. W. G. and H. G. Sol, "Shaping Organizational Information Systems Through Co-ordination Support," Chapter 11 in Ronald M. Lee, Andrew M. McCosh, and Piero Migliarese (eds.), **Organizational Decision Support Systems**, North-Holland, New York, 1988.

Brennan, J. J., and Joyce J. Elam, "Understanding and Validating Results in Model-Based Decision Support Systems," **Decision Support Systems**, Vol. 2, No. 1 (March 1986), pp. 49–54.

Brooks, Frederick P., Jr., **The Mythical Man-Month: Essays on Software Engineering**, Addison-Wesley Publishing Co., Reading, MA, 1975.

Carlson, E., "An Approach for Designing Decision Support Systems," Chapter 2 in John L. Bennett (ed.), **Building Decision Support Systems**, Addison-Wesley Publishing Co., Reading, MA, 1983.

Dantzig, George B., **Linear Programming and Extensions**, Princeton University Press, Princeton, NJ, 1963.

Davis, Gordon B., and Margrethe H. Olson, **Management Information Systems: Conceptual Foundations, Structure, and Development**, 2nd ed., McGraw-Hill Book Company, New York, 1985.

Dennis, Alan R., Joey F. George, Len M. Jessup, Jay F. Nunamaker, Jr., and Douglas R. Vogel, "Information Technology to Support Electronic Meetings," **MIS Quarterly**, Vol. 12, No. 4 (December 1988), pp. 591–624.

DeSanctis, Gerardine, and R. Brent Gallupe, "A Foundation for the Study of Group Decision Support Systems," **Management Science**, Vol. 33, No. 5 (May 1987), pp. 589–609.

Drucker, Peter F., "The Coming of the New Organization," **Harvard Business Review**, January/February 1988, pp. 45–53.

Eom, Hyun B., "The Emergence of Global Decision Support Systems," **OR/MS Today**, Vol. 17, No. 5 (October 1990), pp. 12–13.

Findeisen, Wladyslaw, and Edward S. Quade, "The Methodology of Systems Analysis: An Introduction and Overview,"Chapter 4 in Hugh J. Miser and Edward S. Quade (eds.), **Handbook of Systems Analysis: Overview of Uses, Procedures, Applications, and Practice**, North-Holland, New York, 1985.

Foster, L. W., and D. M. Flynn, "Management Information Technology: Its Effects on Organizational Form and Function," **Management Information Systems Quarterly**, Vol. 8 (1984), pp. 229–236.

Francis, Bob, "Client/Server: The Model for the '90s," **Datamation**, February 15, 1990, pp. 34–40.

Goeller, Bruce F., "A Framework for Evaluating Success in Systems Analysis," Chapter 14 in Hugh J. Miser and Edward S. Quade (eds.), **Handbook of Systems Analysis: Craft Issues and Procedural Choices**, North-Holland, New York, 1988.

Hedlund, G., and D. Rolander, "Action in Hetarchies—New Approaches to Managing the MNC," pages 15–46, in C. A. Bartlett, Y. Doz, and G. Hedlund (eds.), **Managing the Global Firm**, Routledge, London, 1990.

Huber, George P., "Cognitive Style as a Basis for MIS and DSS Designs: Much Ado About Nothing?," **Management Science**, Vol. 29, No. 5 (May 1983), pp. 567–574.

Huber, George P., "A Theory of the Effects of Advanced Information Technologies on Organizational Design, Intelligence, and Decision Making," **Academy of Management Review**, Vol. 15, No. 1 (1990), pp. 47–71.

Information Engineering Management Guide, Pacific Information Management, Inc., Culver City, California, 1989.

Kaula, Rajeev, and Uldarico Rex Dumdum, Jr., "Towards an Organization DSS Architecture: An Open-Systems Perspective," **DSS–91 Transactions**, The Institute of Management Sciences, Providence, RI, 1991, pp. 168–176.

Keen, Peter G. W. and Michael S. Scott Morton, **Decision Support Systems: An Organizational Perspective**, Addison-Wesley Publishing Co., Reading, MA, 1978.

King, John Leslie and Susan Leigh Star, "Conceptual Foundations for the Development of Organizational Decision Support Systems," **Proceedings of the Twenty-Third Annual Hawaii International Conference on System Sciences, Vol. III**, IEEE Computer Society Press, Los Alamitos, CA, 1990, pp. 143–151.

Majone, Giandomenico and Edward S. Quade (eds.), **Pitfalls of Analysis**, John Wiley & Sons, New York, 1980.

Malone, Thomas W. and John F. Rockart, "Computers, Networks, and the Corporation," **Scientific American**, September 1991, pp. 128–136.

McLean, E. R. and H. G. Sol (eds.), **Decision Support Systems: A Decade in Perspective**, Elsevier Science Publishers, Amsterdam, 1986.

Miller, Louis W. and Norman Katz, "A Model Management System to Support Policy Analysis," **Decision Support Systems**, Vol. 2, No. 1 (March 1986), pp. 55–63.

Olson, Margrethe H. (ed.), **Technological Support for Work Group Collaboration**, Lawrence Erlbaum Associates, Hillsdale, NJ, 1989.

Ozsu, M. Tamer, and Patrick Valduriez, **Principles of Distributed Database Systems**, Prentice Hall, Englewood Cliffs, NJ, 1991.

Rash, Wayne, Jr., "Corporate Connections," **BYTE**, September 1991, pp. 215–223.

Reck, Robert H., and James R. Hall, "Executive Information Systems: An Overview of Development," **Journal of Information Systems Management**, Fall 1986, pp. 25–30.

Reich, Robert B., **The Work of Nations**, Alfred A. Knopf, New York, 1991.

Relles, Daniel A., **Allocating Research Resources: The Role of a Data Management Core Unit,** N–2383-NICHD, The RAND Corporation, January 1986.

Simon, H. A., **The New Science of Management Decision**, Harper & Row, New York, 1960.

Simon, H. A., **Sciences of the Artificial**, The MIT Press, Cambridge, MA, 1969.

Sprague, Ralph H., Jr., and Eric D. Carlson, **Building Effective Decision Support Systems**, Prentice-Hall, Englewood Cliffs, NJ, 1982.

Sprague, Ralph H., Jr. and Hugh J. Watson (eds.), **Decision Support Systems: Putting Theory Into Practice**, Prentice-Hall, Englewood Cliffs, NJ, 1986.

Stohr, E. A., and N. H. White, "User Interfaces for Decision Support Systems: An Overview," **International Journal of Policy Analysis and Information Systems**, Vol. 6, No. 4 (1982), pp. 393–423.

Swanson, E. Burton, "Distributed Decision Support Systems: A Perspective," **Proceedings of the Twenty-Third Annual Hawaii International Conference on System Sciences, Vol. III**, IEEE Computer Society Press, Los Alamitos, CA, 1990, pp. 129–136.

Thierauf, Robert J., **User-Oriented Decision Support Systems: Accent on Problem Finding**, Prentice Hall, Englewood Cliffs, NJ, 1988.

Toffler, Alvin, **Future Shock**, Random House, Inc., New York, 1970.

Turban, Efraim, **Decision Support and Expert Systems: Managerial Perspectives**, Macmillan Publishing Company, New York, 1988.

van Schaik, F. D. J., **Effectiveness of Decision Support Systems**, Delft University Press, Delft, The Netherlands, 1988.

Wagner, G. R., "Decision Support Systems: The Real Substance," **Interfaces**, Vol. 11, No. 2 (1981), pp. 77–86.

Walker, Warren E., "Generating and Screening Alternatives," Chapter 6 in Hugh J. Miser and Edward S. Quade (eds.), **Handbook of Systems Analysis: Craft Issues and Procedural Choices**, North-Holland, New York, 1988.

2. Building an EFMS for the USAF

Armstrong, Bruce and S. Craig Moore, **Air Force Manpower, Personnel, and Training: Roles and Interactions**, R–2429-AF, The RAND Corporation, June 1980.

Carter, Grace M., Jan M. Chaiken, Michael P. Murray, and Warren E. Walker, **Conceptual Design of an Enlisted Force Management System for the Air Force**, N–2005-AF, The RAND Corporation, Santa Monica, CA, August 1983.

Walker, Warren E., and the Enlisted Force Management Project Team, **Design and Development of an Enlisted Force Management System for the Air Force**, R–3600-AF, The RAND Corporation, Santa Monica, CA, 1991.

3. The Process of Building an ODSS

Anderson, Robert H. and Norman Z. Shapiro, **Beyond User Friendly**, N–2999-RC, The RAND Corporation, December 1989.

Bergstrom, Leonard P., "Selecting Financial Modeling Software," **ICP Interface: Administrative & Accounting**, Vol. 7, No. 3 (Autumn 1982), pp. 20–26.

Bikson, T. K., C. M. Stasz, and D. A. Mankin, **Computer-Mediated Work: Individual and Organizational Impact in One Corporate Headquarters**, R–3308-OTA, The RAND Corporation, Santa Monica, CA, November 1985.

Boehm, Barry W., "A Spiral Model of Software Development and Enhancement," **IEEE Computer**, Vol. 21, No. 5 (May 1988), pp. 61–72.

Brooks, Frederick P., Jr., **The Mythical Man-Month: Essays on Software Engineering**, Addison-Wesley Publishing Co., Reading, MA, 1975.

Carter, Grace M., Jan M. Chaiken, Michael P. Murray, and Warren E. Walker, **Conceptual Design of an Enlisted Force Management System for the Air Force,** N–2005-AF, The RAND Corporation, Santa Monica, CA, August 1983.

Davis, Gordon B. and Margrethe H. Olson, **Management Information Systems: Conceptual Foundations, Structure, and Development,** 2nd ed., McGraw-Hill Book Company, New York, 1985.

Dennis, A. R., R. N. Burns, and R. B. Gallupe, "Phased Design: A Mixed Methodology for Application System Development," **DATA BASE,** Vol. 18, No. 4 (Summer 1987), pp. 31–38.

Keen, Peter G. W., "Adaptive Design for Decision Support Systems," **Data Base,** Vol. 12, Nos. 1 & 2 (Fall 1980), pp. 15–25.

Keen, Peter G. W. and Thomas J. Gambino, "Building a Decision Support System: the Mythical Man-Month Revisited," Chapter 7 in John L. Bennett (ed.), **Building Decision Support Systems,** Addison-Wesley Publishing Co., Reading, MA, 1983.

Kunreuther, H., J. Lepore, L. Miller, J. Vinso, J. Wilson, B. Borkan, B. Duffy, and N. Katz, **An Interactive Modeling System For Disaster Policy Analysis,** Program on Technology, Environment and Man, Monograph #26, Institute of Behavioral Science, University of Colorado, Boulder, 1978.

Mankin, Don, Tora Bikson, Barbara Gutek, and Cathleen Stasz, "Managing Technological Change: The Process Is Key," **Datamation,** Vol. 34, No. 18 (September 15, 1988), pp. 68–80.

Meador, D. L. and R. A. Mezger, "Selecting an End-user Programming Language for DSS Development," **MIS Quarterly** (December 1984), pp. 267–279.

Miller, Louis W., and Norman Katz, "A Model Management System to Support Policy Analysis," **Decision Support Systems,** Vol. 2, No. 1 (March 1986), pp. 55–63.

Peters, Thomas J. and Robert H. Waterman, **In Search of Excellence: Lessons from America's Best-Run Companies,** Harper & Row, New York, 1982.

Reimann, Bernard C. and Allan D. Waren, "User-Oriented Criteria for the Selection of DSS Software," **Communications of the ACM,** Vol. 28, No. 2 (February 1985), pp. 166–179.

Sprague, Ralph H., Jr. and Eric D. Carlson, **Building Effective Decision Support Systems,** Prentice-Hall, Englewood Cliffs, NJ, 1982.

Thierauf, Robert J., **User-Oriented Decision Support Systems: Accent on Problem Finding**, Prentice Hall, Englewood Cliffs, NJ, 1988.

Turban, Efraim, **Decision Support and Expert Systems: Managerial Perspectives**, Macmillan Publishing Company, New York, 1988.

Walker, Robert G., Robert S. Barnhardt, and Warren E. Walker, **Selecting a Decision Support System Generator for the Air Force's Enlisted Force Management System**, R–3474-AF, The RAND Corporation, Santa Monica, CA, December 1986.

Walker, Warren E., "Models in the Policy Process: Past, Present, and Future," **Interfaces**, Vol. 12, No. 5 (October 1982), pp. 91–100.

4. Decision Support Models

Hillier, Frederick S. and Gerald J. Lieberman, **Introduction to Operations Research**, 5th ed., McGraw-Hill Publishing Company, New York, 1990.

Quade, Edward S., "Predicting the Consequences: Models and Modeling," Chapter 7 in Hugh J. Miser and Edward S. Quade (eds.), **Handbook of Systems Analysis: Overview of Uses, Procedures, Applications, and Practice**, North-Holland, New York, 1985.

Rothenberg, Jeff, **The Nature of Modeling**, N–3027-DARPA, The RAND Corporation, Santa Monica, CA, November 1989.

5. Principles for Building ODSS Models

Hamming, Richard, **Numerical Methods for Scientists and Engineers**, McGraw-Hill Publishing Company, New York, 1962.

Hillier, Frederick S. and Gerald J. Lieberman, **Introduction to Operations Research**, 5th ed., McGraw-Hill Publishing Company, New York, 1990.

Moore, Jeffrey H., and Michael G. Chang, "Meta-Design Considerations in Building DSS," Chapter 8 in John L. Bennett (ed.), **Building Decision Support Systems**, Addison-Wesley Publishing Company, Reading, MA, 1983.

Quade, E. S. (revised by Grace M. Carter), **Analysis for Public Decisions**, 3rd ed., Elsevier Science Publishing Co., New York, 1989.

Rothenberg, Jeff, Norman Z. Shapiro, and Charlene Hefley, "A 'Propagative' Approach to Sensitivity Analysis," in Bernard Zeigler and Jerzy Rozenblit (eds.), **AI, Simulation and Planning in High Autonomy Systems**, IEEE Computer Society Press, Los Alamitos, CA, 1990.

Turban, Efraim, **Decision Support and Expert Systems: Managerial Perspectives**, Macmillan Publishing Company, New York, 1988.

6. How Statistical Concerns Influence Modeling

Box, G. E. P., and G. M. Jenkins, **Time Series Analysis, Forecasting and Control,** Holden-Day, San Francisco, CA, 1976.

Cleveland, William S., Douglas M. Dunn, and Irma J. Terpenning, "SABL—A Resistant Seasonal Adjustment Procedure with Graphical Methods for Interpretation and Diagnosis," in Arnold Zellner (ed.), **Seasonal Analysis of Economic Time Series,** U.S. Department of Commerce, Bureau of the Census, Washington, DC, 1979.

Granger, C. W. J., **Forecasting in Business and Economics,** 2nd ed., Academic Press, San Diego, CA, 1989.

Granger, C. W. J., and R. Ramanathan, "Improved Methods of Combining Forecasts," **Journal of Forecasting** (1984), pp. 197–204.

Harvey, Andrew, **Forecasting, Structural Time Series Models and the Kalman Filter,** Cambridge University Press, Cambridge, England, 1989.

Harvey, Andrew, **The Econometric Analysis of Time Series,** The MIT Press, Cambridge, MA, 1990.

7. Loss Modules in the EFMS

Box, G. E. P., and G.M. Jenkins, **Time Series Analysis, Forecasting and Control,** Holden-Day, San Francisco, CA, 1976.

Cleveland, William S., Douglas M. Dunn, and Irma J. Terpenning, "SABL—A Resistant Seasonal Adjustment Procedure with Graphical Methods for Interpretation and Diagnosis," in Arnold Zellner (ed.), **Seasonal Analysis of Economic Time Series,** U.S. Department of Commerce, Bureau of the Census, Washington, DC, 1979.

Haggstrom, G. W., "Logistic Regression and Discriminant Analysis by Ordinary Least Squares," **Journal of Business and Economic Statistics,** Vol. 1, No. 3 (July 1983), pp. 229–238.

8. Decision Support Models in the EFMS

Carter, Grace M., **Year Of Service Target Generator: Conceptual Specification,** N–3223/1-AF, The RAND Corporation, Santa Monica, CA, 1991.

Carter, Grace M., Deborah Skoller, Stanley Perrin, and Clyde S. Sakai, **An Enlisted Force Management System Model to Predict the Effect of Bonus Decisions,** N–2747-AF, The RAND Corporation, Santa Monica, CA, July 1988.

Rydell, C. Peter, **ALEC: A Model for Analyzing the Cost-Effectiveness of Air Force Enlisted Personnel Policies**, N–2629/1-AF, The RAND Corporation, Santa Monica, CA, August 1987.

9. Data for Analysis and Model Building

Arguden, R. Yilmaz, **Principles for Dealing with Large Programs and Large Data Files in Policy Studies**, P–7409, The RAND Corporation, Santa Monica, CA, February 1988.

Brauner, Marygail, Michael P. Murray, Warren E. Walker, and Elizabeth Davidson, **What's on the Enriched Airman Gain/Loss File**, N–2610-AF, The RAND Corporation, Santa Monica, CA, March 1989.

Murray, Michael P., Daniel Relles, Marygail Brauner, Grace Carter, Leola Cutler, Deborah Skoller, and Warren E. Walker, **What's on the Year-At-Risk File**, N–2744-AF, The RAND Corporation, Santa Monica, CA, March 1989.

Relles, Daniel, **Allocating Research Resources: The Role of a Data Management Core Unit**, N–2383-NICHD, The RAND Corporation, Santa Monica, CA, January 1986.

10. The Use of Prototype Models and Staged Implementation

Alavi, Maryam, "An Assessment of the Prototyping Approach to Information Systems Development," **Communications of the ACM**, Vol. 27, No. 6 (June 1984), pp. 556–563.

Boehm, Barry W., "A Spiral Model of Software Development and Enhancement," **IEEE Computer**, Vol. 21, No. 5 (May 1988), pp. 61–72.

Boehm, B. W., T. E. Gray, and T. Seewaldt, "Prototyping Versus Specifying: A Multiproject Experiment," **IEEE Transactions on Software Engineering**, Vol. SE–10, No. 3 (1984), pp. 290–303.

Cooke, John, Joseph DeSantis, et al., **C-Scape/Look and Feel**, Oakland Group, Inc., 1987.

Dennis, A. R., R. N. Burns, and R. B. Gallupe, "Phased Design: A Mixed Methodology for Application System Development," **Data Base**, Vol. 18, No. 4 (Summer 1987), pp. 31–37.

Hurst, E. Gerald, Jr., David N. Ness, Thomas J. Gambino, and Thomas H. Johnson, "Growing DSS: A Flexible, Evolutionary Approach," Chapter 6 in John L. Bennett (ed.), **Building Decision Support Systems**, Addison-Wesley Publishing Co., Reading, MA, 1983.

Iivari, Juhani and Mikko Karjalainen, "Impact of Prototyping on User Information Satisfaction During the IS Specification Phase," **Information & Management**, Vol. 17 (1989), pp. 31–45.

Jenkins, A. Milton, **Prototyping: A Methodology for the Design and Development of Application Systems**, Discussion Paper #227, Division of Research, School of Business, Indiana University, Bloomington, IN, April 1983.

Rothenberg, Jeff, **Prototyping as Modeling: What is Being Modeled?**, N–3191-DARPA. The RAND Corporation, Santa Monica, CA, July 1990.

Sprague, Ralph H., Jr., and Eric D. Carlson, **Building Effective Decision Support Systems**, Prentice-Hall, Englewood Cliffs, NJ, 1982.

11. Test and Evaluation of ODSS Models and Modules

Abrahamse, Allan, **Middle-Term Disaggregate Loss Model Test and Evaluation: Description and Results**, N–2688-AF, The RAND Corporation, Santa Monica, CA, July 1988.

Carter, Grace, et al., **Middle-Term Loss Prediction Models for the Air Force's Enlisted Force Management System: Specification and Estimation**, R–3482-AF, The RAND Corporation, Santa Monica, CA, December 1987.

Gerjuoy, Herbert, "Validity of Forecasting Systems," Chapter 3 in Wayne I. Boucher (ed.), **The Study of the Future: An Agenda for Research**, National Science Foundation, Washington, DC, July 1977.

Hodges, James S., "Six (or so) Things You Can Do With a Bad Model," **Operations Research**, Vol. 39, No. 3 (May-June 1991), pp. 355–365.

Larson, Richard C. and Amadeo R. Odoni, **Urban Operations Research**, Prentice-Hall, Englewood Cliffs, NJ, 1981.

Miser, Hugh J. and Edward S. Quade, "Validation," Chapter 13 in Hugh J. Miser and Edward S. Quade (eds.), **Handbook of Systems Analysis: Craft Issues and Procedural Choices**, North-Holland, New York, 1988.

Thomas, C. J., "Verification Revisited—1983," Chapter 13 in W. P. Hughes, Jr. (ed.), **Military Modeling**, 2nd ed., Military Operations Research Society, Alexandria, Virginia, 1989, pp. 255–271.

12. Principles for Implementing an ODSS

Brooks, Frederick P., Jr., **The Mythical Man-Month: Essays on Software Engineering**, Addison-Wesley Publishing Co., Reading, MA, 1975.

Clark, David D., **Computers at Risk: Safe Computing in the Information Age**, National Academy Press, Washington, DC, 1991.

Peters, Thomas J. and Robert H. Waterman, Jr., **In Search of Excellence: Lessons from America's Best Run Companies,** Harper & Row Publishers, New York, 1982.

13. Passing the Baton: Implementing New Models

Department of Defense, **Defense System Software Development,** DoD Standard DoD-STD–2167A, April 1987.

Theil, Henri, **Principles of Econometrics,** John Wiley & Sons, New York, 1971.

14. Selecting the System's Software And Hardware

Ananda, A. and B. Srinivasan (eds.), **Distributed Computing Systems: Concepts and Structures,** IEEE Computer Society Press, Los Alamitos, CA, 1990.

Meador, D. L. and R. A. Mezger, "Selecting an End-user Programming Language for DSS Development," **MIS Quarterly,** December 1984, pp. 267–279.

Reimann, Bernard C., and Allan D. Waren, "User-Oriented Criteria for the Selection of DSS Software," **Communications of the ACM,** Vol. 28, No. 2 (February 1985), pp. 166–179.

Sloman, M. and J. Kramer, **Distributed Systems and Computer Networks,** Prentice-Hall, Englewood Cliffs, NJ, 1987.

Sprague, Ralph H., Jr., and Eric D. Carlson, **Building Effective Decision Support Systems,** Prentice-Hall, Englewood Cliffs, NJ, 1982.

Turban, Efraim, **Decision Support and Expert Systems: Managerial Perspectives,** Macmillan Publishing Company, New York, 1988.

Walker, Robert G., Robert S. Barnhardt, and Warren E. Walker, **Selecting a Decision Support System Generator for the Air Force's Enlisted Force Management System,** R–3474-AF, The RAND Corporation, Santa Monica, CA, December 1986.

15. Database Design and Management

Information Engineering Management Guide, Pacific Information Management, Culver City, CA, 1989.

Martin, James, **An Information Systems Manifesto,** Prentice-Hall, Inc., Englewood Clffs, NJ, 1984.

16. Building Applications

Winsberg, Paul, "CASE: Getting the Big Picture," **Database Programming & Design** (March 1988), pp. 54–57.

Yourdon, Edward, **Techniques of Program Structure and Design,** Prentice-Hall, Englewood Cliffs, NJ, 1975.

17. User Interfaces

Anderson, Robert H. and Norman Z. Shapiro, **Beyond User Friendly,** N–2999-RC, The RAND Corporation, Santa Monica, CA, December 1989.

Cooke, John, Joseph DeSantis, *et al.*, **C-Scape/Look and Feel**, Oakland Group, Inc., 1987.

Department of Defense, **Defense System Software Development,** DoD Standard DoD-STD–2167A, 1988.

Francis, Bob, "Client/Server: The Model for the '90s," **Datamation**, February 15, 1990, pp. 34–40.

Stohr, E. A. and N. H. White, "User Interfaces for Decision Support Systems: An Overview," **International Journal of Policy Analysis and Information Systems**, Vol. 6, No. 4 (1982), pp.393–423.

Tsichritzis, D. and F. Lochovsky, **Data Models,** Prentice-Hall, Englewood Cliffs, NJ, 1982.

18. Updating and Maintaining the Models of an ODSS

Murray, Michael P., **Middle-Term Loss Prediction Models for the Air Force's Enlisted Force Management System: Information for Updating,** N–2764-AF, The RAND Corporation, Santa Monica, CA, December 1989.

Index

344